A Digital Gift to the Nation

THE DIGITAL PROMISE PROJECT

www.digitalpromise.org

Sponsored by the Carnegie Corporation of New York, The Century Foundation, the John S. and James L. Knight Foundation, the John D. and Catherine T. MacArthur Foundation, and the Open Society Institute

PROJECT DIRECTOR
Edith C. Bjornson

ASSOCIATES
Henry Geller
Anne G. Murphy
Craig L. LaMay

A PUBLICATION OF THE DIGITAL PROMISE PROJECT

A Digital Gift to the Nation

Fulfilling the Promise of the Digital and Internet Age

Lawrence K. Grossman
and Newton N. Minow

With Background Papers on
Digital Perspectives

July, 2003

*To Bar —
Who's way ahead working on this
dream of ours.   With respect and
admiration.
Larry Grossman*

NEW YORK CITY * THE CENTURY FOUNDATION PRESS * 2001

The Century Foundation, formerly the Twentieth Century Fund, sponsors and supervises timely analyses of economic policy, foreign affairs, and domestic political issues. Not-for-profit and nonpartisan, it was founded in 1919 and endowed by Edward A. Filene.

LIBRARY OF CONGRESS CATALOGING-IN-PUBLICATION DATA

Grossman, Lawrence K.
    A digital gift to the nation : fulfilling the promise of the digital and Internet age / By Lawrence K. Grossman and Newton N. Minow.
        p. cm. "With background papers on digital perspectives"
    Cosponsored by the Century Foundation of New York ... [et al.].
    Includes bibliographical references.
    ISBN 0-87078-466-8 (pamphlet : alk. paper)
    1. Information technology—Research grants—United States. 2. Information technology—Social aspects—United States. 3. Endowments—United States.   I. Minow, Newton N., 1926-   . II. Century Foundation of New York. III. Title. IV. Series.
    T58.5 .G78 2001
    001.4'4—dc21

                                                            2001000628

Nothing written here is to be construed as necessarily reflecting the views of the supporting organizations or as an attempt by them to aid or hinder the passage of any bill before Congress.

FOREWORD

Perhaps the most remarkable thing about the past two hundred years of human history is how, after millennia of episodic and uncertain scientific progress, humans have come to accept and, indeed, take for granted the fact of rapid, technology-driven change. More than that, we have even adjusted to the unsettling and indisputable evidence that major breakthroughs often have unpredictable effects on our lives. No one, for example, foresaw how much the automobile would change communities, jobs, living patterns, national priorities, and warfare. And what the automobile and the airplane did for personal mobility, the later developments of radio and television did for information transfer. It is no exaggeration, in fact, to say that these electronic technologies have changed something truly fundamental: the way most of us experience the reality of the larger world around us.

Technological revolutions even have a way of changing the composition of the "haves" and the "have-nots" in a society. Certainly, the twentieth century was notable in part because of the pace of technological development and its impact on wealth, poverty, status, and power. All were shuffled and then reshuffled in ways that astonished even the most thoughtful observers. That process continues today and, if anything, has been intensified by the characteristics of the modern marketplace.

For the past several years, proponents of digital communications in general and the Internet in particular have claimed that the significance of these breakthroughs will equal or even exceed the impact of the internal combustion engine, the telephone, and radio. To be sure, the new technologies already have evoked remarkable popular enthusiasm. The number of Americans—the global leaders in adopting these technologies—who have access to the Internet has been increasing rapidly; according to one survey, during the six-month period from spring 2000 to the end of 2000, 16 million additional adult Americans gained access, bringing the total of such users to 104 million. Most observers predict similar or even accelerating propagation of Internet usage over the next ten years. Indeed, the potential benefits from this new technology have attracted interest from entrepreneurs, consumer advocates, and policymakers. The new data streams made possible by the release of relatively enormous portions of the electromagnetic spectrum for digital use are thus extremely valuable. A recent auction of additional spectrum rights, for example, brought $17 billion into government coffers.

More than two years ago, Newton N. Minow, renowned former chairman of the Federal Communications Commission, and Lawrence K. Grossman, author and former president of NBC News and the Public Broadcasting Service, had the foresight to recognize that the fruits of the so-called digital revolution would not automatically be shared widely by all the people and institutions in our society. They were especially concerned about the capacity and ability of nonprofit institutions of all types to realize the full potential of the new technologies. At their suggestion, Vartan Gregorian, the president of the Carnegie Corporation of New York, and I convened a meeting of leaders from various nonprofit organizations from around the country. The discussion at that session led directly to the development of the Digital Promise project. The ambitious scope of this effort has been possible only because of the significant additional commitment of the John D. and Catherine T. MacArthur Foundation, the John S. and James L. Knight Foundation, and the Open Society Institute. Minow and Grossman, assisted by Edith C. Bjornson, who is serving as project director, have reached out to specialists and interested parties throughout the nation. They commissioned a large group of papers from a very diverse set of thinkers about these issues. These Digital Perspectives background papers appear after the report and also are posted on the Digital Promise website (www.digitalpromise.org).

This report, outlining the essentials of their proposal, is the centerpiece of the intellectual effort so far. It incorporates the thinking of many about how the nonprofit sector might accomplish a smooth transition to the digital age. The report envisions the creation of a public trust fund from the proceeds of the ongoing public auctions of parts of the electromagnetic spectrum. The Trust could become an important mechanism for the development of intellectual and cultural capital. While America will rely heavily on the marketplace for the dissemination of new digital technologies, we need to see to it that these modern communications systems reach even those individuals and institutions lacking the resources to compete for the newest technologies. In this way, we can ensure the creation of a national digital communications system that works for all Americans.

In the end, there are two overriding public policy questions about the new digital technologies: How can government create a fair and efficient procedure for allocating the public airwaves for digital purposes, and how can it secure access for those institutions that are specifically insulated from the marketplace, such as universities, museums, libraries, and public broadcasting? The authors of this report and of the essays offer comprehensive ideas that answer both these questions. Indeed, they suggest an approach that could add to the nation's stock of critical public capital.

On behalf of The Century Foundation as well as the other foundations that supported this effort, I commend Newt Minow and Larry Grossman for their foresight and leadership.

RICHARD C. LEONE, *President*
The Century Foundation
January 2001

CONTENTS

Preface

We acknowledge with gratitude the nearly three hundred distinguished and diverse citizens who so generously and graciously contributed their experience, ideas, and time to our efforts.* Without their help we could not have fulfilled our important assignment.

We also appreciate the invaluable assistance this significant project received from its project director, Edith C. Bjornson, and our talented and dedicated associates, Henry Geller, Anne G. Murphy, and Craig L. LaMay.

The project's sponsors, the Carnegie Corporation of New York, The Century Foundation, the John S. and James L. Knight Foundation, the John D. and Catherine T. MacArthur Foundation, and the Open Society Institute, have long and outstanding records of public service. They have consistently been leaders in their enlightened concern for the public good. We applaud their interest in the potential of the new telecommunications technologies to serve worthwhile public purposes.

They have given us a free hand to develop our recommendations and proposals, which, of course, are our sole responsibility.

Lawrence K. Grossman
Newton N. Minow

---

* A list appears in the Appendix to this volume.

THE REPORT

by

LAWRENCE K. GROSSMAN

and

NEWTON N. MINOW

EXECUTIVE SUMMARY

I believe we are now entering the Renaissance phase of the Information Age, where creativity and ideas are the new currency, and invention is a primary virtue, where technology truly has the power to transform lives, not just businesses, where technology can help us solve fundamental problems.

Carly Fiorina, chief executive officer,
Hewlett Packard Corporation

In the age of information, the nation's prosperity, its democracy, its culture, and its future will depend as never before on the training, skills, ideas, and abilities of its citizens. The people's access to knowledge and learning across a lifetime in the sciences and humanities must become a national imperative in the emerging knowledge-based economy. In the past decade, information technology advanced the sciences and transformed the economy. In this decade, information technology will serve all of society and transform our daily lives.

At critical turning points in the eighteenth, nineteenth, and twentieth centuries, America's future was transformed by three bold public investments in an educated citizenry. As the United States enters the twenty-first century, it faces social and economic challenges brought on by globalization and vast technological and demographic change. To ensure that the nation can meet those challenges, we propose a fourth bold investment to advance the great legacy of those earlier initiatives.

In 1787, the Northwest Ordinance set aside public land to support public schools in every new state. The Northwest Ordinance helped make a young United States a literate and inventive nation—and a strong democracy.

3

In 1862, in the midst of the Civil War, the Morrill Act led to the establishment of 105 land-grant colleges, which created the preeminent system of higher education and research that has made America's agriculture and industry the most advanced in the world.

In 1944, the GI Bill made the United States "the best-educated country in the world," according to historian Stephen Ambrose. The GI Bill profoundly expanded educational opportunities for the more than 20 million American men and women who fought in World War II. They received an education that only the elite could previously afford and founded the businesses, created the arts, and advanced the sciences that brought about the postindustrial society we now enjoy.

Without any one of these farsighted investments, the United States would not be the great nation it is today. This report, *A Digital Gift to the Nation,* proposes a fourth initiative, one that would advance the legacy of these earlier initiatives into the twenty-first century and open the door to a knowledge-based future for Americans as well as the world. Our report has benefited from extensive discussions with hundreds of leaders of major nonprofit and for-profit organizations (see Appendix). We also commissioned a diverse series of Digital Perspective papers, which have profoundly influenced our thinking, and which are published here. Our findings and recommendations reflect our own views and are, of course, our sole responsibility.

We recommend the creation of a multibillion-dollar Digital Opportunity Investment Trust. We believe that funding for the Trust should come from revenues the federal government earns from its auctions of the publicly owned electromagnetic spectrum, the twenty-first century equivalent of the nation's public lands of an earlier time. The Trust would serve as a venture capital fund for our nation's nonprofit educational and public service institutions. It would be dedicated to innovation, experimentation, and research in utilizing new telecommunications technologies across the widest possible range of public purposes. It would invest in new and promising ideas and prototypes that use advanced telecommunications technologies to deliver public information and education in its broadest sense to all Americans throughout their lifetimes. It would enable schools, community colleges, universities, libraries, museums, civic organizations, and cultural, arts, and humanities centers to take advantage of new information technologies to reach outside their walls and into homes, schools, and the workplace.

The Digital Opportunity Investment Trust would have the potential to strengthen our economy, educate and inform our children, train teachers, improve the skills of workers, serve people with disabilities, and enrich the lives of the growing population of older adults. In the words of Henry C. Kelly, president of the Federation of American Scientists and former White House technology adviser, through advanced technology it is now possible for "any American to learn any subject anywhere at any time (and enjoy doing it)."

Specifically, we recommend that, given the urgent need to bring the benefits of advanced technologies to all citizens, the government should:

- Create a Digital Opportunity Investment Trust on the models of the National Science Foundation and the National Institutes of Health. The Trust would be governed by a board of distinguished and diverse citizens from many fields and disciplines who would set its priorities, oversee its activities, and determine the direction of its research.

- Empower the Trust to commission grants and enter into contracts that stimulate innovative and experimental ideas and techniques to enhance learning; broaden knowledge; encourage an informed citizenry and self-government; make available to all Americans the best of the nation's arts, humanities, and culture; and teach the skills and disciplines needed in this information-based economy.

- Charge the Trust to finance the development and testing of innovative models and materials for job retraining, skills training, and education in the use of new telecommunications and information technologies. As this report demonstrates, throughout the nation, local and regional libraries, museums, school systems, community colleges, universities, arts and cultural centers, and public broadcasting stations need to be able to use advanced information technologies if they are to continue to serve their essential public interest purposes. The Trust should commission the development of online courses, training materials, archives, software, civic information, quality arts and cultural programs, and other digital resources and services of the highest standards to meet the needs of all citizens and help them gain access to the best minds and talents in our society.

- Finance the Trust with the revenues from the auctions of licenses to the publicly owned electromagnetic spectrum. The Congressional Budget Office estimates that the FCC's spectrum auctions will yield

$18 billion over the next several years. In the eighteenth and nineteenth centuries the property sold to foster public education was public land; today, the public spectrum is the valuable natural resource that can provide an "electronic land-grant" for the Information Age.

- Charge the Trust to cooperate with business, industry, philanthropy, and local and national public service institutions and organizations, including the Library of Congress, the National Endowments for the Arts and Humanities, the National Science Foundation, the National Association of State Universities and Land-Grant Colleges, the Corporation for Public Broadcasting, the Institute of Museum and Library Services, the Smithsonian Institution, and others. The Trust should enhance the work of these existing organizations by seeking new ways to put information telecommunications technologies to work in their areas of interest.

- Charge the Trust to take full advantage of public broadcasting's state-of-the-art digital transmission system in carrying out its educational and informational mission. When converted to digital transmission by 2003, as mandated by Congress, the nation's public broadcasting system will have significantly expanded channel capacity and the ability to transmit interactive telecommunications to every community in the nation. In the digital era, public broadcasters should serve their communities by helping to create and distribute distance learning, skills training, civic and health information, and other vital public services.

- Charge the Trust to take risks and be bold. Its emphasis should be on experimentation and innovation. The Internet was originally conceived simply as a new tool that would enable researchers at different locations to exchange ideas and communicate information. No one envisioned that it would open a revolutionary new world of e-business and commerce, chat groups, electronic auctions, personal e-mail, and entertainment, all with global access. The Trust should explore new directions, promote breakthrough applications in advanced technology, stimulate the development and use of new learning techniques, and encourage partnerships and alliances among the nation's and the world's existing institutions and organizations in education, science, the humanities, the arts, civic affairs, and government.

The U.S. government pioneered in the development of information technology that is currently transforming the American economy and much of American society. That technology should now be put to work for the benefit of our society's nonprofit, public service sectors as well as for private companies and individual entrepreneurs. By doing so, we have a remarkable opportunity to meld the Northwest Ordinance and Morrill Act's educational institution building with the GI Bill's benefits to individuals and make lifelong learning available in the twenty-first century to every American. We do not need costly new institutions or large institutional bureaucracies. We should use the extraordinary resources of our existing libraries, museums, and public broadcasting stations, and our local educational, scientific, humanities, and civic institutions. With advanced digital technologies they can work together to reach beyond their walls into every home, workplace, and classroom.

In this century, thanks to dramatic new information technologies, the American people have another opportunity to light a spark that can illuminate and inform the nation and, indeed, much of the world, in ways that were not dreamed of in Justin Morrill's time.

I: THE RECOMMENDATION

"I would have learning more widely disseminated," said Justin S. Morrill, the congressman and senator from Vermont who was a principal founder of the Library of Congress and the sponsor of the farsighted Land-Grant College Act. Morrill's goal for the act was clear; he believed that by its passage:

> A spark will be lighted which may illumine the whole land and lift a cloud from the pathway of the sons of toil, regardless of ancestry or race, that will open to them higher spheres of service and honor, give to republican institutions a more enlightened and enduring support, and make a nation which shall not only deserve to live, but deserve to be immortal.[1]

President Lincoln signed the Morrill Land-Grant College Act in 1862, during the darkest days of the Civil War. One hundred years later, historian Allan Nevins called it "an immortal moment in the history of higher education in America and the world, which gave force to the principle that every child should have free opportunity for as complete an education as his tastes and abilities warranted."[2]

In 1862, the Morrill Act invested in the nation's future by dedicating revenue from the sale of public land to public higher education. The modern-day counterpart to the public land of Morrill's time is our increasingly valuable, publicly owned electromagnetic spectrum. The frequencies that transmit our familiar radio and television signals and an expanding new array of digital information to and from cell phones, computers, satellites, and new wireless devices are a public resource and a significant asset.[3]

Revenue from the sale of rights to use the spectrum, like revenue from the sale of public lands, can become an electronic land-grant gift to the nation—an investment in the future to support lifelong learning both inside and outside the classroom, in a wide variety of public pursuits. The beneficiaries would be the nation's citizens: its children, its young and middle-aged adults, its senior citizens and those who are physically challenged, its employed and unemployed, its poor, and its immigrants.

Today, we are in what Nobel laureate in economics Gary Becker has called, "the age of human capital," an age in which the nation's most valuable resource lies in the knowledge and skills of its citizens. "The essence of life in an information society," wrote political scientist Francis Fukuyama recently, "is the replacement of physical with mental labor." Thus, there is a clear need to expand the knowledge and skills of all Americans. The question is how that best can be accomplished. After thorough analysis, it has become evident that those institutions that have long served as the source of learning in this nation can also play that same role in the Information Age, provided they have access to the resources needed for such an effort. Therefore, we recommend the investment of the revenues from the auctions of the publicly owned electromagnetic spectrum in a multibillion-dollar national Digital Opportunity Investment Trust.

The Trust would serve an essential need, to stimulate the development of innovative projects and experiments in the use of advanced telecommunications technologies to promote formal and informal education and lifelong learning in the broadest sense. It would serve as America's venture capital fund for its vital nonprofit and public sectors. Its purpose would be to help school systems, universities, libraries, museums, and arts, cultural, and humanities organizations transform themselves for the digital and Internet age. Its focus would be on experimentation and the development of prototypes across the spectrum of public services. The Congressional Budget Office estimates that revenues from spectrum auctions over the next few years will be $18 billion. Prudently invested and managed, these revenues would give the Trust more than a billion dollars a year to invest.

Under the direction of a board of distinguished citizens from many backgrounds, fields, and disciplines, the Digital Opportunity Investment Trust could finance worthwhile new ideas, techniques, and technologies to encourage lifelong learning, to broaden knowledge, and to teach the skills essential for success in the Information Age. The Trust's board would set clear priorities and establish provisions for the accountability and review of the research it funds.

The Trust, which would be modeled on the National Science Foundation and the National Institutes of Health, would signal America's commitment to a new national strategy: to take advantage of dynamic new developments in digital telecommunications technology that can provide all Americans access to education in its broadest sense throughout their lives. A major priority of the Trust would be to encourage local and regional public service initiatives. It would work in concert with business, industry, philanthropy, and established public institutions and organizations, including the Library of Congress, the National Endowments for the Arts and Humanities, the National Association of State Universities and Land-Grant Colleges, the Smithsonian Institution, the Corporation for Public Broadcasting, and the Institute for Museum and Library Services, as well as comparable local institutions in communities throughout the nation. To borrow the words of Librarian of Congress James H. Billington, when referring to the Library of Congress's new center for scholars, "It will work in the way America does things best—not with a giant pre-fixed plan that you sit around and debate in the abstract, but by working on the human elements."[4]

Just as the National Science Foundation was established to guide the nation to a better future in the sciences and technology, the Digital Opportunity Investment Trust should guide our schools, universities, libraries, museums, civic organizations, and arts and cultural organizations in the use of advanced telecommunications and information technologies. It would not require building costly and elaborate new institutions or creating vast new bureaucracies. The nation already has a widespread and vigorous network of first-rate educational, civic, and cultural institutions and organizations that contain, in the words of Carnegie Corporation president Vartan Gregorian, "the DNA of our civilization." In the twenty-first century, however, these organizations and institutions all need help in reaching beyond their walls by using new digital telecommunications technologies to reach the nation's living rooms, classrooms, and workplaces. By doing so, they also can make available to the entire world the very best that American society has to offer.

The Trust would be a catalyst for major new partnerships and creative alliances within the nation's educational community and among museums and libraries, public broadcasters, government and nongovernmental entities, and nonprofit community organizations. It would finance research into new approaches to job training, skills training, and lifelong learning. It would stimulate innovation and experimentation in the area of teacher training, as well as offer new dimensions to preschool education, secondary school education, and higher education. The Trust also would seek out the most promising new technologies for disseminating civic and public health education, as well as services to people with disabilities. This report suggests a rich variety of specific educational, informational, and cultural initiatives and experiments—local, regional, and national— that the proposed Trust could support, many in partnership with companies and institutions in the private sector.

Fortunately, the information technologies that have already significantly improved commercial productivity and quality are capable of achieving similar improvements in the nonprofit worlds of education and the humanities. Market forces will continue to determine the commercial winners and losers in the new media order. But market forces alone cannot fulfill all the essential needs of our citizens for formal and informal education, lifelong learning, civic and political information, health information, and arts and culture. These are vitally important to the quality of our society, but they do not normally attract major investment from profit-seeking commercial interests. The Trust can do this efficiently and affordably.

As the bipartisan, congressional Web-Based Education Commission chaired by Senator Bob Kerrey of Nebraska found:

> For education, the Internet is making it possible for more individuals than ever to access knowledge and to learn in new and different ways. At the dawn of the 21st Century, the education landscape is changing. Elementary and secondary schools are experiencing growing enrollments, coping with critical shortages of teachers, facing overcrowded and decaying buildings, and responding to demands for higher standards. On college campuses, there is an influx of older, part-time students seeking the skills vital to success in an Information Age. Corporations are dealing with the shortage of skilled workers and the necessity of providing continuous training to their employees.
>
> The Internet is enabling us to address these educational challenges, bringing learning to students instead of bringing students to learning. It is allowing for the creation of learning communities that defy the constraints of time and distance as it provides access to knowledge that was once difficult to obtain. This is true in the schoolhouse, on the college campus, and in corporate training rooms.

The congressional commission concludes its report, "The Power of the Internet for Learning," with a call to action, to which we subscribe, to provide, among other things, continuous training for educators, new research into how people learn in the Internet Age, the development of high-quality online educational content, and the provision of sustained funding for these efforts. The report says:

> The commission believes a national mobilization is necessary, one that evokes a response similar in scope to other great American opportunities—or crises: Sputnik and the race to the moon; bringing electricity and phone service to all corners of the nation; finding a cure for polio.
>
> It is time we collectively move the power of the Internet for learning from promise to practice.[5]

In the 2000 U.S. presidential election, both major candidates made support of learning, teacher training, skills training, and improvement of the nation's educational standards the centerpiece of their campaigns. In 1999, when the states' governors listed the critical challenges they face, they rated education—lifelong learning, K–12 education, post-secondary education, and early-childhood development—as their number-one priority. The governors' first preference, as reported by the Kellogg Commission on the Future of State and Land-Grant Universities, was "to use technology to deliver more educational offerings" to citizens.

In the same report, the presidents and chancellors of the nation's state universities and land-grant institutions concluded:

> The concept of lifelong learning has been talked of before, but, for the first time, we now have the technological means to make it a reality. . . . [O]ur challenge in our emerging Information Age is two-fold. First, we must ensure that the remarkable growth in demand for education throughout the lifetime of virtually every citizen can be satisfied; second, we must demonstrate that we can meet this need at the highest level of quality imaginable, along with the greatest efficiency possible.[6]

HISTORICAL PRECEDENTS

The goal of education for all citizens has been a major recurring theme of American democracy. Public financing of primary schools had its roots in the 1787 Northwest Ordinance, which declared that "schools and the means of education shall forever be encouraged." Through that ordinance, the struggling young republic made a historic commitment to set aside public land to support public schools in every new state.

Then in the nineteenth century, the Land-Grant College Act revolutionized higher education by making it affordable to Americans who, until that time, could never dream of going to college. The farsighted legislation sponsored by Justin Morrill has left a remarkable educational legacy of 105 public institutions of higher learning, ranging from great research universities like the Massachusetts Institute of Technology, Cornell, the University of California, and Ohio State to small, pioneering two-year colleges like Little Hoop Community College and Bay Mills Community College. The act's successor legislation provided the funds that first enabled newly freed slaves and, later, Native Americans to go to college. It opened the door to higher education for women and for millions of the sons and daughters of working people, immigrants, and the poor, for whom college had never before been thought necessary. Today, America's land-grant educational institutions are among the greatest sources of advanced research in the world, a vital support in the national economy, and a key to the nation's global competitiveness.[7]

In the twentieth century, the GI Bill, passed by Congress during World War II, "made America into the best-educated country in the world," according to historian Stephen Ambrose.[8] It helped more than twenty million veterans attend college, creating incalculable financial and social benefits for the nation's working- and middle-class families and for American society as a whole. Tom Brokaw, in his best-selling book *The Greatest Generation*, calls it "a brilliant and enduring commitment to the nation's future."[9]

In 1952, the federal government made another landmark contribution to education—the reservation by the Federal Communications Commission of 242 channels of broadcast spectrum for noncommercial educational uses. Commissioner Frieda Hennock noted at the time that television could become "an electronic blackboard," "a teaching tool of rare power and persuasion," offering an "unprecedented opportunity for education."[10] Television, however, still has a long way to go to make that a reality. Now, as the medium moves into the digital age, we have the chance to do so at last. (See Part IV.) The conversion to digital technology allows, for the first time, full advantage to be taken of the spectrum reserved for educational purposes. Digital transmission has the potential to provide four or five times the number of public television channels each community now has, which will make possible the widespread delivery of a great variety of educational services. It also has the capacity to make television communicate interactively, like a computer, opening up outstanding possibilities for effective distance learning.

In the midst of the Civil War, the Morrill Act authorized the sale of the federal government's most valuable asset in the nineteenth century, public land, to fill the nation's critical need for widespread technical education that would help American farmers learn how to improve the quality of agriculture and workers to be trained in the new manufacturing trades. In the twenty-first century, the Digital Opportunity Investment Trust, using revenues from the sale of the public spectrum, could support educational innovations that would help today's workforce thrive in our information and services economy, thus improving productivity and maintaining America's preeminent status in an increasingly competitive world. It also could improve the quality of our society and our democracy through support of new initiatives in civic education, the humanities, services to those with special needs, and cultural enrichment.

THE ELECTROMAGNETIC SPECTRUM, A VALUABLE PUBLIC ASSET

Today, in addition to carrying radio and television signals, the spectrum serves a widening variety of valuable telecommunications purposes. Wireless telephony, satellite transmissions, handheld computers, and other wireless digital devices all need spectrum space to function. With the volume of Internet traffic doubling every one hundred days and with that traffic rapidly being made available also on cell phones and handheld computers, the nation's publicly owned spectrum space is now worth many billions of dollars. It is a rich natural resource, as much of an asset in the emerging Information Age as land has been to agriculture and oil and coal to industry.

In 1993, Congress directed the Federal Communications Commission to auction licenses for unused portions of the spectrum, and since that time those auctions have delivered $17 billion to the federal Treasury. As noted earlier, the Congressional Budget Office estimates that auctions of licenses for use of the public spectrum will yield another $18 billion over the next few years.

When such a new source of revenue becomes available, the issue is not only how much money the government will garner, but what will be done with it. A true story makes the point. In 1986, a Florida man named Stanley Newberg died and left $5.6 million in cash to the United States, in "deep gratitude for the privilege of residing and living in this kind of government."[11] Newberg had come to the United States in 1906 as a poor immigrant from Austria but had later succeeded in manufacturing and real estate. In 1994, after Newberg's will was settled, his bequest went directly to the U.S. Treasury, where it was spent in ninety seconds. Then it was gone, disappearing into the $1.5 trillion federal budget. Spectrum auction revenues also are scheduled to go to the Treasury, where, at current spending levels, $18 billion would last less than a week—and then it, too, would be gone.

The short life of Stanley Newberg's gift to his adopted country underscores how extraordinary and fleeting is the opportunity to earmark the spectrum auction revenues for public benefit. Why not make that money last a lifetime, several millions of them, by reinvesting it in an educational "land-grant of the airwaves," thus making it an invaluable asset for the nation's future?

HOW THE DIGITAL OPPORTUNITY INVESTMENT TRUST WOULD WORK

If the Trust were set up, every local, regional, and national institution dedicated to public purposes, as well as talented individuals with promising experimental and groundbreaking projects and ideas, would be eligible to apply for grants or contracts. The Trust's board of directors would set forth the specific standards, criteria, and priorities by which the funds would be awarded. Eligible parties among the institutional applicants would include, but not be limited to, schools; libraries; museums; public broadcasters; community and civic organizations; science and research institutions; institutions devoted to the arts, culture, and the humanities.

A major priority of the Trust would be to stimulate new initiatives for local educational, informational, and cultural collaborations and partnerships. Partnerships and alliances among local public service institutions, such as libraries, museums, and schools, would be encouraged, as well as partnerships and collaborations between public and private organizations and businesses, and between American and international institutions. The products and services that emerge from the Trust's grants and contracts would be available for the benefit of the largest possible number of people not only throughout the United States but also around the globe.

EXTENDING THE WORK OF THE TRUST FUND THROUGH MATCHING GRANTS

In setting criteria for its grants and contracts, the board of the Trust should follow the model of the Morrill Land-Grant College Act, which encouraged states to use their own funds to pay for the costs of building construction and upkeep of their public colleges. The Morrill Act's funds provided financial support largely for content—for instruction, research, personnel, books, and supplies—rather than for buildings and infrastructure. To stimulate local and community involvement, the Trust similarly should encourage, but not require, applicants to pursue financial collaborations with other public interest institutions and to make an effort to raise matching funds from others in the public and private sectors. To ensure that the Trust has a broad reach and general support, the nation's vast network of private foundations, as well as state governments, municipalities, individual citizens, and businesses, should be challenged to contribute matching funds that would extend its efforts and expand its reach.

THE CRITICAL IMPORTANCE OF OPEN ARCHITECTURE

The Trust would help ensure that much of what is most important on the Internet is kept open and readily accessible to all. Whatever the Trust supports should, generally speaking, be widely accessible and in the public domain of knowledge. As Cathy N. Davidson, vice provost for interdisciplinary studies at Duke University, says, "In recent years, scholarly societies and civil liberties groups have argued that the increasing breadth of intellectual property rights and the pressure to protect commercial content on the Internet put both research and speech at risk. Research science and the research university depend on a level of openness, in content and in network architecture, that the current trend endangers. Neither is likely to flourish in a 'pay-per-view' system."[12]

The importance of open source data and software also is emphasized by Thomas R. Martin, the Jeremiah O'Connor Professor in Classics
at the College of the Holy Cross. Not only should "data created by
[grants from the Trust] be freely available for nonexclusive use by anyone,
so, too, would the software code used to organize, present, and manipulate the data be available to anyone."[13]

A NONPARTISAN, FULLY ACCOUNTABLE PROTOTYPE

The National Science Foundation (NSF), which for fifty years has been
ably providing billions of dollars in grants and contracts to stimulate
advances in science and engineering, offers a useful model for the work
of the Trust. The NSF operates under the policy direction of a distinguished nonpartisan board, as should the Trust. Members of the
National Science Board are nominated by the president and confirmed by
the Senate, usually based on the recommendations of blue-ribbon panels of outstanding citizens. Like the National Science Board, the board
members of the Trust should have outstanding competence and experience and distinguished reputations in a wide variety of fields. The Trust's
board should have diverse backgrounds in education, civic affairs, the
arts and sciences, the social sciences, and humanities. In fact, it has been
suggested that the new Trust might operate as a partner agency with
the National Science Foundation, sharing a common administrative
structure.

Marion Fremont-Smith, a senior research fellow at Harvard's Hauser
Center for Nonprofit Organizations, recommends:

> In considering the size and scope of the Digital Opportunity
> Investment Trust and its broad educational goals, a quasi-
> governmental body appears to be the most appropriate form for
> its governance. Placing it within an existing governmental agency
> will limit its scope and ability to innovate; establishment as an
> independent entity would be unlikely to provide the confidence in
> its integrity that members of Congress will need before autho-
> rizing appropriations to it from the sale of federal assets. The
> model afforded by the National Science Foundation, providing
> independence while ensuring accountability to Congress and the
> administration, is well suited for the trust, and the distinguished
> record of the NSF makes it a particularly apt model to follow.[14]

When Congress passed the law creating NSF, it set forth its mission: "To promote the progress of science; to advance the national health, prosperity and welfare; and to secure the national defense." NSF does not conduct research or operate educational projects itself. It has compiled an enviable record as a "catalyst, seeking out and funding the best ideas and most capable people, making it possible to pursue new knowledge, discoveries, and innovation."[15] It is a mission that is perfectly in sync with that envisioned for the proposed Digital Opportunity Investment Trust.

NSF encourages cooperative efforts between public institutions and industry and funds U.S. participation in international scientific efforts. NSF funds education and training programs that benefit students from kindergarten through the postdoctoral level. It conducts research and education via grants, contracts, and cooperative agreements with non-profit institutions of all kinds, working with small businesses and other research institutions. Its grants and contracts are made after a thorough peer-review process. And every three years, independent panels of experts review each NSF program to judge whether the projects funded have succeeded in meeting the foundation's goals. NSF's experience in all these areas would be invaluable in enabling the proposed Digital Opportunity Investment Trust to get off to an effective and efficient start.

Fittingly, NSF was instrumental in administering and developing various uses of the Internet. It fosters networking research and research on advanced information telecommunications technologies. It partners with industry to provide newer and faster network services and allows commercial Internet service providers to have access. NSF managed the Internet network until 1995, then turned it over to the private sector. NSF already has played a key role in providing funds for technological support in helping the Library of Congress digitize those elements in its vast collections that would be most useful for education in school systems throughout the nation. And NSF has been charged with the primary responsibility for encouraging new directions in information technology. It will inevitably play an expanding role in furthering the lifelong learning opportunities the Trust would offer.

WIDENING DISTRIBUTION

The costs of transmission and distribution are rapidly decreasing, thanks to the Internet and other interactive technologies. Congress and the Federal Communications Commission have already recognized the extraordinary new educational opportunities this makes possible. The federal e-rate program has provided the funding to equip more than 90 percent of the nation's schools to gain access to the Internet. Eighty percent of Americans already subscribe to cable or satellite television. The majority of American homes have home computers and more are coming online every day. The digital divide that separates rich and poor, urban and rural, white and ethnic minority groups remains a major factor in this country and more so throughout the world. But the landscape is improving in the United States. The Department of Commerce's most recent report, "Falling Through the Net: Toward Digital Inclusion," released in fall 2000, shows that encouraging progress is being made.

For example, the number of Americans who own a computer or who have access to the Internet, whether from home or other places, has grown impressively. The increases can be seen across geographic regions, income, age, racial, and educational levels. For example, during the last six months of 2000, Internet use by adult Americans grew from about 88 million to more than 104 million, according to a new study released in February 2001 by the Pew Internet and American Life project.[16] Similarly, the number of homes that own computers has risen to 51 percent of the nation from 42.1 percent in December 1998. The gap in Internet use by males and females has all but disappeared.[17]

While still lagging behind other groups, Blacks and Hispanics have shown impressive gains. Black households are now more than twice as likely to have home access than they were twenty months ago, rising from 11.2 percent to 23.5 percent. Hispanic households have also experienced a tremendous growth rate during this period, rising from 12.6 percent to 23.6 percent.[18]

The Internet itself is being transformed through broadband connections into a high-speed, high-capacity transmitter of video, audio, and data. Down the road, the transition to digital broadcasting will enable television sets to function more like personal computers—even as personal computers, with their added features of streaming audio and video, are becoming more like television sets. In the era of digital radio and television, all citizens eventually will have the technological capacity to improve their lives and benefit from the new technologies, even those in the poorest, most remote households. The hardware is becoming increasingly available and affordable. Radio and television are already universally accessible. The urgent need now is for quality content, locally and nationwide, which is what the Trust will help develop.

II: The Need

Fulfilling the Critical Needs of an Information Economy

As the rate of technological change accelerates, creating new jobs and changing old jobs, people's skills must be constantly renewed to meet the demands of the workplace. The need is particularly acute in the critical area of information technology, where one recent study asserts there is a demand for 1.6 million new information technology workers in the United States alone. In fact, the demand for well-educated, highly skilled employees is growing rapidly throughout the economy. In the year 2000, 65 percent of the nation's jobs were classified as "skilled," up from 20 percent in 1950. In 1980, college graduates earned 50 percent more than high school graduates, an earnings gap that increased to 111 percent in 1998.[1]

We are in danger of creating two societies in America—the affluent educated and highly skilled and the poor unskilled. Overcoming that divide in a knowledge-based world is one of the nation's most important priorities. Federal Reserve chairman Alan Greenspan emphasized that point in a speech to the National Governors Association in the summer of 2000. He urged the nation's education system to do more to prepare students for the explosion in information technology. He stressed the need for educational improvement and reform, especially in teaching students how to make use of the new technologies.

As the National Endowment for the Humanities report on "Teaching and Lifelong Learning" concluded, "This is truly an exciting time to be part of education reform. It is a time when more than one-fourth of the population, approximately 72.1 million people, are enrolled in regular schools—nursery through college. It is a time of transition, experimentation, new tools, new players, new partnerships, and, perhaps most important, a recognition by the public that the future of the country lies in the excellence of its schools and colleges."[2]

As people of all ages seek new learning opportunities throughout their lives, the surge of powerful new information technologies is making more porous the boundaries that separate our most important and enduring public service institutions—our schools, community colleges, universities, libraries, museums, cultural and scientific centers, public broadcasting stations, and nonprofit community and civic organizations. The proposed Digital Opportunity Investment Trust will make funds available for worthwhile collaborations and alliances for education, information, science, and the arts, just as the National Science Foundation and the National Institutes of Health have been doing so effectively in their fields. The multibillion-dollar assets of the proposed Trust will help local, regional, and national public service institutions create innovative learning environments designed to harness the power of interactive telecommunications technology to produce an educated, well-informed, economically competitive twenty-first-century nation.

The Trust will finance research, development, and production of new online curricula, courses, training materials, digitized archives, educational and informational software, and arts and cultural content of excellence that use the most appropriate forms of technology for all levels of learning in all communities. It will stimulate learning opportunities that prepare people to lead and participate in our democratic society. It will be responsive to the pressing local needs for quality information and to the burgeoning demands for educational credentials and professional and vocational skills.

- In this new century, younger workers need ongoing training to stay competitive in an economy that sees more than half of all capital investment going into technology. Older workers will need the latest skills to remain productive earners long after their traditional retirement age. The thirty-five to fifty-four age group, the traditional core of the nation's workforce, is expected to decrease while the number of Americans over sixty-five will expand by 80 percent. Many older people are preparing for second or third careers, a trend that is expected to accelerate with the continued shift to an information- and service-based economy. Students over the age of fifty constitute the fastest-growing segment of those in public institutions of higher learning.[3]

- The process of globalization requires constant adjustments and makes this country more vulnerable to world competition. U.S. students now rank last among the top fifty industrialized nations in knowledge of physics and next-to-last in math. Almost a quarter of American children in their last year of high school are functionally illiterate. American pupils start off as good as any in the world, but by the time they are seventeen or eighteen they have fallen far behind those in other developed nations. Students need access to world-class educational resources online to improve their literacy and mastery of basic learning. And preschoolers, especially in poor communities, need additional educational experiences to keep from falling behind.

- While most public elementary and secondary school teachers and administrators believe information technology is an important tool for transforming education, two-thirds of the nation's teachers feel unprepared to use technology in their classrooms. Developing far-reaching new techniques for teacher training is a critical priority.

- Bachelor's degrees still elude large numbers of minority and lower-income Americans. One-quarter of white students who enter kindergarten will earn a bachelor's degree, compared to 12 percent of African-American and 10 percent of Latino students. When examined by income, the educational differences are even more startling: By age twenty-four, 48 percent of men and women from high-income families have been graduated from college, compared to 7 percent of adults from low-income families. The Trust should finance the development of distance learning models that would give low-income adults of all ages easier access to higher education.[4]

- Of even more concern, 40 percent or more of the adult labor force perform at the two lowest levels of literacy, making it impossible for them to carry out the tasks necessary to get and keep good jobs in our increasingly information-based economy. Less than 5 percent of the U.S. labor force score at the highest level of literacy proficiency, according to the National Council of Education Statistics. The development of online literacy programs that take advantage of the new digital technologies should be among the Trust's highest priorities.

- A recent report of the National Research Council, an arm of the National Academy of Science, confirms that foreign workers are needed to help companies in the United States fill vacant technical jobs. In October, Congress voted nearly to double the number of visas for foreign high-tech workers in order to help companies meet their demand for skilled computer programmers and engineers. In addition, as Congress has learned from testimony by the secretary of defense and joint chiefs of staff, we even have a critical need for highly trained foreign technologists to service our own armed force's high-tech weapons and equipment. We urgently need to provide continual skills training for American high-tech workers.

The need, especially in science, math, engineering, and technology, was most clearly stated in a recent "Call for Research and Development in Educational Sciences and Technologies" by Henry Kelly, president of the Federation of American Scientists:

> Full participation in the 21st century economy and culture depends on the widespread availability of quality education, yet too many risk being shut out from educational opportunity. The gap separating the need for education and our collective ability to meet these needs through traditional instructional methods continues to widen. The United States faces a shortage of qualified knowledge workers in all sectors, but especially in science, math, engineering, and technology (SMET). Just in information technologies alone, estimates of the serious shortfall ranged from 1 to 1.6 million qualified workers for the year 2000. Companies face increasing problems in hiring new workers with adequate skills (only 7 percent of seventeen year olds can solve routine problems involving fractions and percents), and it is estimated that 50 percent of all employees' skills become outdated within three to five years. This gap means not only that many people worldwide cannot enjoy the benefits of economic growth; it also threatens the foundations of technology-driven growth itself.
>
> Advances in computers, communication, and other information technology make it possible to significantly increase learning rates for a diverse population of people with widely varying backgrounds, learning styles, and interests. Enlightened use of the new technologies permits a dramatically different approach to learning that fosters and promotes deep and complex understanding. Tomorrow's technologies will provide us with even greater abilities to create new immersive learning

environments that allow learning by doing. These new learning environments will be created over distributed networks and will typically involve model-based simulations, both of physical phenomena and of social interactions. New learning communities could link students, teachers, coaches, and subject-area experts, making learning more compelling, and more relevant, to the interests of teachers, employers, and the learners.

Yet today, most educational uses of computers are limited to re-purposing existing materials and lecture-based teaching techniques, e.g. "publishing" texts, class notes, and videotaped lectures on the web, and adding e-mail and real-time chat rooms. Without additional investment in much-needed research and development, the Net will be little more than hypertext versions of existing material.

A long-term, stable, and large-scale investment in learning science and technology research is needed to help transform education and dramatically improve the educational process and therefore the quality and quantity of educated, skilled workers. To advance the field of education, numerous long-term experiments and project evaluations are essential. However, the proportion of funds spent on basic research exploring the use of new technologies for education is far smaller than any major service or manufacturing enterprise. Billions are being spent on computers and Internet connections for educational institutions, yet startlingly little is being spent to discover how to maximize use of the new information and communication tools and to evaluate their impact on different kinds of students in realistic settings. The cost of missed opportunity is large and international in scope. We can and must do better.[5]

The Trust is not, of course, a panacea in these areas, but it can make a powerful, much-needed contribution to experimentation and also can foster breakthroughs.

III: THE NEW LANDSCAPE FOR LIFELONG LEARNING

FACING "A TECTONIC SHIFT" IN EDUCATION

The rise of the Internet and the convergence of computers, television, radio, satellites, telephone, and wireless are causing "a tectonic shift in academia," Harvard University president Neil Rudenstine said recently.[1] In April 2000, the evaluation of the GI Bill that was submitted to Congress addressed the educational challenges of the new millennium. It concluded that "traditional classroom-based teaching is being augmented and/or replaced with interactive distance learning both within and outside of traditional educational institutions. The bricks and mortar of today's academia will surely evolve into the clicks and mortar of combined traditional and distance learning and may evolve further." The report recommended that any continuation of the GI Bill "should reflect the technology of the next millennium."[2]

The same principle holds true for the education of the nation's children. In the words of a recent *Business Week* special report on "Wired Schools":

> Most of America's 53 million children in kindergarten through 12th grade still attend schools designed for the industrial, if not the agrarian, era. Everything from the school calendar, which still reflects the rhythms of farm life, to chalk-and-textbook instruction are better suited to preparing kids for the past than the future. But from Union City [N.J.] to the suburbs of Silicon Valley and the hollows of West Virginia, dozens of state-of-the-art schools have used technology as a catalyst to reinvent themselves in many ways, creating the blueprint for a new type of

American school . . . schools for the New Economy. . . . [T]he same technologies that have forced corporations to remake themselves for e-commerce hold the potential to similarly transform U.S. education. . . .

[A] decade or so ago, "we had the same controversy about whether the computer would transform work, and critics argued all those investments were a waste," recalls Harvard Business School Professor Rosabeth Moss Kanter. Today, with the New Economy shredding old assumptions about productivity and growth, "it's hard to imagine anyone continuing to say this."[3]

Not only is the digital revolution fundamentally changing how our schools and universities will operate, it is also changing the very nature of the work of our libraries, museums, community institutions, arts and cultural centers, public broadcast stations, and virtually all public service enterprises in every state and every community. "Never before have museums, libraries, and the whole of the non-formal sector of educational institutions faced such challenges and opportunities," said the acting director of the Institute for Museum and Library Services, Beverly Sheppard.[4] No longer confined by bricks and mortar, the nation's public institutions can create new learning environments by moving outside their walls and into homes, schools, and workplaces.

The United States has made a major investment in its public and private noncommercial institutions that stand in every region and virtually every sizable community in the nation. They constitute a treasured part of our life, culture, and heritage. Low-power educational channels programmed by Stanford University and the University of California, San Diego, for example, televise lectures from local museums, performances from regional groups, discussion panels, and dialogues on local history and regional public affairs. They provide health information and education, career information, and science and technology news of special relevance to the regions they serve. The commercial world can turn to venture capital funds in order to exploit the new digital technologies. The nation's public and private noncommercial institutions, on the other hand, need a public service venture capital fund to be able to experiment with new ideas, new initiatives, and new services to their communities. The Internet and other information technologies should serve a higher purpose than simply disseminating information or fueling commerce.

America should harness the new technologies to promote its ideals and aspirations in universal education, enlightened self-government, the humanities, and the arts and culture.

EXPLOITING THE EDUCATIONAL POTENTIAL OF NEW INFORMATION TECHNOLOGIES

The Internet, the rise of virtual schools and universities, and the constant introduction of new communications technologies are generating radical changes in the ways that information is transmitted. Technically, it is now just as easy to deliver instruction on environmental protection and sound health practices to Alaska and Hawaii as it is to provide agricultural extension advice to local farmers in Illinois and Nebraska. Many of our long-standing concepts and ideas about disseminating information and education have become obsolete. Access must be broadened and a wide variety of teaching and learning opportunities made available, from traditional in-school and on-campus instruction to Internet and distance-learning-based educational efforts.

Recently, the *New York Times* reported one example of exactly how effectively new information technology can enhance teaching:

> Last year . . . second graders at the Boeckman Creek Elementary School in West Wilsonville, Ore., went to Mars. For a unit on the solar system, the students first went to the NASA Web site to study the Mars Sojourner. Working in teams, the children built a model of the Mars environment and a computerized robot replica of the Sojourner.
>
> The models were then hooked up to a video camera, and the students moved their modules to mimic the scientists' experience of controlling the space module from Earth. The exercise brought the solar system to life for the young students, who took to referring to themselves as "scientists" at the family dinner table. Many continued to do research about astronomy on the Web throughout the year, sharing their findings with their teacher.[5]

As *Business Week* reported, "new 'digital learning environments' will be geared toward such vital New Economy skills as rapidly finding

and assessing information and working in teams to solve problems. . . .
Teacher quality is even more important to student success."[6] Traditionally,
teachers have been isolated in closed classrooms. But the magazine cited
the new experience of English teacher Nora Dotson at Sherman Junior
High School in Seth, West Virginia, "a poverty-ridden backwater in the
region's coal country." Like most teachers, Ms. Dotson said, "I had to do
all my lesson plans by myself." Then, according to *Business Week:*

> [She] got involved in a . . . project to develop lessons online with
> 11 other English teachers from around the state. She drafted a
> three-week literature unit, online colleagues suggested changes,
> and they tested the plan before submitting it to a jury of master
> teachers. The final product was posted on the Web, where it and
> others like it are expected to be used by thousands of teachers
> statewide. . . . "Now, I have access to the best practices of other
> teachers," says Dotson. "And I have grown enormously."[7]

Already schools in Kentucky, New Mexico, Washington, Wisconsin,
Utah, and Texas that are unable to afford to offer advanced placement
courses are providing them online, outside the classroom, extending
access to students who otherwise would not have been able to take them.
"When you have a course online, you offer students options," said Gaye
Lange, project manager for the Houston Independent School District's
Virtual School program. "You can't have a class with five kids in it. It's
not cost effective. . . . Now we can do it without all the hassle that goes
with it." That is the sort of vitally important educational model, of particular value to the nation's poorest communities, that the proposed
Digital Opportunity Investment Trust will help develop.[8]

Mary Walshok, associate vice chancellor of the University of
California, San Diego, notes that "this new knowledge-based economy
represents an incredible opportunity to build a communications system to
serve the public that is simultaneously rich in local culture, information,
and civic affairs and still connected to globally significant intellectual
and cultural resources." UCSD, she said, is "poised to move into new
forms of communication at the regional level. The only thing limiting
taking the next steps is budget. . . . Television stations . . . could be much
more active producers of enrichment programming that would feed into
the schools and include interactivity in the form of young students asking
questions of experts or performers located on a university campus, in a
museum, or in a library."[9]

DOING WHAT THE MARKETPLACE CANNOT

The business world market has moved with unprecedented creativity, speed, and zeal to exploit the extraordinary commercial opportunities of the new information technologies. As a nation, however, we have yet to focus on what new public policies and financing are needed to enable our not-for-profit public sector to embrace new digital broadband technologies.

Today, our vital educational, civic, and cultural institutions lag behind the private sector in effectively using the new telecommunications technologies. Ironically, as Harvard's Susan Rogers reminds us, it was at these public institutions that the Internet itself was first developed and introduced. Now we need to enable these institutions to exploit other advanced information technologies to serve the public interest. The proposed Trust would help make that possible.[10]

Professor Martin points out:

> It is urgent to act now and to act decisively . . . so the United States will not be left behind in determining what digital information will be created to provide the knowledge capital . . . on which our future prosperity, stability, and democratic values will depend. The world is already at work, and we should be, too. . . . [T]he British government is reportedly planning to spend 170 million pounds on what they are calling the "People's Network." The plan is to install Internet stations as "learning centers" in 4,000 public libraries, with every central library to have at least thirty machines and every branch library at least six. Approximately 60 percent of the money will be spent on infrastructure . . . but, significantly, 30 percent is designated for content creation and 10 percent for training librarians to help the public. . . . Britain is also starting a national "e-university" to serve students in the United Kingdom, especially those who currently do not go on to higher education, as well as students abroad willing to do online courses in English.[11]

PROVIDING MODELS FOR FUTURE DEVELOPMENT

The Trust can serve as a powerful engine for progress by providing information technology models designed for use in remote communities. A good example of the kind of prototype the Trust could adapt for local community use is the Library of Congress's National Digital Library Program. Begun in 1994 with financial support from Congress and private organizations, the program has so far digitized 5 million of the 119 million items in the Library's collection. The digitized works of original archival material are available to the public on the Library's American Memory Website, which receives about 4 million hits per day, most of them from schoolchildren who are able to view items as varied as President Washington's letters, Lewis and Clark's expedition map, suffragist pamphlets, and classic baseball cards. In connection with the project, the Library also operates a fellows program that trains selected elementary and secondary school teachers to use primary research materials and to become master teachers who will train others in their communities and school districts. And yet, as successful as the American Memory project has been, it, like so many public institutions in local communities, still struggles for funding.

The Smithsonian Institution has initiated several distance learning programs that demonstrate the extraordinary potential technology-based educational programs have for enhancing learning and broadening knowledge at all levels and in all communities. For example, the Smithsonian Astrophysical Observatory's MicroObservatory Network of automated telescopes is a unique national resource that provides free access to classroom teachers who wish their students to conduct projects over the web. The network's telescopes make it easy for even ten-year-olds to explore and take pictures of the heavens because the telescopes can be remotely pointed and focused, and filters, field of view, and exposure times can be changed easily. Images are then archived at the website, along with sample challenges and a user bulletin board, all of which encourage collaboration among schools across the nation. The wide geographic separation of instruments (Boston to Australia) provides for access to distant night skies during the day in each locale using the network. The network could be scaled up from its present capacity of 240,000 images each year to one-hundred telescopes, which could provide telescope access for every student in U.S. schools.

In addition, the Smithsonian American Art Museum has an interactive distance learning program that supports the use of museum resources by K–12 students and educators through teacher-developed, activity-based curricular units. The program has featured collaborative partnerships with school systems in Texas, Nebraska, and Ohio. The results include creation of an online Webzine featuring the museum's Latino art, production of web pages in the museum's virtual exhibits designed for the K–12 community, and a major role in the nation's first online K–12 academic conference. The museum is currently creating a virtual community where docents will offer online tours and, in partnership with four school districts in Ohio, will offer similar tours via videoconference.

Sheila Burke, the Smithsonian's under secretary for American Museums and National Programs, endorses the need for the Trust as a means "to encourage the development of exemplary technology-based educational programs."[12]

The National Park Service has similar information technology ambitions and is experiencing much the same kind of gap in fulfilling them as the Library of Congress. The Park Service holds more than 71 million accessioned and backlog items, including nearly 36 million archival documents and more than 35 million museum items in more than three hundred parks. Yet today, the National Park Service's Museum Management Program has fewer than five hundred items in digital form.[13] The Park Service has Ansel Adams's photographs of Yosemite, Thomas Edison's laboratory notebooks and personal papers, archeological collections documenting all of American history, exceptional American military history materials, and the letters and diaries of many major American writers and poets, presidents, explorers, and artists. If these were digitized, students could take virtual tours of the parks, laboratories, archeological sites, battlefields, homes and studios of artists and writers, and so much more. The department needs funds to enhance the availability of its impressive cultural and historical resources and treasures for the benefit of distant schools and those who cannot visit its outstanding museums and parks. The Trust could serve as a catalyst in helping even national institutions like the National Park Service develop the techniques to carry through their ambitious plans.

In this digital and Internet age, the information technology needs are, if possible, even greater for the local and regional civic, educational, and cultural activities of public libraries, museums, school systems, community colleges, universities, public broadcasting stations, arts organizations, community groups, and those who serve the millions of people with learning disabilities. Like the Library of Congress and the National Park Service, these local centers seek to digitize their collections and make them freely accessible to the public on the web. As our digitized collections amass, we are building a national treasure, one that the Trust could help coordinate and develop, and then play a role in making available to all who have access to a computer and the Internet.

Martín Gómez, executive director of the Brooklyn Public Library, warns:

not building the technical infrastructure to support access to these online digital information resources is the kiss of death for libraries in the twenty-first century. . . . Slowly but steadily librarians have begun to transform themselves into public navigators in cyberspace, often providing low- and moderate-income communities with their first instruction in and ticket to cyberspace. In Brooklyn alone, for example, information seekers who visited the public library last year completed over one million public Internet sessions. Nearly 1,600 Brooklyn residents surfed the Internet for the first time by attending our "Internet for Families" instructional programs. Thousands of residents accessed our online databases and subscriptions remotely, from home, office, or on the road, simply by entering their library card number. No other free public institution in New York City can claim the ability to provide access to over fifty databases, including online subscriptions to literally thousands of magazines, twenty-four hours a day, seven days a week! All of these services, like our book-lending program, are provided free of charge. . . .

The only thing holding us back is supportive public policy and adequate public funding. . . . Libraries and librarians must play a critical and necessary role to ensure that people know how to use the networks, can identify qualitative sources of information on the networks, and have access to new learning environments that bring local as well as global institutions together.[14]

CREATING NEW LEARNING ENVIRONMENTS

In the new century, as the recent Kellogg Commission on the Future of State and College Land-Grant Universities pointed out, learning environments must reach beyond the school walls and directly into the home and workplace. Continuous learning for working adults requires technologies that support alternative delivery of educational programs.[15] It also requires flexibility—programs available at the times needed and programs that meet the demands of today's users. Distance education requires that skills and formats be developed to link teacher and students in different geographic locations by means of interactive technologies.

Asynchronous education requires a setting in which teachers and students can move at their own pace at times convenient to learners. As the president's Committee of Advisers in Science and Technology has urged, what is needed is research, experimentation, and pilot projects to develop new environments for learning.

The information technologies that are greatly improving the quality of products and services elsewhere in the economy can fuel a similar revolution in public services. New information tools make it practical to implement many of the insights that have been developed during recent years about the ways people learn most efficiently. Technology can, for example, make it possible for large numbers of students to learn by doing, learn in teams, learn from mistakes, learn by discovery, learn by example, learn through personal tutors, learn through interactive collaboration, and learn through simulation-based explorations. These approaches can make learning more productive and more engaging for all students, including those with special needs, and at the same time tailor instruction to an individual's interests and abilities. Because the science and technology of learning are seriously underfunded, these benefits will be captured far more slowly than our nation can afford. Less than 0.5 percent of the nation's spending on K–12 students goes into education research. Measured as a fraction of the United States' $880 billion spent per year on education, computer chip manufacturers spend two hundred times as much on R&D, and potato chip manufacturers spend twenty times as much. The proposed Trust would help diminish that research imbalance.

"In the Information Age, a new audience—with no direct ties to the university—has tacitly been assumed to be part of the community that a university serves," according to Cathy N. Davidson, who also notes:

> Through public websites, online library resources, and, in more and more cases, courses offered completely on the web (distance learning), the ripple effect of basic research extends even further, to a worldwide community of nonacademic distance learners and lifelong learners. . . .
>
> In the past decade, research universities have absorbed tremendous expenses in both equipment and staffing in order to keep apace with the dizzying changes in all areas of computing, from instructional technology (such as wired and wireless classrooms) to high-speed research computing. . . . Who pays for these additional costs in hardware, software, development, implementation, and technical support staffing? Who devotes

time to making these technologies operational? If faculty are diverted from their core effort of doing research and communicating that research to their students and colleagues, who will be left at the center of the knowledge cycle to do the basic research that ripples outward to many other public educational enterprises?[16]

Both UCSD's Walshok and Duke's Davidson offer a long list of specific and innovative educational, informational, and cultural projects that their universities are ready to undertake, given available resources and qualified personnel. Like-minded institutions throughout the nation have similar ambitions.

The Field Museum in Chicago, for example, according to its president, John McCarter:

> is engaged in researching, experimenting, piloting and assessing applications of new learning technologies that bring out scientists, collections, and scientific research from behind their walls. Over the past two years, the museum has offered "e-field trips," which are multimedia learning adventures that invite K–12th grade teachers and students to join an expedition team exploring the working science of the museum. They visit behind-the-scenes in the museum's research facilities and field sites, interact with its scientists, and work with its collections. In the course of a single school year, students joined a dinosaur dig in Grand Junction, Colorado, participated in environmental science research at the museum's Swallow Cliff research site outside of Chicago, and asked questions of leading Dead Sea Scroll experts as they studied the scrolls in the museum's exhibition. With the Field Museum's focus on maximizing access, it leverages a variety of distribution channels—public TV and radio stations, Webcasts, satellite broadcasts, distance learning networks, and VCR tapes—to ensure that teachers can access its resources regardless of their technology resources or training.
>
> Even leveraging partnerships, it is very expensive for us to pilot e-learning initiatives and then to support and expand models that are proven effective. . . . Although we appreciate the great promise that technology holds, we know first-hand the investment it requires to develop the content that leads to learning outcomes. There are substantial costs associated with the

creation of new learning environments, the development of better assessments to determine the impact of our models, and the communication of these successes to those who can benefit from them.[17]

The role of the Trust would be to support innovation by seeding pilot projects that look promising and then sharing the results with stakeholders throughout the country and the globe.

The good news is that the United States already has in place its own vast networks of public and private not-for-profit educational, informational, and cultural institutions to serve every community. It is essential to give these institutions, as well as talented individuals in communities everywhere, the resources they need to help them do their research, explore new ideas and approaches, and carry out their high public purposes in the digital age. In partnership with businesses, foundations, and others, digital learning centers can be established at universities, museums, libraries, and public television stations to develop and build effective new educational tools.

Henry C. Kelly, president of the Federation of American Scientists, offers graphic examples of how that can be done:

> Computer simulations can let you see a heart beat, look inside to see fluids flowing, and find out what happens when things go wrong. Instead of reading about how the heart works and seeing diagrams on a page, these dynamic tools open extraordinary new possibilities in learning. They bring up-to-date ancient learning techniques based on apprenticeship, problem solving, and mentoring. Imagine developing a digital human model. The human body is the most complex machine we know, and the most fascinating. Mechanical, electrical, fluid, and chemical communications operate at scales from the molecular to gross anatomy. The body has information systems, energy systems, and manufacturing systems. Most of what we know about these systems can be represented in clear visual ways, but doing this requires an unprecedented investment in developing a functioning model—tools more complex than those used to build the Boeing 777. Once built, however, the system could be used to help students from grade school to medical school; help physicians explain procedures to their patients, and serve as a tool for research.

The Digital Opportunity Investment Trust would play a pivotal role as a catalyst in developing such research tools.

Kelly also suggests building interactive simulations of important cities at different periods in their history to understand urban development and needs. He proposes simulating the operation of the most powerful telescopes with online access to databases, to enable students to experience what it feels like to travel on the surfaces of the moon, Mars, and other well-mapped objects. It also would be possible, he says, "just to observe the phenomena of the sky that have been so influential in human culture, but which are mostly 'dead metaphors' to young Americans who see the sky through the thick haze of pollution and city lights. Youngsters could grasp the significance of the solstices, the mystery of the 'wandering stars,' fleet Mercury and sluggish Saturn." Kelly adds that simulation tools

> can let students block their own theatrical performances with avatars speaking lines and moving through virtual sets, or dancers moving through routines. Such new age tools can let students play the world's instruments and hear the results; can make links between the music and science of the instruments and the mathematics of musical notation. Such techniques make learning vastly compelling because each student can make full use of his or her senses. The simulations cross the barrier between abstract representation of concepts in text and numbers and the real world these abstractions seek to describe.[18]

THE SPECIAL NEED FOR CHILDREN'S EDUCATIONAL SERVICES

Children's media specialist Rita Weisskoff reports that 25 million U.S. children age two to seventeen now log onto the Internet, three times the number who were online in 1997. "[F]or some children the computer is competing successfully with TV for their time," she points out. However, "the availability of new technologies does not eradicate the need for educational programming on broadcast television since lower-income children are less likely to have access to these alternative technologies. Even as the interactive media proliferate, we need to understand the importance of television in the mix and continue to find ways to exploit its unique power to support children's learning."[19]

One example of the use of television to support children's learning is "Between the Lions," produced by WGBH in Boston, which teaches early reading skills to preschoolers, kindergartners, and first and second graders. It is the only series on commercial or public television that teaches reading. With the station's outreach partners, it has sent program information to 240,000 first-grade teachers, mailed 40,000 teachers' guides, worked with libraries, held training sessions for 3,000 parents so far, and designed a highly successful website that attracts 4,000,000 visitors per month.[20] The nation needs many more such projects.

For children of middle-school age (nine-fourteen), a group at Caltech, the Caltech Pre-College Initiative (CAPSI), in partnership with Numedeon, Inc., an Internet technology company, has developed an imaginative, interactive, "inquiry-based" educational environment called Whyville.net. Their ambition is to construct a Whyville public television series that will be fully integrated into the education website. With support from the National Aeronautics and Space Agency, they are establishing a site to help children learn Newton's laws by designing rockets and planning a mission to Mars. In partnership with zoos in New England and Los Angeles, they are building a virtual zoo for the protection of endangered species. And in partnership with the Los Angeles Arboretum, the Smithsonian Institution, and Duke University, they are designing a participatory botany segment for young visitors to Whyville. These are the kinds of creative joint efforts and alliances, tied to school curricula and using new technologies, that can significantly enrich the educational landscape for students as well as teachers.

As NSF assistant director Ruzena Bajcsy, in charge of the National Science Foundation's programs in Information Technology and Computers, points out, "Students can learn by following either prescribed instructions or by observing experts' performances using computers and information technology. The advantage here is that the students' mistakes can be immediately corrected. They can ask questions, can discuss and argue, can repeat the experience many more times until they achieve understanding, and can be evaluated on the spot."[21]

NEW ARTS AND CULTURAL EDUCATIONAL INITIATIVES

Wayne Ashley, manager of new media for the Brooklyn Academy of Music, offers other intriguing examples of how local arts and cultural centers like his need support from a source like the Digital Opportunity

Investment Trust to participate in the expansive world of new telecommunications technology:

> [H]igh school students in a suburban area of Illinois and students from rural West Virginia could join Manhattan inner-city students from Martin Luther King Jr. High School in BAM's latest film program, *Screening Prejudice.* After viewing the same American films dealing with the theme of prejudice and race relations in twentieth century America, video conferencing would allow students from spatially dispersed areas to participate in panel discussions with leading commentators from such diverse fields as sociology, history, cinema, journalism, and psychology. At BAM, film critic J. Hoberman, directors Spike Lee and Melvin van Peebles, actor Sidney Poitier, attorney Elizabeth Holtzman, and professor of history and political science Manning Marable would use the films to engage the networked students in probing discussions about the historical and shifting attitudes toward prejudice, stereotyping, and racial interactions. Students would be invited to ask questions and debate issues with their geographically dispersed counterparts.[22]

John Goberman, executive producer for television at Lincoln Center, reflects on the important arts and cultural opportunities reaching far beyond the Center itself that even his relatively prosperous institution cannot take advantage of:

> Obviously, choices must be made, and our philanthropic resources are quite rightly directed at putting operas, ballets, and concerts on the stage, with all else secondary. Of necessity, some important opportunities are necessarily forgone. For example, the extraordinary wealth of material already amassed in our video archives, when combined with the wide-ranging written expertise of program notes from one hundred years of performances, plus the easy availability to us of great artists and teachers, is an exciting and certain basis for the richest website for the performing arts imaginable. Why don't we start tomorrow? Because there is no way to pay for it. What are the costs? First of all, for a website to live, it must be constantly tended and updated—it must keep growing. It cannot be funded by a one-time philanthropic gesture. There must be a regular source of income, most of which . . . will not come from the users of the website and not from corporate sponsors. . . .

Assuming broadband capacity, the Internet offers . . . an ability to offer samples, to try new things without a serious risk of time or money. New music, dance, performers, and so forth made available on a website allows those who are interested to try the new and the talked about.[23]

Maxwell L. Anderson, director of the Whitney Museum, focuses on the exceptional educational potential of the new technologies for the museum world. He describes the new online Art Museum Network (AMN), which he founded and serves as executive producer of, as "the Internet/broadcast arm of the Association of Art Museum Directors." The official website of more than two hundred of the world's leading art museums, including the Metropolitan Museum of Art and the British Museum, AMN is "an essential tool for educational advancement." It is designed "to enrich the educational potential of museums considerably, for the benefit of students and life-long learners alike. . . . AMN is also committed to furthering the educational goals of art museums by promoting distance learning efforts . . . through the combined efforts of education and new media departments across the continent and eventually around the globe."[24] The opportunities for arts and cultural enrichment throughout the nation by means of the imaginative uses of new digital technology are legion.

EDUCATION TO ENHANCE DEMOCRACY AND CIVIC PARTICIPATION

Richard Kimball, president of Project Vote Smart, stresses the unprecedented opportunity to reach out to citizens with civic information and voter education through the new technologies of the Information Age. "[W]e somehow must ensure the people's access to independent, abundant, accurate information about those who govern or those who wish to replace those that do. A loss of that key to our political stability—voter education—is a loss of all we depend upon in our democratic society." Project Vote Smart researches the background and positions of political candidates and issues from local city races through the presidency and puts the information on the Internet for all to have access. "[It] is a library of factual information covering biographical data, voting records, campaign finances, and candidate performance evaluations done by a variety of special interest organizations on over 48,000 holders and seekers of public office in every state of the union."

"The citizens and the young care very deeply. . . . Voters want untainted information," Kimball says. Millions of Americans, from students and schoolteachers to journalists and librarians, use Project Vote Smart regularly, he points out, more than a million a day during the 2000 election campaign. The dilemma is:

> [T]he vast majority of citizens (94 percent) have no idea that Project Vote Smart exists, even though it was unanimously selected by the American Political Science Association as the best political website in existence, and government and news organizations almost universally refer to the project as the ultimate source for accurate, comprehensive information on elected officials and political candidates. We do not have the resources to continue some of our data base collection, and we certainly lack the resources . . . to make the general public aware of the service and its uniqueness.

Many of the Project's most useful online efforts to extend civic information to all—through its K–12 Program, Inclusion Program for Minorities, Youth Inclusion Program, publications for teachers and new immigrants, and publications in a half-dozen different languages—are being cut back or abandoned for lack of ongoing funding. Kimball concludes, "The single most important fight, the one that must be won every single time, is the fight for an educated citizenry. A people that cannot win the battle to maintain their access to independent, abundant, accurate information cannot expect to remain their own governors."[25]

Mark Lloyd, executive director of the Civil Rights Forum on Communications Policy, makes a similar point about the extraordinary potential of information technology to restore and enhance local civic participation and the public's engagement in democracy's affairs:

> Community groups often are unheralded incubators . . . informing the practices and policies of government and business. . . . To the extent that our means of communication with each other and with policymakers requires money . . . democracy is poorer because community groups usually do not have the funds to participate effectively in the "marketplace of ideas. . . ." [We should recognize] that our democracy would be strengthened by protecting and promoting the communications capacity of community groups.[26]

IV: A NEW ROLE FOR PUBLIC BROADCASTING

A KEY PLAYER IN THE INFORMATION TECHNOLOGY ALLIANCE

In the digital world, the nation's multibillion-dollar investment in public broadcasting will yield major dividends. Public broadcast stations, in partnerships with schools, colleges and universities, libraries, museums, and cultural and community institutions, will help develop and distribute to every community the products and services of the Digital Opportunity Investment Trust. Public stations, when converted to digital transmission and production, will greatly expand their capacity as conduits to the people. They will serve as a public freeway on the information superhighway, distributing to homes, schools, workplaces, nursing homes, hospitals, and even prisons many of the innovative products, programs, and services made possible by the Trust. With the help of the Trust's financial support for experimentation and technical innovation in producing content, public stations in many communities can share their production expertise as well as their facilities with other public interest institutions. The nation's public telecommunications system can act as a giant megaphone for each community's schools, libraries, museums, and other nonprofit public and private organizations and institutions.

All public television stations, like all commercial television stations, are required by law to convert to digital transmission and program production within the next few years. The public stations historically have been leaders in developing new technologies for education and public service. From satellite delivery of broadcast signals to use of the Internet, from closed captioning to descriptive video services, public broadcasting has been in the forefront of new media applications. The transition to digital so far is no exception. With digital technology, public television stations will have the capacity to broadcast four or more channels, whereas formerly they had only a single channel, and all of them can be used to communicate interactively with viewers. On any given day, digital public stations throughout the country could use their expanded capacity to broadcast quality fare for preschool children while simultaneously televising high school or college telecourses, teacher training programs, coverage of state and local hearings and town meetings, even as they continue simultaneously to broadcast an eclectic mix of their traditional programming. Eventually, each of these choices would be accompanied by data streams, educational supplements, textual information, and responses to viewer inquiries. Prototypes should be developed that will transform public television, combined with the Internet, into a popular appliance for active learning in every community in the nation.

In the digital world, the public stations, along with the Internet, will be ideally suited to become major electronic transmission points for schools, community colleges, universities, libraries, museums, arts and cultural institutions, and other noncommercial public organizations in their service areas. Through such facilities, secretaries of state in each state can reach citizens with critically important information about voter registration, ballot initiatives, referenda, and other civic activities. With digital transmission, the public stations also soon will have the capacity to make available substantial public service time free of charge to local and national candidates and to devote extensive time to community discussions and debates that bring perspective and depth to current affairs and community issues.

America's public stations are licensed to local universities, school boards, and communities. They are locally owned, locally operated, and locally controlled. In fact, America's public radio and television stations remain the only entirely locally owned and operated broadcasting system in the nation today. And because public stations reach into virtually every home, rich and poor, they can be instrumental in closing the remaining "digital divide" in telecommunications technology.

During the past three decades, the American people have made a multibillion-dollar investment in the nation's public broadcasting facilities. States like Wisconsin, Ohio, Nebraska, South Carolina, Mississippi, and others have massive statewide public broadcasting systems and networks that already link schools, colleges, hospitals, social services, and other public agencies and institutions. In addition, state-, county-, and city-run cable channels, as well as university-licensed low-power stations,

serve as important local sources of informational and educational services. In the digital age, we should capitalize on their existence by developing the tools for them to perform as community telecommunications
centers, dedicated to fulfilling important local public needs.

One example: With seed funding from the Trust, prototypes can be
developed for public stations to use their expanded digital capacity for
C-Span-style local educational and cultural services. In partnerships with
community institutions, the public stations' digital channels can bring
home to those in remote and rural areas, as well as in the inner city, the
wisdom of the nation's leading writers, artists, scientists, economists, historians, medical experts, and professors. They can make available to all
households the stimulating talks, readings, recitals, forums, and discussions
that have until now been confined to the auditoriums of universities,
libraries, museums, schools, arts and cultural centers, and community
centers. In this way, senior citizens, shut-ins, citizens with disabilites, young
people, working people, and those who live in isolated places can enjoy
expanded educational opportunities and can benefit from the best of
American thought and expression.

NEW MODELS FOR PUBLIC TELECOMMUNICATIONS IN THE DIGITAL AND INTERNET AGE

As Richard Somerset-Ward points out in his report for the Benton
Foundation, important initiatives are being launched that begin to demonstrate what the nation's public television stations, in partnership with
others, can do. The Information Age is only just beginning. Considerably
more experimentation, research, and information technology prototypes
are needed.[1]

In Connecticut, the state's public broadcasting network has embarked
on a process it calls "Mapping and Connecting the Assets." It is enlisting
the Yale School of Medicine, the University of Connecticut, Connecticut's
community college system, the Mashantucket Pequot Tribal Museum, the
Discovery Museum in Bridgeport, the Connecticut Children's Commission
and Connecticut Voices for Children, and the Connecticut secretary of
state's office to cooperate in developing experimental educational and
informational telecommunications projects for the entire state.

In Grand Rapids, Michigan, a community media center is emerging
from a partnership of the city's public radio station, community cable

access channel, media advocacy institute, and an organization that helps local nonprofit groups connect to the Internet.

In Nebraska, the state's public network, in partnership with local school boards, is putting online the complete, accredited Nebraska high school diploma curriculum sequence. Aimed primarily at the geographically isolated, the housebound, and the home schooled, it also is designed for students who wish to accelerate their graduation or need supplementary courses to further their secondary school experience. Nebraska parents use the online educational service to communicate with teachers.

In Chicago, public television station WTTW has organized *Network Chicago* to provide nightly local programming and, eventually, local multimedia services for the entire metropolitan area.

In Kansas City, KCPT has joined in the school district's "MoKan Kids Network" to deliver more than seven hundred hours of instructional television a year. It also sponsors an online collection of curricular resources through a service called TeacherLINK, which reaches 340 Missouri and Kansas school districts serving 30,000 teachers.

The Digital Opportunity Investment Trust can play a pivotal role in developing such public service models for community partnerships throughout the nation.

V: Conclusion

An opportunity for a gift to the nation does not often come along. In the history of the United States, three gifts stand out because they enriched the nation not for a day, or a week, or a year, but for many lifetimes. These gifts allowed millions of Americans the benefits of education. The Northwest Ordinance was one such gift. The Land-Grant College Act of Justin Morrill was another. So was the GI Bill. In each case, our country was permanently enriched.

In 2000, at a land-grant college, the Massachusetts Institute of Technology, the chief executive officer of Hewlett Packard, Carly Fiorina, delivered the commencement address. She gave the graduates this advice:

> Now some of you asked me to address the changing role of technology in business and in life. As you draw this first chapter in your life to a close, we are also drawing the first chapter in the Information Age to a close. And I believe we are now entering the Renaissance phase of the Information Age, where creativity and ideas are the new currency, and invention is a primary virtue, where technology truly has the power to transform lives, not just businesses, where technology can help us solve fundamental problems. In this new world we must always remember that technology is only as valuable as the use to which it is put. In the end, technology is ultimately about people. And in this technology Renaissance, we will witness and experience the fundamental transference of power to the people, to the masses. To the individuals who bring their own spark, their own energy to the process, technology becomes not about bits and bytes, but about the celebration of people's minds and people's hearts.[1]

NOTES

I: THE RECOMMENDATION

1. Justin S. Morrill, speech given before the U.S. Senate, December 5, 1872 (Washington, D.C.: Congressional Globe Printing Office, 1872), p. 7.

2. Allan Nevins, *The Origins of the Land-Grant Colleges and State Universities* (Washington, D.C.: Civil War Centennial Commission, 1962), p. 20.

3. For more details regarding the emerging new information technologies, see Les Brown, "The Nascent Age of Broadband," page 55 of this volume.

4. Francis X. Klines, "$60,000 Gift Is Made to Library of Congress," *New York Times,* October 5, 2000, p. A18.

5. Bob Kerrey and Johnny Isakson, "The Power of the Internet for Learning: Moving from Promise to Practice," report of the Web-based Education Commission, Washington, D.C., December 2000, pp. i, iii, vi.

6. Kellogg Commission on the Future of State and Land-Grant Universities, "Returning to Our Roots: A Learning Society," National Association of State Universities and Land-Grant Colleges, Washington, D.C., September 1999, pp. vii–viii.

7. Craig L. LaMay, "Justin Smith Morrill and the Politics and Legacy of the Land-Grant College Acts," page 73 of this volume.

8. Sydney Freedberg, "Beyond the GI Bill," *National Journal,* August 21, 1999, p. 2422.

9. Tom Brokaw, *The Greatest Generation* (New York: Random House, 1998), p. xx.

10. FCC 148 at 591 (1952).

11. Newton N. Minow, "Out of the Wasteland, A Jackpot," *New York Times,* December 4, 1994, p. 82.

12. See Cathy N. Davidson, "Teaching the Promise: The Research University in the Information Age," page 103 of this volume.

13. See Thomas R. Martin, "Fulfilling the Digital Promise in Nonprofit Education on a National Level," page 121 of this volume.

14. See Marion R. Fremont-Smith, "Governance Models for the Digital Opportunity Investment Trust," page 95 of this volume.

15. National Science Foundation Mission Statement, available at http://www.nsf.gov/home/about/creation.htm, and National Science Foundation Act of 1950.

16. Susan Stellin, "Number of New Internet Users Growing," *New York Times,* February 19, 2001, p. C3.

17. *Falling through the Net: Toward Digital Inclusion* (Washington, D.C.: U.S. Department of Commerce, October 2000), Tables I-1, I-2, Figures II-5, II-6.

18. Ibid.

II: THE NEED

1. Michael Moe, K. Bailey, and R. Lau, *The Book of Knowledge: Investing in the Growing Education and Training Market* (New York: Merrill Lynch, 1999), cited in "The Learning Federation," prepared for a conference at the National Science Foundation, November 28–29, 2000.

2. "Report of the Teaching and Lifelong Learning Working Group," National Endowment for the Humanities, Washington, D.C., November 1999, p. 20, available at http://www.neh.gov/pdf/other/tl3.pdf.

3. See Everette E. Dennis, "Older Americans and the Digital Revolution," page 175 of this volume.

4. Kellogg Commission on the Future of State and Land-Grant Universities, "Renewing the Covenant: Learning, Discovery, and Engagement in a New Age and Different World," National Association of State Universities and Land-Grant Colleges, Washington, D.C., March 2000, p. 5.

5. Communication to the authors from Dr. Henry C. Kelly, president, Federation of American Scientists, February 8, 2001.

III: THE NEW LANDSCAPE FOR LIFELONG LEARNING

1. Jodi Wilgoren, "Harvard President Announces Plans to Quit Next Year," *New York Times,* May 23, 2000, p. A20.

2. Department of Veterans Affairs, evaluation summary, Montgomery G.I. Bill Program, Clemm Analysis Group, Washington, D.C., August 17, 2000.

3. William C. Symonds, "Wired Schools: A Technology Revolution Is about to Sweep America's Classrooms," *Business Week,* September 25, 2000, pp. 117–18.

4. Beverly Sheppard, "Museums: The 21st Century Learner," brochure of the Institute of Museum and Library Services, Washington, D.C., November 2000.

5. Bonnie Rothman Morris, "A Day in the Life of the Wired School," *New York Times,* October 5, 2000, p. G8.

6. Symonds, "Wired Schools," pp. 118, 126.

7. Ibid., p. 126.

8. Rebecca S. Weiner, "Educators Turn to Internet for Advanced Placement Classes," *New York Times,* November 8, 2000, available at http://www.nytimes.com/2000/11/08/technology/08EDUCATION.html.

9. See Mary L. Walshok, "The Promise of the Digital Age for the Renewal of Regional Civic Culture," page 135 of this volume.

10. See Susan A. Rogers, "How to Put the Web to Work for Nonprofits," page 155 of this volume.

11. See Thomas R. Martin, "Fulfilling the Digital Promise in Nonprofit Education on a National Level," page 121 of this volume.

12. Letter to the authors, November 16, 2000.

13. Memo to the authors from Dr. Henry C. Kelly, president, Federation of American Scientists, November 2000.

14. See Martín Gómez, "Bridging the Digital Divide: Public Service Telecommunication in the Internet and Digital Age," page 149 of this volume.

15. Kellogg Commission on the Future of State and Land-Grant Universities, "Renewing the Covenant: Learning, Discovery, and Engagement in a New Age and Different World," National Association of State Universities and Land-Grant Colleges, Washington, D.C., March 2000.

16. See Cathy N. Davidson, "Teaching the Promise," page 103 of this volume.

17. Letter to the authors from John McCarter, November 9, 2000.

18. Letter to the authors from Dr. Henry C. Kelly, November 2, 2000.

19. See Rita Weisskoff, "It's 2001. Do You Know What Your Children Are Watching? The Critical Role of Children's Television in the Age of New Media," page 167 of this volume.

20. Letter to the authors from Henry P. Becton, Jr., president, WGBH, November 10, 2000.

21. Memo to authors from Ruzena Bajcsy, assistant director, National Science Foundation, November 2000.

22. See Wayne Ashley, "(Re)Imagining BAM in the Age of Broadband Technologies," page 187 of this volume.

23. See John Goberman, "The Digital Promise of Lincoln Center," page 183 of this volume.

24. "Art Museum Network: The Official Website of the World's Leading Art Museums since 1996," fact sheet, Art Museum Network, July 1, 2000.

25. See Richard Kimball, "You Will Find No Profit in Winning, but If You Lose, You Lose It All," page 199 of this volume.

26. See Mark Lloyd, "Whose Voices Count: A Proposal to Strengthen the Communications Capability of Community Groups," page 207 of this volume.

IV: A NEW ROLE FOR PUBLIC BROADCASTING

1. See Richard Somerset-Ward, "Public Television in the Digital Age," page 239 of this volume.

V. CONCLUSION

1. Commencement address given by Carly S. Fiorina at the Massachusetts Institute of Technology, June 2, 2000, available at http://web.mit.edu/newsoffice/nr/2000/fiorinaspeech.html.

DIGITAL PERSPECTIVES
BACKGROUND PAPERS

1.
THE NASCENT AGE OF BROADBAND

LES BROWN[1]

In a process likened to an ambling stream morphing into a roaring river, the age of narrowband telecommunications is passing swiftly in this decade to one of digital broadband with a force that promises a tempest of socioeconomic change. Happening exquisitely at the start of the new millennium, the shift from the narrowband to the broadband culture is certain to mark an essential difference between life in the twentieth and twenty-first centuries, radically affecting how we learn, work, do business, communicate, are entertained, and practice democracy.

Simply described, digital broadband is the largest communications conduit ever imagined, capable of numerous complex simultaneous transmissions. Its mass deployment is proceeding at a fairly rapid pace since the essential lines are already connected to most households in the form of telephone and cable. Moreover, the providers are able to offer it now at generally affordable rates for the average consumer, when previously it was reserved for corporations and universities willing to pay upward of $1,000 a month. Toward the end of the year 2000 more than four million U.S. residences have fast broadband access to the Internet. By 2002 research organizations expect the number to grow as high as sixteen million, and then with the two-way satellite and wireless forms also firmly in the market and competing for price the build-out should accelerate. These are technologies that use the electromagnetic spectrum, commonly known as the airwaves, and should be especially marketable in parts of the country not serviced by cable or enhanced telephone lines. Coleman Research projects broadband penetration in about one-third of American households by 2004.

With the Internet as catalyst, digital broadband is consummating the long-anticipated convergence of television, computer, and telephone, opening the way to new interactive systems and services that will redefine mass communication and intensify the Information Revolution. Yet few besides the corporate players and technology experts on the front lines recognize the broadband phenomenon's true import. To the consumer public, aware from news reports that it underlies the wave of mammoth telecommunications mergers, broadband is about the bundling of video, phone, and data services by single providers, with speedier access to the Internet as a prime feature. But hardly recognized is the effect of such great bandwidth on content and what the impact of that is likely to be on business, popular culture, and lifestyles. Content will differ markedly from what we have experienced in the analog era because digital broadband is interactive and can support full-motion and high-definition video, multimedia, 3-D images, and virtual reality. And when hitched to the Internet the transmissions are not bound to a locale or a nation but will have a worldwide reach. While most of the planned applications today are in the sphere of electronic commerce, there are also positive implications for education, health care, public safety, civic participation, the arts, and virtually every profession and field of enterprise.

If broadband has not yet fully entered the popular vocabulary it is partly because the term itself, coined by engineers, fails to fire the imagination and verges in fact on the soporific (cable was similarly hobbled at first). A marketing executive observed at an industry conference that "it sounds like a new tire." But mainly it sits on the linguistic fringe because it is hardly understood. For all its significance very little is written about the broadband phenomenon in lay language. Nearly every sophisticated discussion of it in conference papers, technical journals, and Internet chats tends to be laced with esoteric engineering references and arcane acronyms. Any civilian attempting to follow can only get lost in the thicket of IPs, LANs, DOCSIS modems, SMILs, gbps, terabits, LEOs, backbones, and packet switching.

This paper will attempt to describe broadband and its myriad applications and implications in plain English, so that members of industries and institutions outside the communications field may anticipate what is coming and be able to participate in the dialogue on the issues being raised at this stage of the revolution.

THE FAT PIPE

As we leave the Industrial Age and enter the Information Age, it's clear that despite all the technical advances and globalization, the formula for economic success has remained the same: economic prosperity relies on high-speed access to the critical network of information and commerce. That network is the Internet, and the type of access needed is broadband.

—William Kennard, chairman of the Federal
Communications Commission

The main telecommunications media of the twentieth century were narrowband for reasons that were altogether logical. Because the electromagnetic spectrum is limited, radio and television stations were apportioned only so much bandwidth as was needed to transmit their signals to homes. And telephone was able to achieve its two-way voice communication—which was all that it was about—most efficiently and economically with the thin copper wires called "twisted pair."

But in the late 1940s, the wiring of reception-poor valley areas for what was then known as Community Antenna Television, or CATV, required the use of coaxial cable, and a true broadband medium was born. Engineers continually found ways to expand cable TV's channel capacity for the ever-increasing satellite-delivered program services, and the medium spread rapidly around the United States during the 1980s. Bell Laboratories developed T-1 technology in the 1960s as a broadband form of telephony with four wires instead of two, but the high construction costs limited its use to certain businesses. Meanwhile other broadband media emerged, notably Multichannel Multipoint Distribution Systems (MMDS)—so-called wireless cable operating over the air on microwave frequencies—and Direct Broadcast Satellites (DBS). So broadband as a provider of multiple channels (the band referring to bandwidth, or carrying capacity) has been with us a good while in analog form and is often referred to by its nickname, "the fat pipe."

What is making the monumental difference now is that the fat pipe is becoming a huge pipe through its conversion from analog to digital and by continual technological refinements that keep increasing its bandwidth, chiefly with lightwave technology over networks of optical fiber and high-bandwidth parcels of the radio spectrum. The huge pipe allows for the transport of massive amounts of information, in both data and video form, both to the home and from it with lightning speed. Typically it is described in terms of speed.

In its current use, bandwidth usually refers to the rate at which bits of data can move in cyberspace each second, measured in kilobits (thousands of bits), megabits (millions of bits), gigabits (billions of bits), and even terabits (trillions of bits). Internet access has been commonly achieved over analog telephone modems that have a theoretical top speed of 56 kilobits per second (kbps). Most people connect at home at speeds ranging from 14.4 to 33.6 kbps. Broadband modifications of those lines, with telephone technologies known as ISDN (Integrated Services Digital Network), DSL (Digital Subscriber Line), and T-1, can run the data from ten to eighty times faster. Cable modems are faster still. Surfing the net becomes a lot like surfing the cable channels, with the web pages coming up smoothly and instantaneously. Indeed, it is consumer desire for this kind of speed on the Internet that is driving broadband's progress in the mass market.

Advanced broadband technology had existed for decades before the current deployment but was held back because of the huge investment needed in the renovation of infrastructure. The reluctance to spend billions in the hope of finding a sizable residential market was understandable. But the market announced itself with the popularity of the Internet and the growing impatience of users with the slow downloading that has come to be called the "World Wide Wait," and that has been the spur.

Five industries are involved in supplying broadband to answer the demand—those of cable, telephone, satellites, fixed wireless services, and cellular—each with its own particular strengths and weaknesses. Initially the race in the U.S. was mainly between the hard-wire providers, cable and telephone, but a bidirectional satellite, StarBand, entered the consumer market in the fall of 2000 with the ability to reach the entire country. The established direct-to-home broadcast satellite, DirecTV, followed soon after with a technological refinement that allows for full interactivity. Previously it had provided only one-way high-speed Internet access, requiring subscribers to use a telephone connection for the return path.

Meanwhile, the rising consumer enthusiasm for mobile Internet access through the new generation of cell phones and other handheld devices—a contagion in Europe and parts of Asia that has spread here—is creating enormous demands for additional spectrum. Like some governments abroad, the U.S. has been raising billions of dollars from periodic auctions of parcels of the scarce airwaves, causing wireless providers to speak of the spectrum as the most valuable real estate in the world.

Technology has brought prices down for advanced broadband, and the competition among the rival industries is keeping rates at levels—roughly $35–$60 per month—that ensure adoption as the services become available.

Cable, with its superfast modems and its head start in the market, clearly has the edge, especially since AT&T joined its ranks and became, through $120 billion worth of acquisitions in 1999, the largest cable operator in the country. MCI Worldcom and Sprint, AT&T's long-distance competitors, each responded by purchasing large MMDS and Local Multipoint Distribution Systems (LMDS). These are fixed-wireless systems with great broadband capacity for the local connection to homes, or what is called "the last mile" in telecommunications networks—thus easing their dependency on the expensive local loops of the regional telephone companies (telcos). Then in October 1999 the companies agreed to a merger that would have formed another telecommunications colossus, but because it was seen as diminishing competition in the long-distance market the merger failed to gain approval from the European Commission and federal agencies here.

Cable companies were the earliest to deploy because they had begun rebuilding their systems for digital television even before the broadband wars commenced. By mid-1999 cable was able to roll out advanced broadband to twenty-three-million potential residential customers while the telcos, still rebuilding and preparing for major residential deployment in 2000, could offer it to only six million. Research organizations estimate that 63 percent of all cable systems will be converted to broadband by 2001, while the telcos will be able to offer broadband to 70 percent of homes by 2004. Cable modems have a theoretical top speed of 25 megabits per second but in practical terms tend to range between 500 kilobits and 2.5 megabits.

Such is the speed of the cable modem that under optimum conditions it can download a full-length movie in two minutes when dial-up Internet connections would require two hours. But optimum conditions do not always exist, and that points to the most serious shortcoming of the cable modem. In the architecture of local cable systems the main line in an area is shared by a number of households, and when several neighbors are on the Internet at the same time transmission becomes appreciably slower. It can be exasperatingly slow if one of the neighbors is operating a business on the web. Moreover, cable service can be knocked out by storms and blackouts while telephone service remains unaffected. The monthly fee for broadband comes on top of the monthly fee for cable TV, and added to those are an installation cost of around $90 and the purchase of an Ethernet card at around $50.

The regional telcos, or Baby Bells, are entering the residential market primarily with DSL, which cannot match the cable modem's top data rate but has other advantages, not the least of them dependability. Since telephone lines are not shared in the manner of cable but are dedicated to individual users the rate of speed does not vary. Telephone companies also have an excellent reputation for customer service while cable, as an industry, does not and is resented by many consumers, besides, for continually raising its rates. The telcos also have a distinct advantage in rural areas where cable penetration tends to be slight. Still, cable stands to win the immediate battle for households, helped by such services as WebTV and a new generation of set-top boxes that can bring Internet access to the television set without benefit of a PC, promising to gain it subscribers from the ranks of computerphobes.

Telephonic broadband is expected to dominate the small business market, because relatively few offices and shops have had reason to subscribe to cable. Telcos will be offering DSL to households in a range of speeds and prices, but the best seller is expected to be the most economical form, known as G.Lite, which can be switched on from the central office, obviating the need for a service call. G.Lite will also be the standard for the modems that eventually will be available in retail stores and installed by the users themselves. That is when the real mass marketing of DSL is likely to begin. Most of the telcos are giving their broadband products more marketable names; Verizon, for example, is calling DSL "Infospeed" and bundling it with America On Line service for around $42 a month. The downside of DSL is that it is limited by distance, in that subscribers must live within three miles of the telephone switching service in order to be able to receive it.

DSL has a number of variations, but the primary version offered is the "asymmetric" form known as ADSL, achieved on ordinary phone lines that are entirely digitized. The asymmetry refers to the unevenness of speed rates in the two-way system, with much greater bandwidth provided for receiving data ("downstream") than for the user to send data forward ("upstream"). Cable modems are similarly asymmetrical, owing to the belief that subscribers will more often seek material than present their own. Where that is not the case, such as in some corporate situations, telephone offers a symmetrical alternative in HDSL, but cable does not. DSL can provide as much as eight million bits per second (8 Mbps) while the cable modem has a practical upper limit of ten million for PC connections (with a potential 52 Mbps for Internet Service Providers). A comparison with the maximum possible on today's ordinary modems—fifty-six thousand bits per second (56 Kbps)—illustrates the phenomenal expansion of the pipe. Such enormous bandwidth allows for the simultaneous use of Internet, television, and telephone without requiring separate lines, and with a perpetual Internet connection referred to as the "always on" feature.

Although these hard-wire technologies are focal in the broadband revolution, the satellite and terrestrial wireless providers have a fair number of adherents in the U.S. and over time will undoubtedly claim a significant share of the market. Operators of the StarBand satellite, which began as a way to bring Internet and radio service to an Indian reservation situated at the bottom of the Grand Canyon, see their potential market as 50 million households not served by cable or DSL, according to a report in the *Washington Post*. Capable now of offering interactive connections to the Internet, along with being able at last to provide local TV stations, direct-broadcast satellites may finally emerge as serious competitors to cable. They also have the advantage of portability, since the receiving dish can easily be moved with the subscriber to a new address.

The fixed-wireless broadband forms are capable of reaching their customers without the great expense of building and maintaining a vast infrastructure, so they may derive a competitive edge in being priced lower than the others. Teligent, for example, is already offering connections in some cities at rates 30 percent below those of the fiber-based services. In the residential market, wireless services are mainly targeting large apartment buildings, since the cost of equipping a single family home with an antenna and other devices—currently around $5,000—is the same as for an apartment building with dozens of tenants. Other key markets for fixed wireless are high-rise office buildings, condominium complexes, hotels, hospitals, malls, campuses, industrial parks and arenas for trade shows. A chief deficiency of the MMDS and LMDS installations is that they currently allow only one-way communication, although two-way systems are being developed and should be available before very long.

The explosive popularity of cell phones is fueling the market for out-of-home Internet connectivity. The newest digital phones have the ability to send data at 2 megabits per second, which is fast enough for a modified surfing of the web and for brief e-mail correspondence. Cellular connectivity is more expensive than the others, but it is the leading conduit to the Internet in isolated countries like Finland and Iceland and in many parts of Asia where mobile phone penetration is high and wireline telephony relatively scarce. In Japan, the leading mobile broadband service, DoCoMo, had amassed ten million subscribers in 2000 after only eighteen months in the market.

The likely success of satellite and wireless broadband will be a mixed blessing because they are so taxing of the spectrum, which is a finite resource. The scarcity of frequencies was exacerbated when the government allocated an additional channel to each existing television station in 1997 for the development of digital TV. This was done on the misguided assumption that consumers would adopt the new medium so rapidly that the original analog frequencies could be surrendered for auction by 2006. Experts doubt now that wholesale conversion will occur before 2020, if then, and raise the possibility that a spectrum-impoverished U.S. could fall seriously behind other industrialized nations in implementing advanced forms of wireless broadband.

THE FIBER FACTOR

Electronic charges move in wires at nine inches per nanosecond. Microwaves take a quarter of a second to resound for a satellite in geosynchronous orbit. Photons cross a continent in 30 milliseconds.
—George Gilder in *Wired*, January 1998

When speed is the issue nothing succeeds like the speed of light, which is why in the 1990s virtually all cable and telephone networks began rebuilding their so-called backbone infrastructure with fiber optic lines. These cables, containing hair-thin flexible glass fibers conveying light impulses from a laser transmitter, carry far more information than their copper counterparts. But for economic reasons the large optical transmission lines are joined to copper ones at the cable head-end or telephone neighborhood node, where the lightwave transmission is converted back to a lesser electrical signal. This form of construction, called hybrid fiber-coax, is the prevailing one in the United States and generally considered a necessary compromise. Though everyone acknowledges the superiority of all-fiber networks, the expense of pulling fiber to the last mile—the connection to households—is considered prohibitive, not for the cost of the material itself but for the special kind of switching, maintenance, and set-top boxes that would be required.

Still, in pockets of the country, sophisticated fiber optic networks are being built by real estate developers and by the municipal governments of small towns that have been ignored by cable and phone companies for upgraded service because they are sparsely populated. One such rural town, Hawarden, Iowa, built its own $4.5 million fiber loop system and in early 1999 began offering its 2,500 residents cable TV, telephony, and high-speed Internet access superior to what is available in most large cities. Several other similar small communities are following its lead.

A fiber-to-the-home network has been built in a new Houston subdivision by a company called ClearWorks Technologies, which charges the 1,200 homeowners $100 a month for the bundled services. Those include a neighborhood intranet, digital cable, movies-on-demand, telephony, and Internet access with speeds of up to 100 megabits per second. The company points out that all-fiber networks become feasible when built from scratch, and it plans to build others in new communities elsewhere in the country.

Recognizing the importance of fiber to the future economy, and hoping to avoid the disruption that would come from the trench-digging by fiber providers, several major cities are weighing the possibility of using available underground facilities as conduits for networks that would connect fiber to buildings. New York, for example, would make available the ducts of an inactive water system originally built for firefighting that extends for 175 miles throughout Manhattan and much of Brooklyn. Las Vegas would use active water ducts if it proves technologically feasible. In Atlanta and the surrounding region, tests have been conducted on the use of the sewer system as a fiber conduit, reportedly with favorable results. CityNet, the company that would construct the Atlanta network, says the technology is based on one that has been used extensively in such German cities as Berlin and Hamburg. Other cities, among them Los Angeles, are exploring the possibilities with subway system tunnels. Using existing infrastructure would not only expedite the deployment of fiber but would also substantially lessen construction costs and gain the cities additional revenues from leasing the conduits.

Meanwhile engineers are striving for ever-greater speeds, pushing the limits from megabits to gigabits and terabits. In 1998 Lucent achieved the first transmission of a terabit (one trillion bits) of information per second over a single strand of optical fiber. To illustrate what that means, a terabit is enough capacity to carry all the phone calls that take place in the world at any moment. A year later Nortel Networks announced that it had developed the "world's fastest, highest-capacity, most reliable Internet technology," which it claims can move 1.6 trillion bits per second, vastly increasing Internet efficiency. Nortel said the technology, called OPTera 1600G, would be rolled out commercially before very long. Qwest, a Denver-based telephone company, is building a nationwide fiber network with a top capacity of two trillion bits per second. That, according to *Wired* magazine's *Encyclopedia of the New Economy,* would be sufficient "to transmit the entire contents of the Library of Congress cross-country in 20 seconds."

Optical fiber is broadband supreme and vital to the continued health of the Internet, given how its capacity is being taxed by the constant worldwide influx of new users and the tremendous increases in websites and online browsing. A U.S. Department of Commerce report of April 1998 noted that Internet traffic is doubling every hundred days. That rate is likely to accelerate, as the Internet becomes accessible by means other than the personal computer, notably wireless screen phones and TV set-top boxes. All the new mobile phone models being produced by the world's leading manufacturers allow for Internet access today. International Data Corp., a research firm in Framingham, Massachusetts, predicts that eighty-nine million non-PC devices will be connected to the web globally by 2001.

Such demands on the Internet put great pressure on its infrastructure, heightened moreover by the ever-increasing use of bandwidth-devouring video streaming and IP telephony. What prevents a major brownout from occurring is an equally rapid multiplication of bandwidth at the Internet backbone with optical technology. Not only are fiber networks being swiftly and extensively deployed everywhere, they are being enhanced by a laser technology called Dense Wavelength Division Multiplexing (DWDM), which can boost fiber capacity up to a hundredfold.

The Internet on Steroids

Broadband represents a sea change in how virtually any segment of the online marketplace works—from entertainment to education to e-commerce to business data communications.

—Fred Dawson, publisher of *Broadband Commerce & Technology* newsletter

When advanced broadband technology is linked to the Internet the door to the future opens wide. Experts now speak of the Internext, the next generation of the net that will employ superior audio and video streaming, 3-D and virtual reality and will require no dial-up or waiting for pages to download. People may look back on the current data-dominated Internet and equate it with the silent movie era.

Expectations are that within five years of the new century streaming will equal television in technical quality, allowing for live real-time events on the computer. TV and the PC are destined to become so interrelated that each could perform many of the other's functions. Television, which has always been a "push" technology (in the sense of serving the viewer a set menu), becomes as well a "pull" medium, empowering the viewer to customize the programming and to interact with the screen in various ways. Clearly broadband connectivity is going to change both television and the Internet radically, to where it may be difficult to think of them separately, especially since Internet commerce will increasingly be favoring moving images and sound rather than text and fixed graphics. Banner ads will likely give way to commercials of three or four seconds' length.

Sooner rather than later in the twenty-first century television will come from hundreds of sources, with the Internet providing access to networks from every part of the world. New radio stations are already broadcasting on the web without having had to secure licenses from the FCC, and similar unlicensed TV networks are certain to proliferate when the number of U.S. households with broadband connectivity reaches the critical mass of twenty million. That could be as soon as 2005. At least three U.S. companies have been buying up old movies and creating cyber cinemas on the web in anticipation of perfected streaming.

Except for live events like sports and breaking news, cyber television will be exempt from constraints of the clock. Schedules that run in linear time in the broadcast and cable media will exist more or less horizontally on the web, with programs available to be watched at the viewer's convenience. Shows that aired hours or weeks before would be stored in the system and could be accessed as current, so that three episodes of a favorite series could be watched in the same evening. Obviously, commercial television's existing business model stands to be rendered obsolete.

Though certain movies and events will be offered on a pay basis, advertising will be the dominant revenue source for both television and the Internet, and it will of course be interactive. Predictably it will take the form of direct marketing whenever that is practical. Those expensive automobile commercials created in hopes of sending the viewer to the nearest showroom may give way to spots that allow the prospective customer to examine the vehicle thoroughly from the sofa—even virtually test-drive it—and place the order with a click. Advertisers are likely to return to creating their own shows for their own purposes, taking advantage of the viewer's ability to make purchases off the screen in point-and-click fashion while the program is in progress. And with the way user profiles can be assembled on the Internet, advertisements can be presented differently to each demographic group in the audience.

Jupiter Communications, an Internet research firm, projects online advertising sales to reach $11.5 billion in 2003, compared with $2.1 in 1998. That would make it the third-ranked ad medium, after broadcast television and newspapers, ahead of cable TV and magazines.

THE MONEY TO BE MADE

> Broadband Internet access has the potential to turn the current e-commerce trickle into a waterfall.
> —Eric Brown, "Broadband, Narrow Choices,"
> PC World, February 2000

When AT&T purchased TCI's cable systems the price was based on an assigned value of $5,000 per subscriber, an astonishing figure considering that subscribers were valued at $2,000 in such transactions only a few years before. But that was when the revenues from a subscriber came only from cable service. AT&T intended to sell these thirty-three million cable customers local and long-distance phone service, Internet access and, down the line, a good deal more. The rationale for the purchase was that it gave AT&T an immediate broadband connection to consumers.

Indeed, the billions being spent by all the broadband providers to rebuild their systems are not prompted just by the prospect of collecting monthly fees for faster connections to the Internet; that merely creates a market that will be prime for exploitation by all manner of lucrative electronic commerce, ranging from home shopping and banking to advertising and videoconferencing. Cable operators are already selling telephony, movies on demand, and digital video to their existing customer base.

E-commerce is of course already flourishing on the Internet, but many sales are believed lost by the slowness of the process. Powered by broadband's speed and new creative tools e-commerce stands to be a great growth area, expected to soar from an estimated $13 billion in 1999 to $41 billion in 2002 in the U.S. alone. Much of the gain will undoubtedly be attributed to what some are calling b-commerce—the broadband version, which can provide movies, music, CD-ROMs, and DVDs for sale while adding 3-D images and virtual reality to the commercial palette.

There are a number of tempting entertainment markets for broadband providers logically to invade. Among them are the $15 billion video rental business, which can be substantially carved into by genuine video-on-demand (in place of the current "near" video-on-demand) and the $7 billion market for video games, which with the bigger pipe can be offered in 3-D.

Clothing can also be shown in 3-D, on animation models scaled to the user's measurements. The consumer's ability "virtually" to try on the garment should give broadband catalog sales a distinct edge on the paper catalogs whose collective sales are around $52 billion annually. To siphon off only 10 percent of that market would be significant.

Broadband applications extend to nearly every sphere of life. For some examples:

- People in search of houses or apartments can virtually see them room by room, saving needless trips with a real estate agent.

- With IP (Internet Protocol) Telephony, which allows for visual contact, doctors can consult with and examine patients electronically, even over great distances. Telemedicine experiments have been going on for decades but, although successful, were never economically feasible until now.

- With special cameras families can monitor a bedridden aging parent living apart or keep an eye on a child in day care while at work.

- Students attending a broadband university can receive the lectures live and play them back as often as desired. Communication with the instructor can be more frequent and more detailed than in actual school situations, and the courses may originate in other cities or countries.

- Farmers can receive daylong reports on weather conditions and can purchase feed and equipment without having to drive to town.

- Artists can show their work to galleries over the net or mount their own electronic exhibitions. Many may venture into new realms of art with the new electronic canvas and tools that broadband affords.

What all these brief examples have in common is communication eliminating the need for transportation. This raises the possibility that broadband networks linked to the Internet might reverse the social effects of the Industrial Revolution. That was the force behind the growth of cities and the development of new modes of transportation, and the broadband revolution appears pointed in the opposite direction. With communications increasingly taking the place of transportation, people can live at a more comfortable and economical remove from the cities, working in virtual offices and participating in desktop conferences with their bosses. And of course they can buy whatever they need in electronic malls and supermarkets. This vision of telecommuters emptying the cities is not offered as a prediction but merely as an illustration of what could happen to lifestyles in the broadband twenty-first century.

A REGULATORY DILEMMA

We're at a fork in the information superhighway. One way leads to open access, boundless innovation and free expression, the other has us follow the same path that made cable television the closed, unresponsive and overpriced monopoly Americans have grown to hate.
—Andrew Jay Schwartzman, president of the Media Access Project, a public interest law firm in Washington, D.C.

In detailing its proposal for a greater government investment in Information Technology (IT) in 2000, a White House press release dated January 21, 1999, noted that the field now accounts for one-third of the country's economic growth and employs 7.4 million Americans. "All sectors of the U.S. economy are using IT to compete and win in global markets," the release states, "and business-to-business electronic commerce in the U.S. alone is expected to grow to $1.3 trillion by 2003."

Clearly the high-tech communications industry is one of the government's darlings, a shining area where the U.S. holds undisputed leadership in the world and one that vindicates its twenty-year-old policy of regulation by market forces. *New York Times* columnist Thomas L. Friedman observed in an August 20, 1999, article that several European countries have the financial ability to compete and access to all the same technologies but cannot move with our agility because their regulatory policies and stringent labor laws hamper them. He pointed out, by way of illustration, that the world's eight largest high-tech companies are all U.S.-based.

The success of deregulation, at least in this regard, and the government's eagerness for rapid broadband deployment are reasons why most of the mega-mergers of 1998, 1999, and 2000 were readily approved. This was true even when they seemed to transgress the spirit of the Telecommunications Act of 1996, which was to promote competition in every sphere and especially between the industries concerned. Undoubtedly AT&T's acquisition of TCI and then MediaOne, making it both the country's leading long distance company and largest cable operator, received the government's blessings because the telecom giant had the resources to rebuild the systems as needed and immediately roll out broadband in a way that would cause other providers to make haste. In particular, the commission was eager for AT&T to begin offering local phone service through its cable systems and create the competition in local markets called for in the Telecommunications Act.

But issues continually arise that prompt calls for intervention by government, and AT&T's move into cable has raised a number of them. When it followed the TCI merger with the acquisition of MediaOne, the fourth largest cable operator, its coverage extended to nearly half the U.S. cable households, far exceeding the FCC's ownership limit of 30 percent. To gain approval, AT&T promised to meet the cap by divesting the necessary number of systems. Later, however, the company petitioned for a change in the rule that would allow it to retain all its cable properties, indicating that it would otherwise be forced to sell the systems offering the least profit potential, namely those in the rural and inner city areas. This, the company's lawyers pointed out, would have the effect of worsening the broadband Digital Divide, as the imbalance in society of information haves and have-nots is called—an issue of intense governmental concern.

Another key issue is whether AT&T, defined as a cable provider by the regulators though it also offers cable telephony, has an unfair advantage over the traditional telcos. Telephone companies are regulated as common carriers, required to give access to all who desire it, at posted rates on a nondiscriminatory basis, with no control over the content that travels over their lines. They must also make their lines available at wholesale rates to all competing local telephone providers. Cable systems are not common carriers and for the most part are able to govern their content. The regional phone companies complained that with its market power and relative freedom from telephonic regulation, AT&T could overwhelm them as the local competitor. If AT&T uses its cable lines for telephone service, the rival telcos contend, then it should be subject to the same regulations as they. At the time of the announced restructuring of the company, in October 2000, AT&T had only 350,000 cable-telephone customers but indicated that the spin-off company, to be called AT&T Broadband, would continue to compete for telephony in local markets.

Even more serious and more heatedly debated in Washington is the possibility that AT&T Broadband and the giant conglomerate AOL Time Warner, whose $103.5 billion merger was consummated January 11, 2001, might become the principal gatekeepers to the Internet, to the presumed peril of hundreds of Internet Service Providers (ISPs) and companies concerned with content. In absorbing TCI, AT&T had gained not only its cable systems but also its substantial interest in @Home, one of the two main cable ports of entry to the Internet. (It is now known as Excite@Home since its merger with a leading web browser.) At the time of the merger AT&T had signed a contract with @Home as its exclusive ISP on all its systems at least through the year 2002. This was not unusual since other cable systems that have financial stakes in, or contractual agreements with, Excite@Home and its chief competitor, RoadRunner, were not planning to allow independent ISPs to use these ports of entry either, regarding them as cable exclusives.

The issue grew more complex when AT&T absorbed MediaOne, which owned 35 percent of RoadRunner. Public interest advocates maintained that the company's significant stake in both cable ISPs smacked of de facto monopoly. They, along with Prodigy, Sprint, GTE, MCI Worldcom, and AOL (prior to its courtship of Time Warner), petitioned the FCC to require that AT&T provide open access to the Internet, as telcos are required to do, noting that the competition would benefit the consumer with lower prices and greater choice. In its petition, the Media Access Project, a leading public interest organization, warned that to offer Internet service under the model of the closed cable-TV system "will, quite literally, change the character of the Internet," with respect to its openness and diversity and the opportunity it affords for free expression and economic growth.

AT&T's position was that since it would be investing billions to upgrade and deploy it should have the right to determine how its systems are used for Internet access. Addressing the issue, Michael Armstrong, the company's chairman and chief executive, said: "We believe our cable customers should be able to access any portals and content they want to reach. But it should be done on the basis of a sound commercial relationship, not through regulation." One proposal put forth was that customers could have an independent ISP but would have to pay twice, first for the cable entry and then for the ISP they choose.

Throughout the protracted debate, FCC chairman William Kennard asserted his belief in a hands-off approach and trusting to a marketplace in which at least four industries are jousting. "Our goal is to get several broadband pipes built that will compete with each other to carry information to and from customers," he said. "The best way to get pipes in the ground is to guarantee the industry won't be hampered by regulation. If we've learned anything from the Internet, it's that it prospered by being unregulated." As regards AT&T, he said the FCC will continue to monitor its practices, "and if anti-competitive issues arise, we can regulate."

A number of municipalities, asserting their jurisdiction over cable since they award the franchises, have challenged AT&T's position and demanded open access, arguing that preserving competition in the Internet market would lead to lower prices and spur innovation. The FCC, however, contends that its rules for cable supersede those of the municipalities and that nationwide broadband deployment depends on national policy. The question of who has jurisdiction has gone to the courts and on to Congress, so far without conclusive results. Ultimately it may turn on whether the cable modem is defined as a telecom service.

An FCC report in October 1999 argued for a hands-off posture by both federal and local government regulators, noting that broadband is in its infancy, with (then) only 3 percent of U.S. residences having access to it, and needs to be allowed to answer to market forces without interference. Kennard later declared, "We must have fast and ubiquitous deployment of broadband service, and that will only happen if every sector of the industry has incentives to provide it—wireline, wireless, and cable."

But a year later, when the prospective merger of AOL and Time Warner raised other thorny issues, the FCC's position softened somewhat, and it embarked on a study to determine whether some kind of federal regulation was indeed in order. The merger would form the largest communications company in the world, one that owned television and cable networks, a major Hollywood studio, a publishing empire, and vast cable installations while controlling nearly half the market for Internet access, to the alarm of other media giants. In their filings to the FCC such companies as Disney, NBC, Yahoo, and Microsoft stressed the danger that a combined AOL-Time Warner might stifle competition by discriminating against rival program and interactive television suppliers. This time Kennard remarked: "It is unclear . . . whether a marketplace solution will develop absent some form of intervention."

The Federal Trade Commission was first to intervene, satisfying antitrust concerns in approving the merger by requiring Time Warner to open its cable lines to all ISPs offering high-speed Internet connections. A month later— exactly a year and a day after the merger was originally announced—the FCC gave final approval but with more extensive conditions. Most of them centered on AOL's dominance of instant messaging, the popular service that allows two or more parties to meet online for simultaneous back-and-forth communication. AOL's text-based system is deliberately a closed one, not interoperable with those of Microsoft and Yahoo. The FCC has ruled that when AOL begins adding audio and video features to its service—which some believe will give it greater importance than telephony in years to come—the company will have to open instant messaging to its competitors, preferably by adopting an industry-wide standard.

The commission also acted to separate the two cable giants, AT&T and Time Warner, from their involvement with each other. Specifically, it barred exclusive agreements between the two that would affect access for rival ISPs and severed their ownership link by requiring AT&T to sell off its 25 percent stake in Time Warner Entertainment, which had come with the MediaOne acquisition.

Approving the merger was the last official act of the Kennard-led commission, which gave over to Republican domination with the inauguration of President George W. Bush. While the vote for the merger was unanimous, two of the five commissioners dissented from the conditions imposed on AOL Time Warner, arguing that the FCC lacked the jurisdiction to make such requirements. That they were the Republicans on the panel suggested a markedly different regulatory approach in the offing.

Inevitably, the regulators will be faced with other large issues as calls for a level playing field emanate from every industry involved, but the race to deploy broadband and introduce its dazzling by-products is nevertheless sure to proceed apace. There is too much to be gained by the providers who are first to arrive.

NOTES

1. This chapter expands on a paper written in 1999 for the Fordham Center for Communication at the Fordham Graduate School of Business, where the author is an associate professor. The author is grateful to Dr. Everette E. Dennis, director of the Center, for granting permission to use this material.

BOOKS

Abe, George. *Residential Broadband*. Macmillan Publishing, 1997.

Brand, Stewart. *The Media Lab: Inventing the Future at M.I.T.* Penguin Books, 1988.

Dennis, Everette E., and Edward Pease, eds. *The Race for Content*. Media Studies Center, Winter 1994.

Gates, Bill, with Nathan Myhrvold and Peter Rinearson. *The Road Ahead*. Penguin Books, 1996.

Gates, Bill, with Collins Hemingway. *Business at the Speed of Thought: Using a Digital Nervous System*. Warner Books, 1999.

Grossman, Lawrence K. *The Electronic Republic: Reshaping Democracy in the Information Age*. Viking/Penguin, New York, 1996.

Knoll, Roger G., and Monroe E. Price, eds. *A Communications Cornucopia: Markle Foundation Essays on Information Policy*. The Brookings Institution, 1998.

Kumar, Balaji. *Broadband Communications*. McGraw-Hill Series on Computer Communications, 1999.

Maxwell, Kim, and Kimberly Maxwell. *Residential Broadband: An Insider's Guide to the Battle of the Last Mile*. John Wiley & Sons, 1998.

Shapiro, Andrew L. *The Control Revolution*. Public Affairs, 1999.

Wired Magazine's Encyclopedia of the New Economy. Wired, 1998, available at http://www.hotwired.lycos.com/special/ene.

ARTICLES AND REPORTS

Caufield, Brian. "Broadband's Believers." *Internet World*, October 1, 1999.

Clark, David D., et al. "Special Report: High-Speed Data Races Home." *Scientific American*, October 1999.

Dawson, Fred. "Broadband Content and Applications," New World Networks position paper, 1999.

Elton, Martin C. J. "The U.S. Debate on Integrated Broadband Networks." In *Media, Culture and Society*, Vol. 14, Sage Publications, 1992.

"Hooked on Broadband." *The Forrester Report*, July 1999

Kapor, Mitchell. "Where Is the Digital Highway Really Heading?" *Wired*, July/August 1993.

Lambert, Peter. "This Revolution." *tele.com magazine*, April 1998.

Werbach, Kevin. "The Architecture of the Internet 2.0." *Release 1.0*, February 1999.

NEWSLETTERS

Communications Daily - Warren Publishing Co., Washington, D.C.

The Digital Beat – via e-mail, the Benton Foundation.

CNET News.com – via e-mail.

Netscape *Technews* – via e-mail.

WEBSITES

Broadband-guide.com

whatis.com

telecomweb.com

hotwired.com

PERIODICALS

The New York Times

Washington Post

Wall Street Journal

San Jose Mercury

Broadcasting and Cable

Electronic Media

Internet World

The Economist

Television Business International

Strategy & Business

2.
JUSTIN SMITH MORRILL AND THE POLITICS AND LEGACY OF THE LAND-GRANT COLLEGE ACTS

CRAIG L. LAMAY

Justin Smith Morrill, in the style of Vermont politicians, defied easy characterization. He was regarded in his own day as a conservative—he opposed the eight-hour workday, women's suffrage, and direct election of the president and senators—though he is remembered today as a populist. His most notable legacy, the 1862 Land-Grant College Act, extended the possibility of higher education to the masses including such traditionally disenfranchised groups as women and African Americans. By any estimation, the law gave new meaning to equal opportunity and thus to democracy in the post-Civil War period. It gave intellectual force to the human and economic development of the states, and thus of the nation. The law also made the United States the world leader in agricultural production and, coupled with the 1944 GI Bill, established the foundation upon which the nation's defense, diplomacy, and economic competitiveness have relied throughout the latter half of the twentieth century.

Morrill is the subject of two published biographies: William B. Parker's *The Life and Public Services of Justin Smith Morrill*, published in 1924;[1] and more recently Coy F. Cross's excellent *Justin Smith Morrill: The Father of the Land-Grant Colleges*, published in 1999.[2] This sketch of Morrill and his legacy relies on both of those works, as well as several of the hundreds of scholarly essays concerning the Land-Grant Act itself, from the politics surrounding its creation to the technical aspects of land distribution and revenue management under the law. Not surprisingly, there was a large volume of work and commentary in and around 1962, on the centennial of the act's passage. More recently, commentary and scholarship have focused on the unfinished agenda of the land-grant concept, particularly with regard to educational opportunity for minorities[3] and the policy implications of Morrill's idea, both in the nineteenth century and today,[4] as public higher education faces new technological, financial, demographic, and pedagogic challenges to its historic mission.

MORRILL THE PUBLIC SERVANT

Justin Morrill was born in Strafford, Vermont, on April 14, 1810. He had no formal education beyond secondary school. He had wanted to attend college but his father could not afford to send both him and his brothers, so elected to send none of them.[5] Nonetheless, by the time Morrill was elected to Congress in 1854 he had enjoyed a successful career dealing in dry goods in Vermont and also in Maine. Politics was a second career. Morrill had retired from business at the age of thirty-eight, in 1848, and settled down to build his gentleman's farm in Strafford.[6]

Morrill was not a political novice when the Vermont Whig Party nominated him for the state's second congressional district in July 1854, though his experience was limited to New England, and he won his office narrowly—by a total of fifty-nine votes.[7] He came to office at a fortuitous time, given the legislation that would become his legacy. The United States had acquired 500,000 square miles of new territory in the 1848 treaty with Mexico, though the immediate effect of the acquisition was to raise again the question of slavery and whether it would be permitted in the new territories. Within a year of Morrill's election to Congress, many northern Whigs and Democrats, Free Soilers, and other antislavery factions had organized into the Republican Party. The 34th Congress, which opened in December 1855, was one of the most contentious ever; it had 108 Republicans, 83 Democrats (most of them proslavery Southerners), and 43 American Party members, better known as the "Know-Nothings," who were themselves split on the slavery issue.[8] Over the length of his congressional career, which lasted for forty-four years and eleven presidents (from 1855 to 1867 in the House, from 1867 to 1898 in the Senate), Morrill was perhaps best known as an expert on taxes and tariffs. It was largely through his efforts that the Union was to finance the Civil War; Morrill was author of the Tariff Act of 1861 and served as chairman of the House Ways and Means Committee. Later, as a senator, he chaired the Committee on Public Buildings and Grounds and served on the Finance Committee.[9] In those positions he was influential in creating, if not singularly responsible for, the modern Library of Congress—its site, its funding, and its architectural design. Until 1897 the congressional reading room was a fairly unimpressive business tucked away in the Capitol building.

EVENTS LEADING TO PASSAGE OF THE 1862 ACT

Morrill, his biographers note, regretted his own lack of formal education and, as a Vermonter, saw the need for practical education in agriculture and mechanics for the working people with whom he identified. In the mid-nineteenth century 80 percent of Americans lived in rural areas, and about 60 percent of Americans were farmers (compared to 23 percent and 2 percent, respectively, today), most of them eking out a subsistence living.[10] In 1860 one farm produced only enough food to feed five people, compared to today's production level of about 140 people per farmer.[11] Agricultural societies had formed in the United States after the Revolutionary War (the first of them, the Philadelphia Society for Promoting Agriculture, founded by Benjamin Franklin and still in existence), and they pushed, with small success, for agricultural colleges that would improve farming methods and productivity. The first American school devoted to agriculture was Gardiner Lyceum, in Maine, established in 1823.[12] Pennsylvania established the first agricultural high school in 1855, which in 1862 became the state's Land-Grant college and eventually Pennsylvania State University. Michigan established the first agricultural college in 1855, followed by Maryland in 1856.[13] All of these schools suffered from a lack of quality teachers and curricula and shaky finances, but they provided fertile ground for the idea that Morrill would carry to the House floor.

Not coincidentally, the farmers and workers whom Morrill championed were the same people who, by 1862, were dying by the thousands in places like Bull Run, Shiloh, and Cold Harbor. Speaking in Congress in 1858, Morrill decried the fact that such people had to "snatch their education, such as it is, from the crevices between labor and sleep. They grope in twilight. Our country depends upon them as its right arm to do the handiwork of the nation. Let us, then, furnish the means for that arm to acquire culture, skill, efficiency."[14]

Historians generally agree that Morrill's vision for Land-Grant colleges had its origins elsewhere—in Europe, which by the mid-nineteenth century had its own workingmen's colleges, and in the work of an Illinois College professor, Jonathan Baldwin Turner, a Yale graduate who had proposed providing liberal education to farmers, factory workers, and others as early as 1850.[15] Specifically, it was Turner who proposed the public lands appropriation as the basis of an endowment to support the creation of new colleges. The Illinois legislature formally proposed the idea to Congress in 1853, asking that each state get $500,000 worth of public land to "endow a system of industrial universities."[16] More generally, of course, the idea for government-sponsored colleges was, in the United States, at least as old as 1618, when King James granted ten thousand acres to Virginia for a college.[17] Public schools in the United States had won federal financial support as early as 1785, when the then quite weak federal government had reserved one section of each township in the country for their maintenance.[18]

A college education in the mid-nineteenth century was generally reserved for white men preparing for careers in theology, medicine, or law, and above all for the well-to-do (since neither medicine nor law called for much advanced training in those days, and such training as existed was often perfunctory).[19] It was anything but practical, and, Morrill thought, obsolete. Many others agreed with him, among them Turner in Illinois and in the East businessmen Ezra Cornell and Thomas Clemson and newspaper publisher Horace Greeley.[20] By 1850, wrote Allan Nevins, the industrial revolution was well under way:

> For Americans in particular, every fresh invention, from sewing machines to telegraphs, every new application of power, from locomotives to liners, every industrial innovation, from oil wells to Bessemer steel, opened stirring vistas. . . . Against this background the college education of earlier times seemed hopelessly antiquated; it had to be wrested out of the ruts in which it had so long traveled.[21]

By 1855, however, there were only a very few institutions around the country that taught something other than the classics. (As late as 1860, according to census data for the year, only 3 percent of the nation's 397 colleges had departments of science or agriculture.)[22] One of them was Norwich University in Vermont, just twelve miles from Morrill's home in Strafford. Norwich had been founded by a former West Point commandant, Captain Alden Partridge, and Partridge had urged Congress in 1841 to establish a national system of higher education that included in its curriculum courses on farming, engineering, and business. To finance the system, Partridge urged a federal appropriation of $40 million, to be paid for by the sale of public lands. Morrill became a trustee of Norwich in 1848 and served in that role until his death in 1898.[23]

Morrill introduced the peoples' college idea to Congress in 1856 (three months after taking his seat in the House), but without the land-grant component. He asked the House Committee on Agriculture to establish "one or more agricultural schools upon the basis of the naval and military academies."[24] One student from each congressional district could then receive a free education at these institutions. A committee member from South Carolina killed the idea.[25]

On a second attempt, Morrill incorporated the idea of federal land grants as a means of finance, and thus re-introduced (following Turner and the Illinois legislature) the land-grant concept to Congress. He introduced the Bill Granting Lands for Agricultural Colleges on December 17, 1857. In it he proposed that each state receive twenty thousand acres of public land for each representative and senator, a proposal for which there was ample precedent.[26] By the mid-nineteenth century the federal government had awarded approximately 45 million acres of public land to veterans, another 25.4 million acres to states and territories for the construction of railroads, and another 67.7 million to states and territories for schools and universities. By Morrill's estimate, his bill would give about 5.8 million acres to the cause of agricultural colleges, leaving more than 1 billion acres of public land still in government hands.[27]

Morrill's bill went to the House Committee on Public Lands, where opposition focused on the bill's constitutionality and, secondly, on the idea itself. On the first score, Morrill defended his proposal under the commerce clause, likening his idea to the government's financial support for lighthouses, harbor construction, and the service academies and railroads, all in the service of commerce and trade. On the second, he marshaled impressive statistics with which he was able to show that European farmers produced far greater yields on smaller plots of land than did their American counterparts, a feat born of scientific methods largely unknown in the United States. Morrill attributed the Europeans' success to their agricultural colleges, though he noted that these colleges were, in European style, for the privileged few. Morrill argued that any American counterpart to these colleges should be "for the use and benefit of all."[28]

The House passed Morrill's bill 105 to 100 on April 20, 1858. It then went to the Senate, where it ran into strong Southern opposition led by Clement Clay of Alabama, James Mason of Virginia, and Jefferson Davis of Mississippi. The South, in fact, opposed the bill with virtual unanimity, and Democrats everywhere opposed the bill for its implications about federal power. Some unionist Southerners supported the bill for its agricultural significance, which spoke directly to their self-interest. Many westerners opposed it for its easy susceptibility to land speculation and because they thought the idea of educating farmers and working class people quixotic. Only New Englanders supported the bill strongly. Nonetheless the bill passed, twenty-five to twenty-two, on February 7, 1859.[29] President James Buchanan then vetoed the bill at the urging of Louisiana senator John Slidell. Buchanan said he thought the bill unconstitutional, though he commented with some favor on its intent:

> Under this bill, it is provided that scientific and classical studies shall not be excluded from [the colleges]. Indeed, it would be almost impossible to sustain them without such a provision; for no father would incur the expense of sending a son to one of these institutions for the sole purpose of making him a scientific farmer or mechanic. The bill itself negatives this idea and declares that their object is "to promote the liberal and practical education of the industrial classes in the several pursuits and professions of life." This certainly ought to be the case.[30]

Morrill tried again after the election of 1860 and the secession of the South. He assumed his chances were good, as thirteen states had instructed their representatives to approve the measure should it come up again. He reintroduced his bill on December 16, 1861, this time increasing the land allotment from twenty thousand to thirty thousand acres for each representative and senator and, importantly, including a provision for teaching military skills (all this excluding the rebellious Southern states, of course).[31]

As with the earlier bill, the new one did not exclude the liberal arts from its curricular prescription. Speaking years later before the Vermont legislature, Morrill said, "It was not provided that agricultural labor in the field should be practically taught, any more than that the mechanical trade of a carpenter or blacksmith should be taught."[32] Rather, Morrill said, he had wanted to bring intellectual instruction to the many—the 1862 bill's exact language proposed colleges that while practical would be broad, "without excluding other scientific and classical studies."[33] In Morrill's words, "The fundamental idea of this legislation was to offer an opportunity in every state for a liberal and larger education to larger numbers, not merely to those destined for sedentary professions, but to those much needing higher instruction for the world's business, for the industrial pursuits and professions of life."[34]

The bill again went to the Committee on Public Lands, whose chairman, John Potter of Wisconsin, recommended against its passage. Western congressmen generally disliked the bill, since of course much of the public lands to be given away and sold were theirs, the benefits (as they saw them) to accrue to eastern states. Western states also feared that the bill would lead to land speculation, a fear that later would prove to have merit. Earlier land grants had benefited those who lived nearby or in the same state, and almost always new states; the Morrill Act, with its national system of distribution based on congressional representation, favored smaller, established, and more populous states, mostly in the east.[35]

While the bill languished in the House, Morrill asked a colleague to introduce it in the Senate, where it met resistance on the same grounds as in the House but nonetheless passed thirty-two to seven on June 10, 1862.[36] The House then approved the bill ninety to twenty-five on June 17, and President Lincoln signed it into law on July 2, 1862.[37] Only two months before, Lincoln had signed into law the Homestead Act, which gave settlers in western states and territories 160 acres of federal land and would eventually give away seventy million acres. Several historians offer the comment that the Morrill Act, with its terms so favorable to the East, might not have passed but for the countervailing terms in the Homestead Act, which were so favorable to the West. In any case, it is notable that the first debate over the Land-Grant Colleges bill had been fought over North-South divisions; the second debate, in 1862, had been fought over East-West divisions, which were sharp but far less bitter or deep. Indeed, one historian describes the 1862 act rather glowingly as "one of many Republican efforts to cement an alliance between east and west, between industry and agriculture."[38]

A day before the Morrill Act became law, on July 1, Lincoln had approved a transcontinental railroad bill that gave approximately 130 million acres of public land to the railroads. These giveaways followed on earlier legislation, preceding Lincoln, which had given 61 million acres of public lands to veterans of the Mexican War and various Indian wars. Because so much federal land was suddenly available, the states' response to the Morrill Act was fairly slow. Eventually the 1862 colleges received 17,430,000 acres—the tiniest portion of the federal lands given away in this period,[39] but in economic and historical terms, as it would turn out, the investment with by far the greatest return.

THE 1862 ACT IN OPERATION

The mechanics of the 1862 act were straightforward. Western states that still had public land to sell would actually select parcels of land that they could either sell immediately or hold until prices went up. Eastern states with no federal public land remaining within their borders (which was most of them) were given scrip, which they then had to sell to assignees to prevent any state from owning land in another. Assignees could redeem the scrip for land. States were then to invest the proceeds from sales into the "stocks of the United States or of the States, or some other safe stocks, yielding not less than five per centum."[40] This fund was to remain untouched, and the income was to pay for the "endowment, support and maintenance of at least one college" in each state.[41] States had their own role to play in this, since the interest from the land-grant funds was not to pay for buildings, but only for books, supplies, instruction, and so on. The states themselves had to provide the land and the buildings, though the law provided that as much as 10 percent of the capital could be used for the purchase of sites.[42] Some states built from scratch, while many others invested in existing colleges (such as New York did with Cornell, Massachusetts with MIT, New Jersey with Rutgers, and Michigan with its agricultural college, later to be known as Michigan State University). In 1864 Congress amended the act, requiring the states that wished to participate in the program to agree to the law's terms within two years[43]; in 1866, Congress required the participating states to establish a college within five years.[44] A large number had difficulty meeting the 5 percent return requirement and so found various ways to make up the difference. A few (Illinois, and later North Carolina and South Carolina) lost their endowments through "defalcation or dishonesty" and their state legislatures issued bonds to restore them.[45]

Because the monies made available through the 1862 act were so often insufficient to its aspirations, the colleges developed slowly. The first three states to act on the law were Iowa, Vermont, and Connecticut, in 1862. A year later fourteen states had adopted the act, and by 1870 thirty-seven states had instituted some kind of program for teaching agriculture, mechanical arts and, as the act stipulated, military tactics. Nonetheless the Land-Grant College Act might well have been perceived as a bust in its early years. Land prices were low. Total receipts on the 17.4 million acres came to a fairly meager $7.5 million.[46] Many Eastern states sold their scrip quickly and earned less than a dollar an acre for it (Kentucky did the worst, at fifty cents per acre).[47] Only nine states received more than the $1.25 per acre that the act had mandated as a minimum return; New York held its grant the longest and managed to earn a whopping $5.82 per acre.[48] States had little money for buildings, few qualified teachers, and not many applicants.

Morrill tried repeatedly—first in 1872 and eleven more times through 1890—to win additional land grants or financial support for the colleges, and by 1890 he could boast that forty-eight colleges had been created as a result of his 1862 legislation.[49] That year he succeeded: President Benjamin Harrison signed the second Land-Grant Act into law on August 30, 1890, granting states an additional $15,000 a year initially, and rising to $25,000 per year.[50] Morrill tried again in 1897 and 1898, just before his death, to win additional funding. Where Morrill failed others followed. The 1887 Hatch Act added funds to support agricultural extension stations; the Adams Act of 1906 and the Purnell Act of 1925 both provided for research grants at the extension stations; a 1907 amendment to the 1990 act added another $25,000 per year per college for salaries and operating funds (bringing each state's yearly total to $50,000); the Smith-Lever Act of 1914 established the Co-operative Agricultural Extension Service and made federal funds available to pay part of its costs; and the Bankhead-Jones Act of 1935 added still more federal funds, $1 million to be distributed in flat grants of $20,000 to each state.[51] (For a list of the Land-Grant colleges, see page 85; for a list of federal legislation supporting Land-Grant education, see page 90.)

THE LAND-GRANT ACT AND THE
TRANSFORMATION OF AMERICA

The social and economic impact of the Morrill Act and related legislation is impossible to measure, but a few quantitative measures are suggestive. Today the largest of the Land-Grant programs is the University of California, which enrolls approximately 150,000 students on its nine campuses; the smallest is Kentucky State University, with about 2,500 students. All together the Land-Grant colleges enroll about three million students annually and award about 500,000 degrees each year, including one-third of all bachelor's and master's degrees, 60 percent of all doctoral degrees, and 70 percent of the nation's engineering degrees. Since 1862 they have awarded more than twenty million degrees.[52]

There are in addition so-called sea-grant colleges, authorized by the federal Sea Grant Act of 1966. Base funding for the sea grant comes from the National Oceanic and Atmospheric Administration in the Department of Commerce, and the idea is to promote better understanding and use of the nation's coastal, ocean, and Great Lakes resources. There are now twenty-nine sea-grant programs, one in every coastal and Great Lakes state and in Puerto Rico.[53]

Other benefits of the Morrill Act have to be measured qualitatively. Above all, as Morrill had hoped, the land-grant colleges have benefited "those at the bottom of the ladder who want to climb up, or those who have some ambition to rise in the world but are without the means to seek far from home a higher standard of culture."[54] The colleges made higher education available to women and to blacks, both of whom had traditionally been excluded from educational opportunity. The 1862 law, of course, denied its benefits to Southern states until they re-entered the Union after the war, and in the politics of Reconstruction many of the first land-grant colleges in the region were for blacks. The first was Alcorn State University in Mississippi, founded in 1871. Hampton University followed in Virginia in 1872.

The 1890 act denied funds to any school "where a distinction of race or color is made in the admission of students," and essentially required Southern states to open their land-grant facilities to blacks or open separate institutions for them. They did the latter, of course. It can hardly be denied that the effect of the law was to entrench separate-but-equal as educational policy, the effects of which were made more insidious by the fact that black colleges typically received an amount equal to about 10 percent of the funds states made available to their white-only counterparts.[55] Still, Morrill had successfully argued the principle that education should be available to all for the greater good. Speaking in the Senate in 1876 he said:

> Having emancipated a whole race, shall it be said that there our duty ends, leaving the race as cumberers of the ground, to live or to wilt and perish, as the case may be? They are members of the American family and their advancement concerns us all. While swiftly forgetting all they ever knew as slaves, shall they have no opportunity to learn anything as freemen?[56]

Among the schools for African Americans founded after the 1890 act were the Colored Normal, Industrial, Agricultural and Mechanical College of South Carolina in 1896 (now South Carolina State University) and, in 1897 in Kentucky, the State Normal School for Colored Persons (now Kentucky State University). Today there are seventeen historically black land-grant colleges and universities, and they have awarded approximately 700,000 degrees. All of the historically black colleges have been co-educational from the beginning.[57]

Most recently, it is Native Americans who have benefited from the land-grant program. The National Agricultural Research, Extension and Teaching Act of 1994 (a provision of the Elementary and Secondary Education Reauthorization Act) authorized a $23 million endowment, to be built up over a five-year period, to support twenty-nine tribal colleges on Indian reservations throughout the United States.[58]

There were other, less immediately obvious or even foreseeable benefits of the 1862 law. With its nonsectarian foundations the Morrill Act helped to separate religious doctrine from higher education and, particularly in the period after World War II, when huge numbers of returning servicemen swelled the rolls of land-grant colleges, helped to establish research as a core function of the American university. At the outbreak of the war, the act's provision for military training at the land-grant institutions was instrumental in meeting the demands of mobilization. Morrill had presumably included the provision in response to the woeful record of Union officers in the Civil War, particularly as compared to the performance of the Confederate officer corps,[59] but it was World War II where the land-grant military training program proved invaluable. When the war began, the U.S. military was very small, and it relied on about fifty thousand Reserve Officer Training Corps officers from the land-grant colleges and universities to train hundreds of thousands of civilians over a very short time.[60] As Army chief of staff General

George C. Marshall put it, "Just what we would have done . . . without these men I do not know."[61]

Justin Morrill himself could not have foreseen that the institutions he established would in time become the preeminent system of higher education in the world. Indeed, higher education is one of the few areas in which the United States enjoys a consistent and favorably lopsided balance of trade— relatively few American students travel abroad to study for degrees, while thousands of people come to the United States from virtually everywhere to study, most commonly at the land-grant colleges, and especially for advanced degrees in science and engineering. In this respect, the Morrill Act still functions as its creator hoped it would, making higher education available to those who otherwise would not be able to obtain one, and broadly diffusing its benefits.

What Morrill probably did foresee—indeed, the rationale that compelled him in 1862 and throughout his career—was the role the land-grant institutions would play in carrying American democracy into the next century. At one level the act accomplished that purpose by virtue of its design: The institutions it created, while rising to international prominence, have remained deeply rooted in the needs of their states and regions, as the 1862 act supposed they would be. The United States, unlike many European nations, would have no "national" university; rather. the flexibility of the federal-state partnership permitted each state to find its own way. The act thus enabled the colleges it created to meet the changing needs of a changing country in a manner consistent with the aspirations of a free and open society.

The democratic faith that Morrill made his cause was no certain thing in 1862. As Lincoln would say at Gettysburg a little more than a year later, it was an open question whether a nation dedicated to liberty and equality could endure the bitter strains of separatism. Beyond his role in financing the Union's prosecution of the war, Morrill ensured the outcome of the struggle for freedom by making education the most potent weapon in the contest. Further, Morrill saw to it that the Land-Grant Colleges Act, through the endowments it created, would not be static but dynamic, carried on in perpetuity for the benefit of generations yet unborn.

NOTES

1. William B. Parker. *The Life and Public Services of Justin Smith Morrill.* Boston: Houghton Mifflin Co., 1924.

2. Coy F. Cross II. *Justin Smith Morrill: Father of the Land-Grant Colleges.* East Lansing, Mich.: Michigan State University Press, 1999.

3. See, for example, Frederick Humphries. "1890 Land-Grant Institutions: Their Struggle for Survival and Equality," *Agricultural History,* Vol. 65, No. 2, 1991.

4. See, for example, Scott A. Key, "The Origins of the Land-Grant Universities: An Historical Policy Study." Unpublished Ph.D. dissertation, University of Illinois-Chicago, 1995.

5. Cross, 5.

6. Ibid., 10–12.

7. Ibid., 26.

8. Ibid., 26–27.

9. "Justin Smith Morrill," *American National Biography*. New York, Oxford University Press, 1999, 883.

10. "Events leading to the establishment of Land-Grant universities," website of the University of Florida Institute of Food and Agricultural Sciences (http://gnv.ifas.ufl.edu/www/ls_grant/whatislg.html), May 23, 2000, 1–2.

11. Ibid., 3.

12. Ibid., 4.

13. Ibid. See also Lee C. Deighton, ed. "Land-Grant Colleges," *The Encyclopedia of Education*. New York: Macmillan Co. and the Free Press, 1971, 319.

14. Justin Smith Morrill. *Speech on the Bill Granting Lands for Agricultural Colleges*. United States House of Representatives, April 20, 1858. Washington, D.C.: Congressional Globe Printing Office, 8.

15. See, for example, William David Zimmerman. "The Morrill Act and Liberal Education," *Liberal Education*, Vol. 50, No. 3, 1964, 396–400.

16. Allan Nevins. "The Origins of the Land-Grant Colleges and State Universities." Washington, D.C.: Civil War Centennial Commission, 1962, 6–21; Cross, 78; Zimmerman, 397.

17. Harold M. Hyman. *American Singularity: The 1787 Northwest Ordinance, the 1862 Homestead and Morrill Acts, and the 1944 G.I. Bill*. Athens, Ga.: University of Georgia Press, 1986, 18–34.

18. Ibid.

19. Nevins, 11.

20. Ibid., 6.

21. Ibid., 8.

22. Deighton, 319.

23. Cross, 78–79.

24. Parker, 82.

25. Ibid., 12. See also Cross, 79.

26. Cross, 80–81.

27. Ibid., 81–82. See also Deighton, 319.

28. Cross, 81–82.

29. Ibid., 82–83.

30. *Congressional Globe*, 35th Congress, 2 Session, 1413.

31. Cross, 83.

32. John T. Fey. "Morrill's Concept of Education." *Vermont History*, Vol. 31, No. 2, 1963, 157.

33. *Morrill Land-Grant Act of 1862: An Act Donating public lands to the several States and Territories which may provide colleges for the benefit of agriculture and the mechanic arts.* 12 Statute 503, July 2, 1862.

34. Fey.

35. Simon, 105–109.

36. Ibid., 106.

37. Ibid.

38. Ibid., 110.

39. Sauder, 34–37; Cross, 85.

40. *Morrill Land-Grant Act of 1862.*

41. Ibid.

42. Ben F. Andrews. *The Land Grant of 1862 and the Land-Grant Colleges.* Washington, D.C.: Department of the Interior, Bureau of Education, 1918, 10.

43. *Act of 1864 to Extend the Time for Accepting the Grant,* April 14, 1864.

44. *Act of 1866, Extending the Time within which Agricultural Colleges May Be Established,* 14 Statute 208, July 23, 1866.

45. Ibid., 56–57.

46. Cross, 85.

47. Andrews, 19.

48. Ibid., 35–36; Cross, 85.

49. Cross, 86.

50. Ibid.

51. Roland Renne. "Land Grant Institutions, the Public and the Public Interest." *The Annals of the American Academy of Political and Social Science,* Vol. 331, 1960, 47. See also Deighton, 320.

52. Cross, 88–89.

53. "Land-Grant and Sea-Grant Acts, History and Institutions," Web page of the University of Florida Institute of Food and Agricultural Sciences (http://gnv.ifas.ufl.edu/www/ls_grant/index.html), May 23, 2000, 3–4.

54. Justin Smith Morrill, *Speech on the Educational Bill.* United States Senate, December 15, 1880. Washington, D.C.: Congressional Globe Printing Office, 4.

55. Jenkins, Robert L. "The Black Land-Grant Colleges in Their Formative Years, 1890–1920." *Agricultural History,* Vol. 65, No. 2, 1991, 63–72; see also Humphries, 3–11.

56. Justin Smith Morrill, *Speech on the Educational Fund.* United States Senate, April 26, 1876. Washington, D.C.: Congressional Globe Printing Office, 10.

57. Cross, 86.

58. "Events leading to the establishment of Land-Grant universities," 6.

59. Richard M. Abrams. "The U.S. Military and Higher Education: A Brief History." *Annals of the American Academy of Political and Social Science,* Vol. 502, 1989, 15–28.

60. Cross, 88.

61. Herman R. Allen. *Open Door to Learning: The Land-Grant System Enters its Second Century.* Urbana: University of Illinois Press, 1963, 171–72.

THE LAND-GRANT COLLEGES

* Indicates historically black institutions
** Indicates Native American institutions created since 1994
*** The 30 tribal colleges created in 1994 are included individually in this list but are represented as a system by the American Indian Higher Education Consortium.

ALABAMA
Alabama A&M University*
Auburn University
Tuskegee University*

ALASKA
University of Alaska system

AMERICAN SAMOA
American Samoa Community College

ARIZONA
University of Arizona
Navajo Community College**

ARKANSAS
University of Arkansas, Fayetteville
University of Arkansas, Pine Bluff*

CALIFORNIA
University of California system
D-Q University

COLORADO
Colorado State University

CONNECTICUT
University of Connecticut

DELAWARE
Delaware State University*
University of Delaware

DISTRICT OF COLUMBIA
University of the District of Columbia

FLORIDA
Florida A&M University*
University of Florida

GEORGIA
Fort Valley State College*
University of Georgia

GUAM
University of Guam

HAWAII
University of Hawaii

IDAHO
University of Idaho

ILLINOIS
University of Illinois

INDIANA
Purdue University

IOWA
Iowa State University

KANSAS
Kansas State University
Haskell Indian Nations University**

KENTUCKY
Kentucky State University*
University of Kentucky

LOUISIANA
Louisiana State University system
Southern University and A&M system*

MAINE
University of Maine

MARYLAND
University of Maryland, College Park
University of Maryland, Eastern Shore*

MASSACHUSETTS
Massachusetts Institute of Technology
University of Massachusetts

MICHIGAN
Bay Mills Community College**
Michigan State University

MICRONESIA
Community College of Micronesia—FSM

MINNESOTA
University of Minnesota
Fond du Lac Community College**
Leech Lake Tribal College**

MISSISSIPPI
Alcorn State University*
Mississippi State University

MISSOURI
Lincoln University*
University of Missouri system

MONTANA
Montana State University
Blackfeet Community College**
Dull Knife Community College**
Fort Belknap Community College**
Fort Peck Community College**
Little Bighorn College**
Salish Kootenai College**
Stone Child College**

NEBRASKA
University of Nebraska system
Nebraska Indian Community College**

NEVADA
University of Nevada, Reno

NEW HAMPSHIRE
University of New Hampshire

NEW JERSEY
Rutgers, the State University of New Jersey

NEW MEXICO
New Mexico State University
Crownpoint Institute of Technology**
Institute of American Indian and Alaska Native Culture Arts Development**
Southwest Indian Polytechnic Institute**

NEW YORK
Cornell University

NORTH CAROLINA
North Carolina A&T State University*
North Carolina State University

NORTH DAKOTA
North Dakota State University
Fort Bethold Community College**
Little Hoop Community College**
Standing Rock College**
Turtle Mountain Community College**
United Tribes Technical College**

NORTHERN MARIANAS
Northern Marianas College

OHIO
Ohio State University

OKLAHOMA
Langston University*
Oklahoma State University

OREGON
Oregon State University

PENNSYLVANIA
Pennsylvania State University

PUERTO RICO
University of Puerto Rico

RHODE ISLAND
University of Rhode Island

SOUTH CAROLINA
Clemson University
South Carolina State University*

SOUTH DAKOTA
South Dakota State University
Cheyenne River Community College**
Ogalala Lakota College**
Sinte Gleska University**
Sisseton Wahpeton Community College**

TENNESSEE
Tennessee State University
University of Tennessee

TEXAS
Prairie View A&M University*
Texas A&M University

UTAH
Utah State University

VERMONT
University of Vermont

VIRGIN ISLANDS
University of the Virgin Islands*

VIRGINIA
Virginia Polytechnic Institute & State University
Virginia State University*
American Indian Higher Education Consortium***

WASHINGTON
Washington State University
Northwest Indian College**

WEST VIRGINIA
West Virginia University
West Virginia State College*

WISCONSIN
University of Wisconsin-Madison
College of the Menominee Nation**
Lac Courte Ojibwa Community College**

WYOMING
University of Wyoming

FEDERAL LEGISLATION SUPPORTING LAND-GRANT EDUCATION

1787 - Northwest Ordinance is passed, authorizing the sale of public land for support of education, thus establishing the land-grant principle.

1862 - First Morrill Act is passed and signed by President Abraham Lincoln, donating public lands to the several states, the sale of which is for the "endowment, support, and maintenance of at least one college where the leading object shall be, without excluding other scientific and classical studies and including military tactics, to teach such branches of learning as are related to agriculture and the mechanic arts, in order to promote the liberal and practical education of the industrial classes in the several pursuits and professions in life."

1887 - The Hatch Act is passed, mandating the creation of agricultural experiment stations for scientific research.

1890 - The Second Morrill Act is passed, providing further endowment for colleges. Part of this funding is to be used for institutions for black students, leading to the creation of seventeen historically black land-grant colleges.

1907 - Nelson Amendment to the Morrill Acts of 1862 and 1890 is passed, providing further increased appropriations to land-grant institutions.

1908 - Benefits of Second Morrill Act and the Nelson Amendment extended to Puerto Rico.

1914 - The Smith-Lever Act is passed, providing federal support for land-grant institutions to offer educational programs to enhance the application of useful and practical information beyond their campuses through cooperative extension efforts with states and local communities.

1924 - Clark-McNary Act. Section 5 of this act provides funds (on a matching basis by the individual states) for cooperative farm-forestry work.

1928 - Capper-Ketcham Act. This provides for the further development of agricultural extension work at the 1862 land-grant colleges and stipulates that future funds be allocated "in addition to and not a substitute for" those made available in the Smith-Lever Act of 1914.

1929 - Alaska Act of 1929. This extends the benefits of the Hatch Act and the Smith-Lever Act to the Territory of Alaska.

1931 - Puerto Rico Act. This coordinates the agricultural-experiment station work and extends the benefits of the Hatch and Smith-Lever Acts to the Territory of Puerto Rico.

1934 - Congress creates the National Youth Administration to enable college students to earn money by performing educationally useful tasks and to continue their studies.

1935 - The Bankhead-Jones Act adds to annual appropriations for land-grant institutions. This extends the scope of research conducted under the Hatch Act and provides for the future development of Cooperative Agricultural Extension work and for the further endowment and support of 1862 and 1890 land-grant colleges.

1942 - The General Equivalency Diploma (GED) program and the Military Evaluations Programs for veterans who left school to serve in World War II are established.

1944 - The Servicemen's Readjustment Act (GI Bill of Rights), Public Law 346. This provides for the higher education of veterans.

1945 - The Bankhead-Flannagan Act furthers the development of cooperative extension work in agriculture and home economics.

1946 - Congress passes the Fulbright Act (Public Law 584) to enable Americans to study and teach abroad.

1946 - The United Nations Educational, Scientific and Cultural Organization (UNESCO) is established, which, among its many other activities, provides international exchange opportunities for American scholars and administrators.

1946 - Agricultural Marketing Act. This furthers authorized extension programs in marketing, transportation, and distribution of agricultural products outside the Smith-Lever formula, but states are required to match federal funds.

1948 - The U.S. Information and Educational Exchange Act (the Smith-Mundt Act) provides for the international exchange of teachers, students, lecturers, and other specialists.

1949 - Clarke-McNary Amendment. This authorizes the U.S. Department of Agriculture to cooperate with land-grant colleges in aiding farmers through advice, education, demonstration, etc., in establishing, renewing, protecting, and managing wood lots and so forth, and in harvesting, utilizing, and marketing the products thereof.

1950 - Point Four Program is enacted by Congress (the Foreign Economic Assistance Act, subsequently called the International Cooperation Administration, then renamed the Agency for International Development, or AID).

1950 - Congress creates the National Science Foundation (NSF).

1950 - The Land-Grant Endowment Funds Bill protects federal and private endowments from unilateral federal action to divert them from the purposes for which they were granted.

1952 - Veterans' Readjustment Assistance Act (Korean GI Bill of Rights) is passed.

1953 - Smith-Lever Act Amendment. This simplifies and consolidates ten separate laws relating to extension. Establishes new funding procedures based on rural/urban population formula and amounts. Repeals the Capper-Ketcham Act and the two Bankhead-Jones Acts of 1935 and 1945. Inserts "and subjects relating thereto" after agriculture and home economics and makes reference to necessary printing and distribution of information.

1955 – Smith-Lever Amendment. This authorizes work with disadvantaged farms and farm families and authorizes funds for extension outside the traditional funding "formula."

1958 - National Defense Education Act (NDEA) provides college student loans, graduate fellowships, and aid for the improvement in the teaching of science, mathematics, and modern languages.

1960 - Land-grant status for the University of Hawaii establishes a new precedent. Since there is no longer adequate federal land to donate for the creation of an endowment, the University of Hawaii is given a $6 million endowment in lieu of land scrip.

1961 - Report of the U.S. Commission on Civil Rights, "Equal Protection of the Laws in Public Higher Education: 1960," recommends that federal funds be disbursed "only to such publicly controlled institutions of higher education as do not discriminate on grounds of race, color, religion, or national origin."

1963 - The Higher Education Act (HEA) of 1963 recognizes federal responsibility for aid to colleges and universities in the form of grants and loans for the construction of academic facilities.

1964 - The National Defense Education Act Amendments authorize major changes to expand and strengthen the graduate fellowship program and eliminate discriminatory institutional limitation on loan-fund grants.

1965 - The Higher Education Act of 1965 is passed, funding many higher education programs, including student aid.

1965 - The Housing and Urban Development Act of 1965 establishes a maximum interest rate of 3 percent for the College Housing Loan Program to provide relief for students from the high cost of college attendance.

1966 - The National Defense Education Project is passed to coordinate the federal role in international education. Later, this project is incorporated as Title VI of the Higher Education Act.

1966 - National Sea Grant College and Program Act. This establishes a program (under the U.S. Department of Commerce) to provide for applied research, formal education, and advisory (extension) services for development of marine and Great Lakes resources. About two-thirds (of the thirty coastal and Great Lakes states involved) have integrated this effort with that of cooperative extension.

1967 - The District of Columbia Post Secondary Education Reorganization Act gives land-grant status to Federal City College, now the University of the District of Columbia. This establishes a precedent for federal trust areas to participate in the land-grant system.

1968 - The Navajo Community College Act creates the first tribally controlled college.

1968 - District of Columbia Public Education Act. This designates Federal City College as the land-grant institution for extension in the District of Columbia and authorizes funds for this work.

1972 - Rural Development Act of 1972 - Title V. This authorizes rural development and small-farm extension programs, requires that administration of programs be associated with programs under the Smith-Lever Act, and establishes State Rural Development Advisory Councils.

1972 - University of Guam, Northern Marianas College, the Community Colleges of American Samoa and Micronesia, and the College of the Virgin Islands secure land-grant status through the Education Amendments of 1972 (Public Law 92-318).

1978 - The Tribally Controlled Community College Act stimulates the development of a variety of technical, two-year, four-year, and graduate colleges currently located on or near tribal reservations.

1979 - The U.S. Department of Education is established.

1980 - Congress passes the Education Amendments of 1980 (to the Higher Education Act of 1965).

1991 - National Security Education Act (Boren Bill) is enacted to provide support for undergraduate study abroad and graduate work in foreign languages and area studies.

1992 - President Bush signs the Higher Education Act Amendments, reauthorizing the 1965 Higher Education Act.

1993 - The National and Community Service Trust Act establishes a corporation to coordinate programs through which students receive minimum wage stipends and tuition benefits in return for community service.

1993 - The federal government begins "direct lending," a program that enables colleges and universities to provide loans using federal funds directly to students, thus avoiding private lenders and streamlining the process.

1993 - The American Indian Higher Education Consortium (AIHEC), supported by the National Association of State Universities and Land-Grant Colleges, launches a campaign to secure land-grant status for twenty-nine Native American colleges located in twelve states and serving sixteen thousand students.

1994 - National Agricultural Research, Extension and Teaching Act of 1994. Land-grant status is conferred on twenty-nine Native American colleges as a provision of the Elementary and Secondary Education Reauthorization Act. The bill authorizes a $23 million endowment for them, to be built up over five years. The colleges are to receive annual interest payments from the endowment. This act also provides grants for a pilot project to coordinate food and nutrition education programs of states, and it provides for demonstration grants for extension and nonprofit disability agencies to offer on-the-farm agricultural education and assistance directed at accommodating disability in farm operations.

1994 - The Department of Agriculture Reorganization Act of 1994. This establishes the Cooperative State Research, Education, and Extension Service (CSREES) to coordinate U.S.D.A. and state cooperative agricultural research, extension, and education programs. It also establishes the CSREES to consolidate cooperative research and agricultural extension and education programs with state agricultural experiment stations and extension services within land-grant and related universities.

3.
GOVERNANCE MODELS FOR THE DIGITAL OPPORTUNITY INVESTMENT TRUST

MARION R. FREMONT-SMITH

The purpose of the Digital Opportunity Investment Trust is to enhance learning, broaden knowledge, support the arts and culture, and teach skills necessary for the emerging Information Age. It would accomplish these purposes by providing financial support to institutions in local communities, states, and nationwide, acting in cooperation with the states and other sources of public and private financial support by distributing funds appropriated by Congress. The governing board of the trust would be charged with establishing priorities and criteria for funding, facilitating partnerships and alliances, and assuring broad dissemination of the products and services that result from its funding. This paper summarizes the potential organizational forms for the administration and distribution of these funds and the patterns that could be adopted for its governance and operations.

From a legal perspective, the educational purposes of the Digital Opportunity Investment Trust place it in the separate branch of the law of trusts that deals with those whose purposes are considered of broad benefit to the general public, in contrast to those established for the private benefit of individuals. These purposes are denominated as "charitable" and were codified in 1601 in the Statute of Charitable Uses, also known as the Statute of Elizabeth. The statute was enacted to encourage the establishment of charitable gifts and to institute procedures for remedying abuses that had arisen in the administration of charitable funds by private individuals. Among the purposes considered in the act to be charitable were support of "schools of learning, free schools, and scholars in universities." Trusts established for purposes enumerated in the act were exempt from many of the restrictions applicable to trusts established for private purposes.

The principle of favoring gifts for charitable purposes was accepted in the colonies and appeared in the laws of each state. The most widely accepted legal restatement of the common law definition of charity in the United States appears in a case decided by the Massachusetts Supreme Judicial Court in 1867:

> A charity, in the legal sense, may be more fully defined as a gift . . . for the benefit of an indefinite number of persons, either by bringing their minds or hearts under the influence of education or religion, by relieving their bodies from disease, suffering or constraint, by assisting them to establish themselves in life, or by erecting or maintaining public buildings or works or otherwise lessening the burdens of government.[1]

This same definition of charity was accepted by Congress in 1894 when, in the first income tax act, it granted exemption from income tax to any corporation or association organized exclusively for religious, educational, or charitable purposes. Although this act was subsequently declared unconstitutional, each subsequent enactment contained nearly identical exemptions. Similar exemptions appeared in the estate and gift tax laws, and the same definition was adopted in the provisions permitting taxpayers to deduct gifts to exempted organizations from their income tax. The federal tie to common law appears in treasury regulations applicable to exempt organizations in which the term *charitable* is defined "in its generally accepted legal sense, not limited by the separate enumerations in the Internal Revenue Code." Thus, the purposes of the Digital Opportunity Investment Trust, regardless of the legal form that it takes, will be protected by concepts of public benefit well defined in the law.

There are three categories of organizational forms that could be employed to operate the Digital Opportunity Investment Trust: it could be established as a separate agency in one of the branches of the federal administration; it could be given a quasi-governmental status as a public corporation or trust that would operate independent of any governmental agency but be subject to state oversight and, in some cases, fiscal control; or it could be established as a separate and independent charitable and educational organization, exempt from tax, subject to a degree of oversight by a state or federal agency, but operating independent of governmental agencies. Examples of organizations falling within each of these categories are described below.

GOVERNMENTAL ENTITIES

Governmental entities established to carry out charitable purposes are found within any department of government whose mission is to carry out those purposes, principally departments of education and health or social welfare. Such an entity is an integral part of the government, subject to policy and fiscal control by the head of the agency, staffed by civil servants, and funded by appropriations from the legislature. A pertinent example is the federal programs establishing and supporting the Land-Grant Colleges, where Congress directed the distribution of land or land scrip by the Department of the Interior to the individual states to be used to establish new educational institutions, with requirements to report annually to the department on the status of their programs.

Delegation of the duty to carry out the purposes of the Digital Opportunity Investment Trust to a department of the federal government would greatly limit its flexibility and its ability to devise innovative responses to educational needs. Congress may demand this close connection to the administrative branch as a condition for creation of the trust, and the trust could function in this framework, but it would not function as freely as envisioned.

QUASI-GOVERNMENTAL ENTITIES (PUBLIC CORPORATIONS)

The first public corporations were established shortly after the formation of the United States to meet the new country's need for a national banking system. It was not until the twentieth century that this form of organization was widely utilized to accomplish other purposes. Starting in the mid-1930s, public corporations were created for a broad range of social purposes, primarily designed to answer needs created by the Depression. Many of these corporations were disbanded during the Second World War or in the years immediately thereafter, but the form has continued to be used for the administration of federal and state programs that provide public funding to private organizations and individuals to accomplish "charitable" purposes.

THE NATIONAL SCIENCE FOUNDATION

A prototype for the Digital Opportunity Investment Trust is the National Science Foundation (NSF), which was created by Congress in 1950. It is governed by a board consisting of twenty-four individuals appointed by the president with the advice and consent of the Senate to serve six-year terms. Board members are required under the statute to be eminent in their respective scientific fields and are selected on the basis of their record of service and to reflect geographic diversity. In addition, the president is "requested" to give due consideration to nominees submitted by the National Academy of Sciences, the National Academy of Engineering, the National Association of State Universities and Land-Grant Colleges, the Association of American Universities, the Association of American Colleges, the Association of State Colleges and Universities, or by other scientific, engineering, or educational organizations. Members of the board serve part-time and are unpaid. A board member who has served for twelve consecutive years is ineligible for appointment for a two-year period following the twelfth year of service.

The board elects a chairman and a vice-chairman who serve for two-year terms. It also elects four of its members to serve on an executive committee. The chairman and vice-chairman, by tradition, have been members of the executive committee, but this is not a requirement. Members of the committee may not serve more than six consecutive years. The executive committee exercises "such powers and functions as may be delegated to it by the Board." It is required to render an annual report to the board and such other reports as it deems necessary. The board is empowered to appoint standing and temporary committees and to delegate many of its tasks to them. In addition to the annual meeting, regular meetings are set by the chairman of the board, and he also must call a meeting if requested by one-third of the members. Traditionally, the board meets five times a year, with the mandated annual meeting being held on the third Monday in May.

The NSF is staffed by a director and a deputy director. The director is appointed by the president with the advice and consent of the Senate, after affording the board an opportunity to make recommendations for the position. The position is full-time and salaried, and the director serves for a six-year term unless removed earlier by the president. The director serves as an ex officio member of the board and the executive committee, with the power to vote on all matters other than compensation and tenure. He is also eligible for election as chairman or vice-chairman of the board. The director exercises all of the authority granted to the NSF, as well as any powers or functions that may be delegated to him by the board. The current director is Dr. Rita Colwell who, before her appointment, served as president of the University of Maryland Biotechnology Institute. She had previously served as a member of the board.

The deputy director is also appointed by the president with the advice and consent of the Senate. The president is requested in the statute to afford the board and the director an opportunity to make recommendations for this position. The deputy director exercises such powers as the director prescribes.

The mission of the NSF is to "promote the progress of science; to advance the national health, prosperity, and welfare; and to secure the national defense." In carrying out these purposes, it supports a number of other National Research Centers and provides financial support through grants, contracts, and cooperative agreements with more than two thousand colleges, universities, and other education/research institutions throughout the country. It supports more than twenty thousand research and education projects in science and engineering, accounting for 20 percent of all federal funding for basic academic research in these fields. It had 1,300 employees and a budget of almost $4 billion in FY 2000.

THE SMITHSONIAN INSTITUTION

The Smithsonian Institution is another quasi-governmental entity with charitable purposes and with a governance structure somewhat similar to that of the NSF. A principal difference between the two organizations is that the

Smithsonian was established by act of Congress in 1846 in acceptance of a testamentary gift to the United States from James Smithson of London to create an institution for the "increase and diffusion of knowledge among men." Like the NSF, the Smithsonian is governed by a board of regents, but this board is comprised of the vice president of the United States, the chief justice of the U.S. Supreme Court, three U.S. senators, and three U.S. representatives, together with nine citizen regents who are not members of Congress, two of whom reside in the District of Columbia and the others in seven different states. The senators are chosen by the vice president for terms co-terminus with their terms of office; the representatives are chosen by the speaker of the House for two-year terms. The nine other citizen regents are chosen by joint resolution of Congress for six-year terms. All members serve without pay.

The board is empowered to elect a chancellor who serves as the presiding officer, and three members of an executive committee. The board also appoints regents to various standing committees. The executive officer of the Smithsonian, called the secretary, is chosen by the board and serves at its pleasure. The statute defines his duties to include taking charge of the building and property of the institution, serving as secretary of the board, and discharging the duties of librarian and of keeper of the museum. He may, with the consent of the Board of Regents, employ assistants. The Smithsonian currently employs a number of other nonstatutory executive officers, including an under secretary, a provost, a director of government relations, and a general counsel. The Smithsonian employs over 6,500 people to staff its sixteen museums and five research institutes.

The Smithsonian is unique among the many other public corporations established by act of Congress in that its initial funding was from the Smithson gift and not from appropriations and it was financed in its early years with income from the endowment. Today the trust corpus produces only a small portion of the Smithsonian's annual support. Operating revenues for FY 1999 totaled $869.6 million, with 59 percent coming from federal appropriations, 23 percent from donors/sponsors, 10 percent from government contracts, and 7.5 percent from income from its endowment.

THE MASSACHUSETTS ENVIRONMENTAL TRUST

A third example of a quasi-governmental body with charitable purposes can be found in trust funds established within the last twenty-five years by the legislatures in Maryland, California, and Massachusetts to administer funds earmarked for environmental education. The Massachusetts Environmental Trust is typical. It was created by special act of the legislature in 1988 to administer funds that the state would have been required to pay to the U.S. government as fines for its failure to clean up the pollution of Boston Harbor. Under the terms of an order of the federal court that found the state in violation of the federal law, in lieu of payment to the U.S. Treasury the state was permitted to establish what is in effect a charitable trust that would receive the payments (a total of $2 million) and administer them as directed by the court to ensure compliance with its orders and to provide education on the environment to the citizens of the state. During the period in which the court-directed payments were being made, interest earned on the corpus was to be distributed at the direction of the trustees to accomplish its broad general purposes so that the trust would be operated as a grant-making foundation. Since its initial funding, the trust has been the recipient of court-directed penalties arising from other federal and state suits, and in 1995 the legislature designated that it would receive revenue from the sale of special automobile license plates. The license plate fees now provide the principal source of revenue for the trust.

The trust is governed by a board of trustees appointed by the secretary of environmental affairs. The trustees serve for unlimited terms. They elect a chairman and vice-chairman and appoint a director who operates with two staff members. All funds are invested by the state and all expenditures are made at the direction of the secretary with the advice of the trustees, thus subjecting the trust to greater direct state control than the Smithsonian. In the twelve years since its creation, the trust has made total grants in excess of $5 million to governmental entities and nonprofit organizations in the state. Its current budget anticipates annual grants of approximately $1.3 million, primarily reflecting revenue from the sale of license plates.

INDEPENDENT CHARITABLE TRUSTS AND CORPORATIONS

There are two forms of legal entity that can be utilized to administer funds for charitable purposes independent of the government—trusts and nonprofit corporations. As noted above, charitable trusts are established by the independent acts of individuals who agree to hold and administer funds for certain purposes of benefit to the general public. No governmental action is required to create them; all that is needed are people who agree to serve as trustees and funds donated or appropriated to them to administer. If the purposes fit within the common law definitions of charity and the beneficiaries constitute a broad class of people, rather than specific individuals, the law grants perpetual existence to the trust, releases it from restrictions on accumulations of income, and entitles it to exemption from a wide range of federal and state taxes. However, it is the laws in the states and the District of Columbia that afford these privileges; the Federal Code contains no provisions upholding the validity of trusts, charitable or private, so that it would not be possible to create a trust under "national law," although a trust created in the District of Columbia or any of the states could be the recipient of federally appropriated funds.

Unlike charitable trusts, which are established by act of the parties creating them, corporations can be established only by grant of a legislative body. The earliest corporations were created by special act of Parliament in England, and later by special acts of the state legislatures in America. In the mid-1800s, the widespread acceptance of the advantages of the corporate form for conducting business led to the enactment of general incorporation laws, under which individuals could obtain charters from the state without the need for a specific act of the legislature. Some states enacted separate laws governing creation of corporations for charitable purposes; in others the business corporation statute governed these entities. In almost all cases, however, the definition of charity was that found in the common law of trusts, and the rules of construction applied in interpreting the validity of gifts for charitable purposes followed the common law precedents. Similarly, the tax law provisions do not distinguish between trusts and corporations in regard to eligibility for tax exemption.

From 1889 to 1907, Congress by special act granted corporate charters to thirty-four charitable organizations, including the Carnegie Institution of Washington, the American Academy in Rome, and the American Historical Association. Following this precedent, in March 1910 a bill was introduced in the U.S. Senate to incorporate The Rockefeller Foundation. It was in almost all respects identical to the charter granted without protest by Congress in 1903 to the General Education Board, and Rockefeller and his advisers anticipated that it would be treated in a similar fashion. Instead, it became a subject of intense controversy, and, three years later, the bill was withdrawn and the foundation was subsequently incorporated without protest in the state of New York.

It has been rare for individuals to seek federal charters since that date. Thus, as a practical matter, establishment of an independent, voluntary organization to govern the Digital Opportunity Investment Trust could best be accomplished in one of the states or in the District of Columbia, either under the statute governing creation and administration of nonprofit corporations, such as the New York Membership Corporation Act, or under the general incorporation act applicable to business and nonprofit corporations, such as that in Delaware, under which there would be no shareholders or else a provision that shareholders have no pecuniary rights in the stock they receive.

The governance of a charitable trust is in the hands of trustees, who may be appointed by outside agencies or be self-perpetuating. There is no legal requirement that they name officers or adopt procedural rules, but there is no impediment to their doing so. Unless otherwise specified in the trust document, voting is by majority and the trustees may be given the power to delegate trust duties to others. Governance of charitable corporations is entrusted to directors (often designated, however, as trustees to distinguish them from directors of a business corporation). The purposes of the corporation and the requirements for membership, if any, are specified in the founding documents, usually called Articles of Organization, and the directors operate according to the provisions incorporated in by-laws they adopt regarding terms of office and elections, the method for calling meetings, and other provisions to ensure orderly administration and operation. The directors differ from those of an ordinary business corporation only in regard to the role of shareholders. In fact, the governance of a charitable corporation differs from that of a public corporation only in the method of appointment of its directors and the provisions ensuring accountability to the president and Congress.

A trust or corporation would be an eligible recipient of congressional appropriations, as a grant or contract fee, with the monies paid directly or through a federal agency. It would also be eligible to receive funds through an intermediary such as a public corporation. In several states, the directors or trustees would be required to submit annual financial accounts to the attorney general. In all states but one, the attorney general is empowered to seek correction of misbehavior by trustees or directors from an appropriate state court. However, the degree of regulation among the states varies widely, and in some there is no effective government role in assuring proper administration of either charitable trusts or corporations.

At the federal level, charitable trusts and corporations may obtain rulings from the Internal Revenue Service that they are entitled to exemption from federal taxes and to receive contributions from members of the general public, which may be deducted for income, gift, and estate tax purposes. The charities, in turn, are required to file annual financial reports with the Internal Revenue Service; failure to comply with federal rules prohibiting private inurement and excess benefit can lead to loss of exemption and/or personal liability for receiving excess monetary benefits at the expense of the charity.

Charitable organizations receiving federal grants and contracts are in most cases accountable to the granting or contracting organization so that there is an additional layer of control over their use of federal funds. This degree of accountability is sufficient in many instances for Congress to permit nongovernmental entities to administer public funds, particularly in the case of social welfare programs and funding for public housing.

CONCLUSION

In considering the size and scope of the Digital Opportunity Investment Trust and its broad educational goals, a quasi-governmental body appears to be the most appropriate form for its governance. Placing it within an existing governmental agency will limit its scope and ability to innovate; establishment as an independent entity would be unlikely to provide the confidence in its integrity that members of Congress will need before authorizing appropriations to it from the sale of federal assets. The model afforded by the National Science Foundation, providing independence while assuring accountability to Congress and the administration, is well suited for the trust, and the distinguished record of the NSF makes it a particularly apt model to follow.

NOTES

1. 14 Allen 539, 556.

4.
TEACHING THE PROMISE: THE RESEARCH UNIVERSITY IN THE INFORMATION AGE

CATHY N. DAVIDSON[1]

THE MISSION OF THE RESEARCH UNIVERSITY

It is hard not to sound platitudinous when speaking of the research university, arguably the single major intellectual accomplishment of what has been termed "the American century." Nearly 50 percent of America's high school graduates go on to a college or university, and the result is an incomparable national resource. The shared rite of passage for these citizens is immersion in a complex and diverse community whose mission is the discovery and communication of knowledge. Whether the student is an eighteen-year-old worried about whether she or he can make the grade, a nontraditional student juggling the demands of job and family, or a postbaccalaureate in a graduate or professional school seeking to learn and to produce cutting-edge research in a specialized field, all have made a special commitment. They have cordoned off space and time from the adult world of paid labor in order to make a judicious, long-term investment in their own education.

It has been argued that this educated citizenry is both directly and indirectly responsible for the dominance of the United States in the current era of new global information technologies. We have moved from the Industrial Revolution, which depended on the mobilization of physical and financial resources, to what Gary Becker, Nobel laureate in economics, has called "the age of human capital." In this current era, the most valuable resources we can possess are the knowledge, skills, and social values taught by postsecondary education.

103

As useful as all of this may sound, the single defining quality of the modern university is *not* its preparation of students for the labor market. On the contrary, the purpose of the research university is not vocational so much as it is inspirational— to convey to students the excitement of creativity, imagination, research, and experimentation. It is also transformational, since it provides students with life- long tools for a better understanding of the world. The college or university is one of the only places where our society permits the exploration of knowledge for its own sake. Government and industry are rife with the production of new knowl- edge, but the university, in its mission, decrees itself a place where ideas may be generated free from ideology or the profit motive. The university preserves its claims to intellectual freedom through tenure, a complicated process of collective evaluation and rigorous scholarly peer review, that guarantees that no academ- ic, once tenured, can be fired for writing controversial material (including cri- tiques of the university itself) or doing research in areas that may not be ideal for federal or corporate funding.

This extraordinary mandate of academic freedom allows research that is future-oriented or whose use-value is uncertain at best, on the assumption that often the most important use is the one that could never have been predicted. At the same time, universities, like other enterprises, must operate within strict budgets. Especially in areas where research requires expensive equipment, there is a balance between theoretical and applied work, between future-oriented and use-inspired projects. Higher education involves a constant negotiation between the timeless and the timely, the new and that which is most prized from the past. It is responsive to current needs, forever creating new fields of intellectual endeavor and expertise, while preserving and fostering inquiry into other areas that remain important for how they define and bind a culture. Even the heated debates for which the acade- my is notorious (such as the recent "Culture Wars" and "Science Wars") yield a productive dialectical process of idea-sorting and sifting that is as old as Socrates. The debates that bubble up and become known to the public are symptomatic of the dynamism that constantly reshapes academic fields and preserves them.

Research is at the core of the modern university. As we see in Figure 4.1, scholarly research has a "ripple effect," expanding outward to an ever-widening audience. Traditionally, academe has communicated the fruits of its research in the ways indicated by the two concentric circles closest to the basic research core: teaching and scholarly publication. Teaching transfers new ideas to students through a quirky but dexterous combination of lecturing, class discussion, read- ing and writing assignments, feedback, dialogue, laboratory partnership, men- torship, peer exchange, and other forms of intellectual modeling that, together, constitute the tool kit of campus-based pedagogy. Interactive websites, syllabi and assignments posted on the web, and class chat rooms are the latest (and, some insist, the most time-consuming) additions to that arsenal. Scholarly publica- tion (including scholarly books, journals, and databases) is rigorously refereed and reaches a worldwide community of specialists in the field.

FIGURE 4.1. RIPPLE EFFECT: FROM BASIC RESEARCH TO THE PUBLIC

Other ways of disseminating ideas are important but have laid less of a claim on the everyday functioning and the budget of the university. Outreach to local teachers and their students, for example, has been a tertiary mission of some universities (and especially state universities), but is rarely central to the overall mission (except in schools of education). The ripple effect of translating cutting-edge research to the general public has been accomplished not by the researchers themselves, but mostly by trained journalists and public intellectuals working through a variety of print and broadcast media as well as through the expansive, national network of libraries, museums, arts organizations, and other community-serving nonprofits.

THE EXPANDED ROLE OF UNIVERSITIES IN THE AGE OF NEW TECHNOLOGIES

In the Information Age, a new audience—with no direct ties to the university—has tacitly been assumed to be part of the community that a university serves. As we see in Figure 4.1, this new audience occupies the circle furthest removed from the basic research mission. Through public websites, online library resources, and, in more and more cases, courses offered completely on the web (distance learning), the ripple effect of basic research extends even further, to a worldwide community of nonacademic distance learners and lifelong learners. This seems, in many ways, like the logical extension of the educational mission of the research university. Certainly such direct, unmediated communication to the general public is a good thing. Yet here we have a difference from the previous rings in the diagram since, for public outreach to succeed in the Information Age, the university must be not only the creator of basic research but also, in a sense, a public broadcaster. This communication imperative—and the hardware, software, and human resources it requires—has silently added to strained university budgets, imposed a new layer of responsibility on the academic organizational structure, and made new demands on the time of professors.

The question here is, at what point will the various demands of the Information Age begin to compete with the basic research mission of the university? In the past decade, research universities have absorbed tremendous expenses in both equipment and staffing in order to keep pace with the dizzying changes in all areas of computing, from instructional technology (such as wired and wireless classrooms) to high-speed research computing. At many research universities (including my own), the cost of educational technology rose over 100 percent in the last three years, and rose the same amount in the previous period. Who pays for these additional costs in hardware, software, development, implementation, and technical support staffing? Who devotes time to making these technologies operational? If faculty are diverted from their core effort of doing research and communicating that research to their students and colleagues, who will be left at the center of the knowledge cycle to do the basic research that ripples outward to many other public educational enterprises?

Paradoxically, the information era can make it difficult and costly to create new knowledge. An example will clarify this paradox. We know that it is possible to take archival sources (data and documents) that have been preserved in one location (let's say, a parish church in Maine or a state records office in North Dakota) and make those machine-readable and accessible throughout the world. Genealogists, historians, and epidemiologists are only some of the myriad possible users, both in the scholarly community and in the general public, who can now, in a matter of hours, find accurate information that, in the past, could have taken a lifetime of laborious, costly, and often frustrating work. What is the downside of such bounty? Simply, it is extremely costly and labor-intensive to put resources online, and there is no way to recoup such costs from those who receive their benefits.² To charge for the services (1) limits access and thus potentially curtails the production of knowledge that digitization was designed to promote; and (2) rarely repays the prodigious investment in hardware, software, and meticulous human labor necessary to create a digital archive since there is no way to know, in advance, how popular or valuable an archive will turn out to be.

Costly and labor-intensive as digitization is, the new knowledge made possible by new tools and new archives is extraordinary. Fields from art history to zoology are being transformed. We need trained researchers with advanced educations to be able to understand the wealth of new data available because of new computational tools. In science and engineering, especially in the area of nanoscience, the tools have become so sophisticated that they create information researchers could not have predicted. In some cases, the data necessitate the creation of new explanatory theories. In unexpected fields—such as epigraphy (the study of inscriptions carved on ancient stones) or telemedicine (where dime-sized video cameras scan diseased organs)—new tools for visualization have transformed the body of knowledge itself. In fact, it is hard to imagine a field untouched by the new technologies, from computer science and engineering, to the new economics and global marketing strategies, to sociology, psychology, political science, anthropology, and other fields in the social sciences that help to explain and make policy for a rapidly changing world.

No one can predict what intellectual areas will open up because of the new technologies. Interestingly, after a decade of declining funding to the arts in public schools and higher education, suddenly the new technologies are making us aware of how short-sighted was society's verdict that the arts were inessential to the Information Age. Distance pedagogy, global marketing, mass communications, and the array of new media (from special effects movies, to virtual reality games, to medical visualization) have replaced the charisma of human contact with visual, auditory, performative, graphic, kinetic, and other aesthetic appeals. As economic competition increases, so does competition for the relatively small pool of artists, designers, film and video makers, and musicians. There is also an increasing need for language training and understanding of other cultures. English may be the dominant language of the Internet (something which has caused legitimate outrage throughout the non-English-speaking world), but globalization ultimately results in interdependence that cannot operate in one direction alone. Globalization requires more rather than less cross-linguistic and cross-cultural communication since the preponderance of goods and ideas around the world are produced, transported, and exchanged by people who do not use the web and certainly do not speak English.

Nor will seemingly impractical fields such as philosophy, history, religious studies, or literature disappear. We know from the history of past technologies that there is always a resurgence of interest in spiritual and metaphysical issues at the moments of greatest modernization and change. We need the humanities, now, to help think through the nature of human-ness just as high-speed computing, as a tool of biotechnology, most makes us question what a human being is. Now that we have cracked the genetic code, what decisions will we make with our valuable and potentially terrifying new information? Ethicists, historians, anthropologists, and moral philosophers need to work side by side with scientists and engineers to help us consider the implications of the choices we make.

Focusing too much funding and energy on the technology itself—and not on technology as a tool essential for the knowledge it conveys, the services it provides, or the social interactions it makes possible—is another way that knowledge and information can be at odds. Universities should never be so dazzled by the technology that they become blind to their original mission to create knowledge. Nor should universities become mere technical colleges for the present moment. As John Seely Brown (one of the visionary scientists of the Information Age) and Paul Duguid put it in *The Social Life of Information*, some of the most brilliant "digital innovation has come from people who spent their time on campus wandering around in the arts, theater, psychology, and the humanities"—not just in the predictable worlds of computer science or e-business.[3]

Without question, the glorious and unpredictable assemblage known as the research university is being changed in our era of the ethernet, Internet 2, distance learning, and web-based curricula. However, the recent prognosis by a popular magazine that "college professor" is one of the ten occupations that will disappear because of the Internet is ludicrous. Indeed, the opposite is true. If there is a crisis in higher education today, it is not that universities face their own demise. The crisis is that—at current levels of funding and public support—universities cannot begin to respond to the multiple and growing demands placed upon them.

SOME HISTORICAL PERSPECTIVE ON NEW TECHNOLOGIES

Right now, much of the rhetoric about new technologies is hyperbolic. Technology is a bane or a panacea, portending apocalypse or utopia. *Either* the university will disappear because of web-based, distance education *or,* because of this new form of education, the American university system will educate the world, leading to global dominance of American ideas, values, education, technology and commerce, and the disappearance of all other languages except English. The claims are as ludicrous as they are ubiquitous.

They are not surprising, either. We know from the history of technology that, whenever we are at the advent of a new form of technology, predictions about its application and its effects are both wild and wildly inaccurate. What we also know from this history is that as soon as a new technology becomes fully operational, it is virtually invisible. Do I spend time thinking about the wondrous technology that brings light or heat to my home? After a new technology is accepted, what remains is the content it conveys, the products it makes and distributes, and the social relations that it transforms by its applications as well as by its inequities. These are lessons that are difficult to remember since, at its moment of origin, technology fools us into thinking that it exists for, in, and of itself.

One of the previous great eras of technological innovation—the end of the nineteenth century—saw rapid developments in electricity, telephony, telegraphy, photogravure, and mass printing that allowed people to communicate faster and to a wider audience than ever before. As with our own era, these new communications technologies evolved at the same time as vast changes in biotechnology (primarily microscopy and, subsequently, bacteriology). Finally, the invention of the automobile and Taylorized mass production changed the way humans migrated, traveled, dressed, ate, lived, and died. Many people have suggested that this last technology revolution caused dramatic changes in business practices, leading to the creation of the corporation in America, just as our own era's technological innovations are leading to new rules for global e-commerce.

The social perils of the late nineteenth century are well known (including poverty among immigrants living in unhealthy squalor in American cities, violence against and persecution of African Americans in the legal system and on the streets, and unsafe and exploitative labor conditions). Mark Twain dubbed it, with all the irony intended, the "Gilded Age" and Thorstein Veblen called it an era of "conspicuous consumption." At the same time, it was an era of philanthropy, with many of the major industrialists supporting institutions that would improve general public knowledge and creativity. Across the nation, cities unveiled new libraries, opera and ballet companies, and art museums. The late nineteenth century saw the burgeoning of the Land Grant and state college system of education and the founding of numerous liberal arts colleges and major private research universities (among them Stanford and the University of Chicago). Additionally, this was the foundational era for graduate and professional school education in America and, it must be added, a prime time for distance education, then carried out through the mail as "correspondence schools." The Yale classics professor who would become the first president of the University of Chicago, William Raney Harper, came to the post from his previous position at the helm of one of these correspondence schools, the Chautauqua College of Liberal Arts. The need for a more educated citizenry for the modernized nation was as pressing then as now—and the rhetoric was equally agitated.

History repeats itself—and so does the aspiration toward universal, lifelong education to be pursued at one's own pace. The last century's utopian vision for distance education had mixed results. Many universities created extension programs that continue to provide an invaluable service to the community beyond the campus. On the other hand, the same desire for lifelong education led to a proliferation of correspondence schools, many of which depended more on hucksterism than expertise. By the 1930s, major national commissions on correspondence schools derided the poor education offered even by the programs sponsored by universities such as Chicago, Columbia, and the University of Wisconsin. By the time of the G.I. Bill in 1944, veterans were discouraged from wasting their federal funding on correspondence schools, many of which depended on revenue from "dropout money" to survive.[4] Surely there is a warning to be heeded here as more and more web-based, for-profit, and university-sponsored educational enterprises spring up over night.

At the same time, most major public universities continue to offer extension courses with success, serving a community of learners who either live too far away to attend classes on a regular basis or who have work or family obligations that require flexible scheduling. Several universities have transformed former extension outreach into web-based courses, called Asynchronous Learning Networks (ALN), that include self-paced exercises, chat rooms for peer learning and connection, and individualized e-mail feedback from instructors. Some universities are forming consortia, such as the Southern Regional Education Board (SREB), an alliance of fifteen state universities into what they call an "academic common market" and an "electronic campus" that offers for-credit courses in everything from "Modern Japanese History" to "Introduction to Physics." Enrollment in a SREB course also gives students password access to Galileo, a collection of databases created by the University System of Georgia in 1995 from scholarly periodicals and publications in state and university archives.

A 1999 Sloan Summer Workshop on ALNs reports that, in many of these university-based programs, student satisfaction among those who complete the course is very high. In some classes, over 90 percent of the students report that they "believe they learn as much or more than they would in a classroom-based course." Additionally, the dropout rate among these students is lower than that in the same campus-based courses. Finally, in a number of key studies of ALNs, instructor satisfaction was reported as high, although the increased expenditure of time (especially for developing such courses) was cited repeatedly as a cause for dissatisfaction.[5]

It is clear that, for certain students in certain situations, reputable distance learning offerings can have important benefits. What is also clear is that, at present, most distance education attempts to approximate (with better or worse results) the standard pedagogy of the lecture or seminar room. The visionary potential of the new educational technologies has not yet been fully tapped. A historical perspective again is useful here. We know from the history of technology that, at first, established organizations have a difficult time comprehending the full potential of new technologies. Railroad companies, for example, could see themselves only in the railroad business, not the transportation business, and missed opportunities brought by the automobile and the airplane. At present, education is rather in the position of the railroad companies, still trying to figure out a way to lay new tracks to far-flung locales, instead of thinking about versatile ways to capitalize on the full possibilities of exchange and collaboration in the midst of a transportation revolution.

New Technologies, New Universities

Most research universities have not yet used the new technologies to transform the basic structure of education. To date, most distance learning operates on the familiar unidirectional pedagogical model: from educators outward to students and then to the various circles of a paying public. There are few ripples back from those outer circles, inward to the core areas of the university's mission. The exceptions are key medical and nursing schools as well as a number of progressive (and expensive) executive education programs in business schools where new pedagogical models are being explored. These professional schools are using new technologies to revitalize education, creating virtual learning communities among students, fostering outreach between students and clients (patients or fledgling businesses), and experimenting with a fruitful combination of distance learning and face-to-face interaction.

It is intriguing to think about what might happen if this professional school model could be transferred to the general research university. The challenge is to understand how such a transformation could happen without jeopardizing the essential core of basic research that, as we have seen, cannot be duplicated anywhere else. That is a formidable challenge. However, if one were to think expansively for a moment, one could envision ways that the interactivity of new technologies could transform our organizational model for the university. Setting aside the issue of costs (in seed and start-up money, infrastructure, and support staff), what could a university gain if the ripple effect worked *both* ways? What would happen if we reconceived distance education as an exchange of up-to-date cultural and technological knowledge (held by the conventional student population) for real-life experience (offered by alumni and distance learners)? A combination of distance learning, campus residencies, business or community-serving internships, and formal mentor/apprentice relationships could extend the lessons learned in the college classroom and make educational use of lessons learned in the world beyond.[6]

Educational technologies might also be used to help close the "digital divide" that separates social "haves" and "have-nots." As in the past, the creation of a new technology tends to highlight the gap between the affluent and the impoverished—whether within a nation or between rich and poor nations. Reconceiving the campus could help here. Mentorships between college students and children from disadvantaged backgrounds could become a service component in courses from math to sociology. Technology could facilitate these interactions, which would have a variety of social and educational goals. We also know there is a technology gender gap. Similar mentoring relationships between female college students and young girls could help here, too, as could a "technology Peace Corps" where college students would travel abroad to help bring students in other countries into the worldwide educational network.

Rather than facing obsolescence, the university faces enormous strains on its limited resources and on its basic research mission because it is *too* central to the needs of our society. Technology is not free. All over America, the operating costs of universities are soaring faster than tuition fees—and no one is sanguine about the high price of a contemporary education. If the university is going to be a model facility with information technologies; if it is going to use state-of-the-art technology to augment communication in the classroom and to pioneer better methods of communicating outside the classroom; if it is going to invest in the expensive and indispensable new tools necessary for high-speed computing, nanoscience, and other technology-intensive research; and if it is going to do all of this while not detracting from its fundamental and irreplaceable mission to create new knowledge and communicate it to the next generation, then we need an action plan for how to support the research universities in the wisest, most creative, most flexible and visionary way.

A public trust fund of the kind we are proposing in these papers would allow support for the best information technology, its creative development and application, high-end computing needs, and the dissemination of knowledge to a larger public—for free. It could support the open source mission championed by leading thinkers because it leads to ever more creative innovations. It could work toward the sometimes conflicting ideas of both privacy and open access. We are in one of the most promising and perilous moments in the history of higher education. There is no better time than now to make a major investment in the long-term future of ideas in America.

RECOMMENDATIONS

Information technology changes so rapidly that recommendations for the best ways to use and support that technology tend to look dated almost as soon as they are written. The following suggestions are thus offered tentatively and with that caveat in mind. Underlying all of these specifics are a few overarching principles guiding the operation of a public trust to support the information and communication functions of research universities: (1) allocation of funds should be highly competitive and based on rigorous, scholarly peer review processes (similar to those at the National Science Foundation, the National Institutes of Health, the National Endowment for the Humanities, or the National Endowment for the Arts); (2) funds should be awarded where they will increase an organization's internal incentives to innovate; and, most importantly, (3) the purpose of the public trust is to subsidize expensive technologies that are necessary to make the particular knowledge of the research university available to the widest possible audience.

"SPUTNIK"-STYLE SCHOLARSHIPS FOR GRADUATE AND PROFESSIONAL SCHOOL STUDENTS IN INFORMATION SCIENCE, INFORMATION SYSTEMS, AND INFORMATION STUDIES

Rather than pursue advanced graduate or professional training, many college students with expertise in the various aspects of information studies (from computer science to sociology to commerce) are being lured away into business by higher salaries. We are seeing a decline in applications to graduate and professional schools similar to that in the 1960s, especially in the sciences, engineering, and business. The positive side is that the drop in admissions has allowed U.S. universities to open their doors to many more foreign students than ever before. We have much to learn from the experiences and perspectives that international students bring. Nonetheless, it is a topsy-turvy commitment to knowledge if a country's own citizens are too shortsighted to take full advantage of its own educational system. We have reached a crisis point in some fields, including in computer science. We face a brain drain out of the university and a knowledge drought. This is especially important since, before the information revolution, much of the exciting computing innovation occurred in research universities. Now the excitement is in industry, which does some things extremely well, but then bypasses other research areas where the profit-potential is unclear. We need the equivalent of the cold war support for postgraduate education to reverse a trend that, in the long run, will have deleterious effects on our society.

A COMPETITION TO FIND THE MOST CREATIVE AND SIGNIFICANT USES FOR WEB-BASED INSTRUCTION

An annual competition for innovative uses of web-based instruction that truly can serve the public good both could provide support for winning proposals and could make those proposals public, in order that other nonprofit institutions could adapt the most interesting new models to their local situation. This is necessary in order to think of creative new ways to deliver knowledge via the web.

Web-based instruction is not a substitute for face-to-face education, but an enhancement to the already complex set of pedagogical tools available. These technologies are expensive and, at present, many have been taken over by for-profit corporations that recoup their research and development costs by selling their services at high prices. Too many of these companies depend on cheap instructors (as tutors and online graders), who are undertrained, underpaid, and overworked. Some also depend on a no-refund tuition policy and high dropout rates (up to 80 percent at some distance learning institutions). Yet distance general education has an enormous potential for public good. We have not begun to explore the full ramifications of educational technology for true, lifelong education or for the transfer of those experiences back into the classroom.

SUPPORT FOR NEXT-GENERATION MEDIA TECHNOLOGIES IN EDUCATION

We have the capacity to move well beyond the current uninspired and uninspiring "talking heads" version of distance education. Now, too much web-based learning lacks the fire of face-to-face communication—the teacher walking among the students, noticing a furrowed brow, stopping and engaging that student in debate as the rest of the students brim with excitement. Even in a lecture course, the best teachers speak from notes rather than a full script and rarely deliver the same lecture twice. They are alert to the temperature in the room, aware of events happening outside the classroom that may have a tremendous impact on how the material is received, and attentive to new developments in the field or in ancillary fields that make a particular point vital or irrelevant. Distance education lacks this flexibility and spontaneity. Right now, it takes on both a simplified and static form of the content and an impoverished rendition of the method. Yet, with the right collaborative energies between education, media specialists, and corporations, technology could *enhance* the learning experience in other ways that are unique to its capacities. Some of the remarkable tools of the entertainment industry, robotics, virtual reality, and other technologies could create, for example, the sights, sounds, smells, and feel of New York in 1890—uptown and down, on Fifth Avenue and the lower East Side. This is already happening in medicine, where virtual patients react in individualized ways to specific medications, allowing for another pre-screening tool that is noninvasive and safe—and extremely expensive. A public trust fund could help ensure that such modern wonders are not limited to blockbuster movies.

RENEWED FUNDING FOR THE ARTS AND TECHNOLOGY

The nineties witnessed declining federal arts funding on every level, from support for elementary and high school arts programs to universities. Yet the new information and media technologies require heightened sensitivity to all of the arts in a way that we have never experienced before. The universities that are savviest about technology often understand the symbiosis of art and technology (think of M.I.T., the California Institute of Technology, and, indeed, most of the universities in California, within a stone's throw of the entertainment industry). However, other research universities, facing the expenses of technology, have been forced to set tough priorities, and, often, the arts have suffered. Additionally, most academics at research universities, who are of a generation where education was primarily text-based, ethnographic, or lab-based, have not kept pace with the student interest in the arts nor appreciated the way new information and media technologies have given urgency (as in the MP3/Napster debates) and primacy (as in the renaissance of television and movie animation) to the arts, both the traditional ones and film, video, and other media forms.

Understaffed and underfunded, art, music, dance, theater, and film and video departments turn away far more students than they are able to serve. Support for the range of the arts in research universities could have an enormous future impact on the media that dominate our lives more and more and could help close the gap between C. P. Snow's "two cultures" at a time when, sadly, this gap is imposed by legislators and educators on students who do not experience this separation in their daily, web-based lives.

CREATIVE INTEGRATION OF TECHNOLOGY INTO STUDENT RESEARCH

The research paper, the thesis, and the dissertation are the primary mechanisms by which students demonstrate their mastery of subject matter. New eras require new modes of expression. It would be an exciting challenge to allow the final product of a student's education to be a collaborative effort that communicated the fruits of basic research in a form other than or supplementary to a final, written document. This creation, realized in some new technological form, could then become a pedagogical tool for future students in a course or program. The range of options here is endless. The obstacle is support for the production costs of such a venture.

SPONSORED DISTANCE RESEARCH COLLABORATIONS

Just as different government organizations and private foundations support conferences now, we need a public trust supporting global teleconferencing that could open access to ever wider groups of participants, including in third-world countries, and that could be recorded, archived, and distributed via the Internet to an even wider audience. In October 2000, "Mega-Conference 2" took place worldwide with "no one at the podium." At locations around the world, video-streamed real-time conversations occurred on the topic of how to use new technology to transfer research into the classroom. This new, expansive, global model for sharing knowledge is truly exciting. At Duke, at the John Hope Franklin Center for Interdisciplinary and International Studies, we have been fortunate to build a new facility with state-of-the-art technologies that make such conferencing possible. We are planning, for example, a conference on the impact of immigration patterns on local populations. We will partner with a number of universities around the country and the world to make comparisons in precise ways in order to cut through the excessively glib and broad generalizations rampant about "globalization." At the Franklin Center, we are also developing an accounting system to keep track of how much we have gained from our distance collaborations and how much they cost (in money and human time). Such cost-benefit analyses are almost nonexistent in either academe or industry. We need funding both to *study* the value of these distance collaborations and, when they are worthwhile, to facilitate them.

EXTENDING GLOBAL COMMUNITIES THROUGH NETWORKED STUDY ABROAD

The study abroad experience that is a hallmark of undergraduate education is ripe for digital enhancements. Only a few universities take technology abroad with their students. Recently, Stanford and SUNY Buffalo pioneered a distance learning program with their students on exchange in France that both helped the students keep up with their classwork at home (especially important to students in engineering and the sciences) and allowed them to use their experiences in France to video-broadcast a course of their own creation back to students in the United States. Additionally, the web allowed for a continuing and productive relationship between the students in the United States and France after the semester abroad ended. This adds another expense to the already expensive proposition of studying abroad, but adds to the international networking vital to global community.

TRANSFORMING THE CAMPUS THROUGH THE CREATION OF LIFELONG LEARNING COMMUNITIES AND COLLABORATIONS

Campus-based college experiences create the closest communities many people experience in their lifetime. Later, career pressures force moves that disrupt friendships and community. Similarly, in the busy life beyond college, it is hard to keep up with new developments in one's field or with basic education that helps to keep one in touch with a changing world. Lifelong, alumni-based learning opportunities both can serve the objective of fostering ongoing, interactive alumni communities and can help members of those communities keep up with the rapid changes brought about by the information revolution. Universities could develop intergenerational learning communities that link alumni to current students in a way that could prompt an exciting reconfiguration of traditional university organization and traditional forms of learning. Distance mentors (alumni) and distance technology tutors (current students), for example, could exchange ideas and expertise. These virtual exchanges could be shaped into face-to-face experiences, including service-learning and internships facilitated by alumni, and thereby make the university even more integral to the world beyond—and vice versa. Seed money could help stimulate ways of using technology to rethink existing academic organizational structures and to connect the academy to the world beyond.

CLOSING THE DIGITAL DIVIDE THROUGH EDUCATIONAL PARTNERSHIPS

Many first-tier state universities have the support for their media and information technologies necessary to engage in top-rate new research. Prestigious liberal arts colleges have, in many cases, realized that training the next generation of computer-literate students is part of their mission and use their excellence in this area to attract students. Private research universities often lag behind, as do second-tier state institutions. But, not surprisingly, the biggest digital lag—in hardware, software, and, most significantly, in trained personnel—is in under-funded, historically black colleges and universities. A public trust fund could support collaboration, mentoring, resource-sharing, internship programs, and other shared ventures between wealthier and less affluent institutions.

K–12 OUTREACH

Many universities, historically, have seen educating *future* college students as part of their community-service mission. There are rich traditions of this type of support, such as the Lab School at the University of Chicago, or the Talent Identification Program (TIP) at Duke, which identifies gifted students early on and brings them to campus for a summer of intensive and advanced learning that may not be available in their local high schools. Other universities have targeted special needs students, disadvantaged students, or children with learning disabilities. Many of the new technologies could be vastly helpful in making resources available, in allowing for networking support for local teachers and university professors, in mentoring relationships between college students and K–12 students, and in other ways, serving to make stronger links between universities and primary and secondary schools.

EDUCATIONAL SUBSIDIES FOR INVENTING BASIC RESEARCH TOOLS

We are at a moment where the tools are so complex that even the smartest researcher often cannot predict what will happen when a certain tool is put to work on a problem. Especially in the area of nanoscience, the tools don't quite "think," but they reveal entirely new forms of knowledge that force scientists to rethink some of their most time-honored concepts. In an August 2000 interview in *Wired* magazine, when John Seely Brown, principal scientist at Xerox Palo Alto Research Center, was asked, "What gets you more excited, knowing you can find a charismatic young leader or a charismatic young tool?" he first answered "tools," then added: "The real key is how to create a charismatic milieu that combines leading-edge designers with leading-edge tools." At present, many research universities have the right "milieu" but lack the resources to bring together the best tools and the best leaders. Microsoft and other high-tech innovators build "campuses" and try to approximate the diverse educational, social, and recreational facilities of a campus to create the right milieu—but corporations lack the mandate for the intellectual freedom of an actual university campus. They have no motivation to pursue "useless" knowledge (including that which may turn out to be enormously useful in the near or distant future). For-profit education providers will apply cutting-edge existing technologies to their enterprise but have little research and development funding or expertise to create new technologies. To truly explore possibilities, we need resources to bring the right tools to the right people in the right place.

EXPLORING THE BEST METHODS FOR PUBLISHING
REFEREED SCHOLARLY RESEARCH

Nowhere is the gap between "knowledge" and "information" clearer than in the contrast between the refereed scholarly publication and the ad hoc, individualized website, where there are no checks and balances to ensure accuracy or fairness. The careful process of adjudication and meticulous scholarly evaluation that leads to scholarly publishing is the foundation for the value system (including rankings, hierarchy, and professional standards of excellence) upon which the research university is based. Yet scholarly publishing is an expensive venture. For the last decade, the Mellon Foundation has heroically led the charge in trying to make the fruits of scholarly labor available digitally, but this has turned out to cost far more than anyone anticipated. On the other hand, in many areas of the sciences, commercial publishers dominate the field and charge astronomical prices that drain library budgets. A cohort of forward-thinking university presses is exploring online science publishing that will cost less than trade publishers and be available quickly yet preserve the standards of scholarly peer review. Both a competitive subsidy fund and a venture competition for innovative ideas could support traditional scholarly publication and provide incentives for developing new ways of disseminating information to a worldwide intellectual community.

DEVELOPING AND PROMOTING INTELLECTUAL PROPERTY NORMS

We need a corps of legal scholars and advisers who can serve as national consultants—the equivalent of our other legal aid services—to nonprofit organizations to help develop the right legal norms for their institutions and also to help them negotiate legal disputes over fair use (both what they use and what of their own property is used). What knowledge should be available to all? What should be copyrighted or patented? Where are the boundaries between "use" and "theft"? Nonprofits cannot afford to engage in the extended legal imbroglios that are becoming ever more commonplace in the Information Age. Without support, they could be both exploited by others willing to transmit their knowledge in a haphazard fashion (as with the student note-takers who publish sloppy and unauthorized lecture notes on the web) and hampered by the expense of obtaining, sharing, and collaborating on research projects with others.

KEEPING THE ARCHITECTURE OF THE INTERNET OPEN SO KNOWLEDGE CAN
BE SHARED WIDELY[7]

Another function of a Digital Opportunity Investment Trust would be to help support the Internet as an open, free, and public domain of knowledge. This is not to advocate the abolition of specific commercial sites on the Internet, but, rather, to reinforce the idea that open access to the Internet as a worldwide information-sharing and communication tool should be preserved as an invaluable social good. In recent years, scholarly societies and civil liberties groups have argued that the increasing breadth of intellectual property rights and the pressure to protect commercial content on the Internet put both research and speech at risk. Research science and the research university depend on a level of openness, in content and in network architecture, that the current trend endangers. Neither is likely to flourish in a "pay-per-view" system.

FUNDING TO PRESERVE OUR HISTORY

Paper has been around a long time, and we have learned what we need to do to preserve it. Very little research has been done on the archiving and preservation of materials only available on diskettes, computer chips, CD-ROMS, websites, databases, or hard drives. We know from the movie industry what a disaster it has been for the historical record that celluloid is so fragile. Will historians of the future be able to write the history of the Information Age? It would be ironic indeed if the Information Age left no trace. We need funding for research on how to save, archive, and preserve the fruits of this remarkable era in the history of ideas. And we desperately need funding that will allow us to conserve ephemera such as web pages that otherwise disappear without a trace.

FUNDING FOR THE FUTURE: AN INNOVATION COMPETITION

The single greatest gift the research university offers to society is intellectual freedom. The campus is a rare place where ideas can be tried out because, in the future, their particular form of knowledge *may* prove key. As many of the most brilliant innovators of the new technologies insist, without the freedom to think, the web would not exist right now. It was a wild gamble, supported largely by universities such as M.I.T. that were in a position to invest in a possible future. Research universities should be supported in the mission to think large and to think loose. An "innovation competition" for research universities, with the widest possible disciplinary parameters and the challenge to think outside the box, would be an enormously far-sighted public funding project—a "MacArthur" not for individual genius but for brilliant collective projects by networks of scholars with diverse expertise, from diverse institutions. The watchwords of such a competition would not be "technology use" but "creative experiment." Such a bold competition would mark a national investment in the most precious knowledge of all—"useless knowledge," which holds the potential to change the world.

NOTES

1. Many colleagues, at Duke and elsewhere, have contributed to this paper. I especially thank Ellen Mickiewicz for the idea for the figure and for her original energies on behalf of Digital Promise and Duke University. Thanks go as well to

Katharine Bartlett, James Boyle, Tyler Curtain, Richard Danner, Gerardine DeSanctis, David Ferriero, Christoph Guttentag, John Harer, Alice Kaplan, Robert Keohane, Betty Leydon, Richard Lucic, Christopher Newfield, Michael Pickett, Molly Renda, Rob Sikorski, Sim Sitkin, Brian Cantwell Smith, and Ken Wissoker. I am grateful to the staff of Duke's new John Hope Franklin Center for Interdisciplinary and International Studies (and especially Mark Olson) for designing innovative media and communications technologies as well as an important plan for a cost-benefit analysis of the Center's distance research and teaching collaborations.

2. In September 2000, the National Endowment for the Humanities and the National Science Foundation joined forces to award more than $4.8 million in grants for five new digital projects in the humanities, an impressive beginning that draws attention to how great the funding needs are in the humanities alone. The five projects are: "Digital Music Library" ($3,056,913); "Creating Standards and Procedures for Online Encyclopedias" ($528,896); "Cuneiform Digital Library Initiative" ($650,000); "Classical Chinese Digital Database" ($146,859); and "Indexing Handwritten Manuscripts" ($450,000).

3. John Seely Brown and Paul Duguid, *The Social Life of Information* (Boston: Harvard Business School Press, 2000), p. 218.

4. One of the few archival studies of correspondence schools is by the distinguished social historian David F. Noble, "Digital Diploma Mills, Part IV," published in the Internet journal *First Monday*, November 1999, http://www.communication.ucsd.edu/dl/ddm4.html. Unfortunately, this key study lacks footnotes so it is not possible to track its sources. It should be noted that Noble has been an important voice not only as a historian but also as an activist and polemicist cautioning against the university's headstrong rush into digital education. He took part in the first labor action, at York University in Canada, by university faculty refusing to comply with their university's demand that they make all of their instructional materials available on the web. UCLA, too, has faced opposition from faculty and has dropped its stated goal to have 100 percent of its courses web-based by the year 2000.

5. John Bourne, ed., *On-Line Education: Learning Effectiveness and Faculty Satisfaction*, proceedings of the 1999 Sloan Summer Workshop on Asynchronous Learning Networks, Alfred P. Sloan Foundation, 2000.

6. I am indebted to Brown and Duguid, *The Social Life of Information*, pp. 204–41 (the chapter "Re-Education"), for some of these ideas, and also to feedback from Richard Lucic and Brian Cantwell Smith. Gerry DeSanctis, Sim Sitkin, and other colleagues in Duke's pioneering executive, distance-learning programs at the Fuqua School of Business were also very helpful.

7. My special thanks to my colleague, legal theorist James Boyle, for his contributions and insights on the centrality of open-source architecture to the goals of this project.

5.
FULFILLING THE DIGITAL PROMISE IN NONPROFIT EDUCATION ON A NATIONAL LEVEL

THOMAS R. MARTIN

The information technology revolution presents unprecedented opportunities and challenges for nonprofit education in this country. By education, I mean not only schools, colleges, and universities, but also all the other institutions and organizations that add value to society by performing an educational mission—libraries, museums, learned societies, music associations, historical societies, public broadcasting, and so on.

Broadly speaking, the opportunities are to extend broader and deeper educational experiences both in learning and in creating content to a greater number of people than ever before in history, to lead the way in explaining and promoting an open-source approach to creating and distributing digital information, to create a framework for new ways of credentialing content in the increasingly diverse and fast-expanding world of digital data, and to devise ways to maintain the social dimensions of learning in an increasingly technological environment.

It is particularly pressing that action be taken for the humanities and social sciences because currently they lag behind the natural sciences in recognizing the promise of the information technology revolution. For example, the National Science Foundation reportedly has received very significant funding to work on the science, mathematics, engineering, and technology education section of the Online National Library, an ambitious digital information project that was announced early in 2000 by Senators Fred D. Thompson (R-Tenn.) and Joseph I. Lieberman (D-Conn.) of the Senate Governmental Affairs Committee on their website at http://gov_affairs.senate.gov. Furthermore, the United States Army has made public its plans to provide a laptop computer and distance-education opportunities to every soldier, presumably concentrating on technical, scientific, and business subjects. In the nongovernmental sector, the privately owned University of Phoenix, which enrolls the largest number of college and post-graduate students in the nation, offers technology-based instruction in technical and business subjects. I imagine that the same curricular emphasis was to prevail in Rupert Murdoch's ambitious plan, now apparently dissolved, to join his News Corporation with eighteen universities around the world, in a network called Universitas 21, to try to capture the lion's share of the fast-growing global market for online education. No project of even remotely comparable scale exists for the humanities and social sciences in this country.

In planning for such a project, the challenges are to create mechanisms for nonprofit institutions to agree on common goals, to find and organize people to do the work in defining and promoting the goals, and to secure the permanent funding that will be necessary to keep nonprofits from being bankrupted by the expense of achieving these goals in the high-cost environment of today's information technology, in which the costs are soaring, not only for acquiring and categorizing data but also for installing technical infrastructure and hiring and keeping competent personnel.

It is urgent to act now and to act decisively on behalf of the humanities and social sciences so the United States will not be left behind in determining what digital information will be created to provide the knowledge capital (in the same sense we speak of social capital) on which our future prosperity, stability, and democratic values will depend. The world is already at work, and we should be, too. To speak only of the English-speaking countries, the British government is reportedly planning to spend 170 million pounds on what they are calling the "People's Network." The plan is to install Internet stations as "learning centers" in 4,000 public libraries, with every central library to have at least thirty machines and every branch library at least six. Approximately 60 percent of the money will be spent on infrastructure ("stringing wires"), but, significantly, 30 percent is designated for content creation and 10 percent for training librarians to help the public. (See the People's Network site at http://www.peoplesnetwork.gov.uk.) Britain is also starting a national "e-university" to serve students in the United Kingdom, especially those who currently do not go on to higher education, as well as students abroad willing to do online courses in English.

The United States simply cannot afford to miss this competition to shape the future, but we are morally bound by the traditions of our country to have our efforts conform to the highest standards of democratic ideals and conduct, striving to maintain a balance between community responsibility and individual initiative. In this spirit, I will recommend information technology principles and goals for nonprofit education, thought of in the broad sense defined above and organized in a coalition of the kind being proposed by Digital Promise. To try to provide some concreteness to my arguments, I will include a few thoughts about the kinds of pilot projects that might take place if Digital Promise's recommendations for a coalition of nonprofits and public funding bear fruit.

The ideas and observations in this paper stem from my nearly two decades of creating content in digital form and using it in teaching and research in my academic field of Classics, which encompasses the literature, history, and archaeology of ancient Greece and Rome. Above all, my experience comes from working as one of the original collaborators on The Perseus Project: Interactive Sources on Ancient Greece (www.perseus.tufts.edu). Perseus has won national and international recognition, garnering laurels such as an award from the higher education association EDUCOM and inclusion in the top websites recognized by the National Endowment for the Humanities. From the beginning, Perseus had as its goal creating electronically accessible versions of primary sources, the building blocks of knowledge. In the context of ancient Greek studies, primary sources include original ancient texts (in Greek and in English translation) and visual data on art and archaeology, complemented by diverse and complex reference tools to help users conduct searches and investigations of these building blocks in pursuit of a wider understanding of the subject.

My experience with Perseus has spanned a time of great change in information technology. The tremendous dimensions of that change make me optimistic that digital dreams can come true, even ones as grand as those outlined in this paper. When we first started work on what would eventually become Perseus, personal computers did not yet exist, the Internet was used only by computer experts who could worm their way into the national network originally created by the Defense Department for communication during a nuclear attack, and the promise of cheap, mass storage was still a fantasy, with CD-ROM technology still only a rumor instead of a reality. When we first began using Perseus in the classroom, the requisite hardware was expensive, balky, and slow, and the constant technical problems with the technology of the day were discouraging to teachers and students alike.

Most problematic of all, however, was the radical social novelty of using electronic technology and promoting a research-based model of student-faculty interaction in humanities classes. As believers in the vision of Perseus, we were no longer willing in our teaching to confine ourselves to dispensing predigested information to students, but now insisted that they learn to use technology to ask questions of the primary sources in Perseus, organize the results, and explain the significance of what they had discovered. This was what content creation meant in the new digital world, we kept saying, and it was a necessary part of learning.

In the beginning, many students and colleagues alike resisted this new approach, but, over time, the situation has changed dramatically. Today, both technology and attitudes are vastly different. The speed of computers and the low cost of data storage (roughly ten thousand times less expensive than when we started) has meshed with the communication possibilities of networks small and large to change education in my field forever. Perseus is widely taken for granted in teaching, and it is now having an impact on professional research (the slowest part of the field to accept change). I think it is accurate, and I hope not unduly immodest, to say that Perseus has succeeded and has set a precedent that could be followed, enlarged, and improved upon to the benefit of nonprofit education in this country.

The success of Perseus did not come cheap—creating content has always been expensive. Even though the main collaborators in Perseus supported themselves by holding down jobs as professors rather than by taking salary from the project's funding, it still cost several million dollars to produce the first versions. The difficulty in continuing to find funding or create a sufficient revenue stream in a humanities field as small as ancient Greek studies has meant that Perseus in recent years has had to branch out into areas far from its original one (for example, Shakespeare) in order to find the money to keep operating. The only viable hope for humanities content creation projects such as Perseus in the future is to be part of a national project of the kind envisioned by Digital Promise.

THE OPEN-SOURCE PRINCIPLE

The governing organizational principle for the coalition of nonprofits being suggested by Digital Promise should be to use and create only "open source" data and software. That is, not only would data created by the coalition be freely available for nonexclusive use by anyone, so, too, would the software code used to organize, present, and manipulate the data be available to anyone for free. This principle is essential to preserve the democratic values of a publicly supported project.

The open-source movement is becoming increasingly prominent in contemporary technological development, boosted most recently by the growing importance of the LINUX operating system and associated application software. Michael Jensen, director of publishing technologies at the National Academy Press, offers a convincing justification for an open-source approach in an editorial piece on open-source computer programming in the *Chronicle of Higher Education,* in which he explains that "research and scholarship are fundamentally open-source enterprises. The research on which scholarship builds is always cited; the methodology of any study is explained as a repeatable framework; and theoretical presumptions are made clear as part of any published argument. Those principles generally lead authors to be careful, and help other scholars to test an author's conclusions."[1] He defines open-source as meaning "that the source code—the programs, readable by human beings, that are compiled to make executable programs—can be viewed, modified, and then recompiled for one's own purposes." And, he might have added, the programs cannot be claimed as proprietary, as "owned" and thus charged for.

As Jensen says, open source is the kind of software that aligns with the mission of nonprofit institutions. This point, for example, underlies the principles and goals described in the websites that best explain the significance of an open-source approach for research in science and technology, www.opensource.org and www.openscience.org. Additional information and justification for the open-source approach are also available from the nonprofit group Software in the Public Interest (www.pi-inc.org) and the Free Software Foundation, which is developing the GNU Scientific Library (www.gnu.org) to produce a collection of open-source programs for mathematical and scientific computing uses. It is time for the humanities and social sciences to adopt the same principles for creating content for nonprofit educational use.

THE BUILDING BLOCKS OF NEW CONTENT CREATION

A publicly funded coalition of nonprofit educational institutions could make a great contribution to the knowledge capital needed for a healthy future by using an open-source approach in organizing a national inventory of primary source materials. This inventory would be an interactive archive of the building blocks of knowledge, freely available for individual and institutional initiatives in electronic content creation. Since no single official project, no matter how large, could ever come close to covering the range of significant subjects in the humanities and social sciences, it is crucial to begin to create a wide-ranging inventory of online textual and visual materials that will be in the public domain and serve as components for projects done by individuals or groups or institutions. The foundation for the inventory will be searchable and "queryable" databases of primary sources that will be created as the background for use in interactive projects of all kinds, from static online materials to streaming video. Texts and pictures will be freely downloadable, whether for use in schools, individual research, or reading in e-books.

The national inventory of electronic primary sources in the humanities and social sciences would cooperate with existing projects to avoid duplication, as, for example, in putting full, searchable texts of the writings of the American Founders on line. It would also try to leverage existing collections of print primary sources by putting them into tagged digital form, such as the comprehensive collection of pre-twentieth-century imprints of U.S. material held by the American Antiquarian Society, works that have the advantage of being out of copyright.

The digital data of words, pictures, and video to be made available in the inventory created by the coalition of educational nonprofit institutions would remove a major roadblock to entrepreneurial initiatives in creating content in the humanities and social sciences. At present, potential content creators are regularly frustrated in turning their ideas into online reality because it can be so difficult and expensive to gain permission to reproduce materials of all kinds. Nonprofits joining this initiative would agree to make as many of their materials freely available as possible, consistent with their obligations to other copyright holders. One main reason nonprofits have so far been reluctant to do this is financial. Fearing that they would lose a revenue stream, they restrict access to their materials. Like the music industry confronted by the implications of online exchange of songs, it is time for nonprofits to acknowledge that a different business model is needed. For one thing, a national fund of the kind being recommended by Digital Promise perhaps could be used to provide compensation to nonprofits that provide materials to the national open-source inventory. For another, nonprofits could be encouraged to seek revenue by "value added" enhancements of freely available primary materials, following the model of the growth of the LINUX operating system in the open-source software world. They could, for example, sell enhancements to their primary materials, such as guides or courses.

This idea is admittedly ambitious and open-ended in terms of what materials would be entered into the inventory of primary sources and in what order. Without underestimating the difficulties of organizing such a project, I nevertheless believe, based on my experience with Perseus, that it is important to begin with a very broad vision, even in the face of uncertainty and lack of unanimity about what might be the full of panoply of primary sources that should be included and even exactly where to begin. As with Perseus, we need to make a start and then overcome the inevitable difficulties by continuing to review what turns out to be feasible and desirable.

One good possibility for making a start might be to conduct a circumscribed pilot project by entering a set of materials with an obvious relevance to the history of democracy and government in the United States but with wider implications, such as primary sources on the Bill of Rights or the other amendments to the Constitution. This project could promote an educated citizenry and meet a perceived need of our democracy. Frank Newman, for example, the former president of the Education Commission of the States, has faulted education in our country because students "are graduating these days with very limited knowledge of how American government works. This is one factor in the slow erosion of voting in this country."[2] At the same time, public interest in online materials on our history and culture is high, as shown by the millions and millions of "hits" that constantly bombard the Library of Congress's website, "American Memory" (memory.loc.gov), which provides primary sources and archival materials.

In my own field, associated projects could be created to explore the background of democracy, such as the creation in ancient Athens of the first democratic government, society, and tradition of freedom of speech. The DEMOS project, currently underway at STOA (www.stoa.org) as part of the planned project POLITEIA: From Athenian Democracy and Roman Republic to These United States, provides an example of the scholarly resources that could be marshaled in a cooperative effort. (Information on POLITEIA is not yet available on the STOA website. In the interests of full disclosure, I should say that I am a member of the board of advisers of this project.) POLITEIA plans to build on the experience of previous projects, such as Perseus, in providing state-of-the-art electronic tagging and database structure for primary sources and explanatory essays on the democracy of Athens, the republic of Rome, and the lessons that the American Founders took from these ancient precedents.

Another possible associated project would address the need for understanding the power and dangers of what is usually and inadequately called "oral communication," which will become the norm in society as technology makes it possible to communicate with computers through speech instead of typing. It seems certain that speech-controlled computers, hitherto the stuff of science fiction, will become standard and that "oral communication" via technology will become ubiquitous. This form of communication actually includes much more than the sound of speech, because it communicates meaning visually, too, by tone, gesture, deportment, and so on. In a very real sense, we will be going "back to the future," to a world of communication of the kind experienced by the Greeks and Romans. Over hundreds of years, they developed concepts and techniques—the discipline of rhetoric—to inform, enrich, and control the complex factors of "oral communication." For a democratic society such as ours, it is imperative to prepare our citizenry in what is sometimes called "media literacy," so that they can understand and control the full complexity of the new world of oral communication that technology will inexorably create. The best guide to how to go about getting ready for this change lies in the vast experience of the ancients, who lived in just such an "oral" environment.

Finally, if I can be excused for proposing a very expensive and ambitious dream, I would even go so far as to propose that the coalition of nonprofits might sponsor a project to illuminate American history and government by using the emerging technology of interactive streaming video, which is the most enticing, flexible, and extensible form of information technology yet invented. Interactive streaming video, linked to databases of explanatory primary sources, provides today's most exciting prospect for attracting widespread interest in educational information technology projects.

This dawning medium turns watching video from a passive viewing experience into an interactive one. In interactive streaming video, viewers "trigger added graphics and content, animation programs and other applications as they watch," in the words of Jim Bodor, describing the commercial software products being developed by a company called Media 100 (Media 100's goal naturally is to promote commerce). As he says, "someone watching a trailer for the recent movie 'Mission: Impossible 2' would be able to click on Tom Cruise's sunglasses, and order a pair."[3]

An interactive streaming video pilot project on United States history and government would promote learning instead of shopping. Imagine, for example, watching the musical film 1776 (Columbia Pictures, 1972), which depicts with cinematic verve the Continental Congress of that year and the signing of the Declaration of Independence, and being able to click on Benjamin Franklin, not to buy a pair of his famous granny glasses but to be linked to searchable databases in the national open-source archive of relevant primary sources (for example, newspapers and pamphlets on Franklin's role at the congress, Franklin's own writings on the American Revolution, art showing how Franklin was represented, and so on, perhaps even information on the technology of making spectacles in the eighteenth century). These sources would in turn be linked to others on related topics. Rather than watching passively, viewers could ask and seek answers to questions such as "What did he really say?" or "What were other people saying about what was going on?" or "Where can I look for more information about something interesting to me in the video?" In other words, the powerful lure of our time's leading form of video entertainment—moving pictures—would be employed in promoting active learning about U.S. history and government.

Whatever the nature of the projects that the coalition might sponsor to build on the national open-source inventory of primary sources, all such projects should emphasize providing open-source and user-friendly access to as comprehensive as possible a set of relevant building blocks of knowledge in the humanities and social sciences. To try to minimize disputes over partisan selection and presentations of evidence, the amount of interpretation provided for the primary sources in officially supported projects would be kept to the minimum necessary to air differences of opinion and controversies. Provisions also could be made for recording and making accessible criticisms of the materials as presented in the projects.

PROVIDING FAIR OPPORTUNITY TO ALL TO CREATE CONTENT

If we truly want to be democratic in leveraging the united power of educational nonprofit institutions in furnishing building blocks of knowledge, we have to try to provide a fair opportunity for everyone to learn how to build with the blocks. That is, it is not enough only to provide electronic versions of primary sources. We also have to provide ways to learn how to use the software needed to employ these building blocks in creating content and then provide a way to store and preserve what is created. This recommendation and the one following are meant to address these concerns by recognizing the disparity between technological "haves" and "have nots" in access to the information technology revolution's true engines of power—knowledge of software and storage capacity for digital data.

Nonprofit education is currently failing to address the need of students (of all ages) to learn to use software for content creation, not just for passive computing tasks. Federal Reserve chairman Alan Greenspan, in a speech to the National Governors Association on July 11, 2000, has emphasized that the nation's education system needs to do more to prepare students for the explosion in information technology by going beyond mere infrastructure and establishing guidelines on the best way to teach students how to make use of all the new technologies. He stressed the need to provide teachers with the training they will need to instruct their students on how to do more than just type on computers and search the Internet.

This idea has been expressed in more technical terms by Lawrence Snyder, a computer scientist at the University of Washington, who chaired the committee that issued the report *Being Fluent with Information Technology* for the National Research Council.[4] It concludes that students today need more than simple computer skills (such as using e-mail, browsing the web, and so on) to be successful. They should be taught a deeper understanding of information technology, what the report calls an ability to understand and do "algorithmic thinking." The way to learn this is by doing real-world projects, the report says, that require skills, an understanding of relevant concepts (how a computer works, what a network does, how information is digitally encoded and transmitted), and the production of an end result that is based on algorithmic thinking (and can thus tell a computer what to do). Snyder gives as an example of such a project "formulating an H.-I.-V. tracking system for a hospital or a doctor's office."[5]

Some work related to this goal is in fact under way. Most promising so far are specific examples, such as *An Introduction to Structured Markup* by Anne Mahoney, available (along with introductions to other subjects) through STOA (www.stoa.org/guides). Also relevant are efforts such as the three-year, $2.2 million grant that the U.S. Department of Education has given to The International Society for Technology in Education, a nonprofit group located in Eugene, Oregon, to develop national standards and recommendations for colleges to consider in preparing teachers to use technology effectively in their teaching, to develop curriculum, assess students, and increase their professional knowledge. Bell Atlantic has given $300,000 to support The Virtual Resource Site for Teaching with Technology, developed by the University of Maryland's University College (www.umuc.edu/virtualteaching). There are also other sites with similar purposes, as well as numerous print publications on the subject.

Despite these admirable projects, what is still missing in this country is a coordinated effort to leverage the open-source software movement in the public interest by providing comprehensive, free, online instruction in how to use the rapidly growing set of open-source software tools available for content creation. (Compare the British plan to spend tens of millions of pounds to train librarians for the People's Network.) I am not sufficiently informed about the "technology education" segment of the National Science Foundation's project for the Online National Library to know whether it includes a project similar to this one. (I was unable to locate any further information by searching for this project on the foundation's website at www.nsf.gov.) If it does not, it is past time to plan to offer suitable online instructional materials to the U.S. public in using open-source tools, such as the project called Squeak, a framework for developing web-ready multimedia. This new tool is being developed by a team at Disney Imagineering headed by Alan Kay and supplemented by volunteer programmers around the world. As Michael Jensen says, "Squeak is free, open-source software that is likely to improve the world."[6] But that "improving the world" will not happen in an appropriately democratic way unless we make available the knowledge of how to use such exciting technological tools.

It is beyond the budgets and expertise, and even outside the mission (as presently and, in my opinion, inadequately defined), of nonprofit higher education to provide this training. This deficiency will cost our country dearly in diminished opportunities for the creation of knowledge capital. Fortunately, a solution is possible—publicly funded, free online tutorials that teach open-source software, complemented by a metasite on the Internet that would guide people to online tutorials already in existence elsewhere. The coalition that Digital Promise is recommending should agree to support this solution.

NATIONAL SERVER FARMS FOR STORING NEW CONTENT

Storage capacity for digital data and technical maintenance of its organizing software (such as databases) are the complements to knowledge of open-source software for the creation of knowledge capital in the national interest. Server farms—large collections of computers storing digital data at centralized facilities and delivering it to multiple customers over the Internet—are an explosive area of business growth, which should tip us off to the importance of this model for hosting, managing, and distributing data and web-based applications to widespread locations in higher education. One recent estimate, by Michael Turits of Prudential Securities, is that 58 percent of all business sites were remotely hosted in 1999 and that this penetration could rise to 80 percent by 2003. In addition to application service providers and hosting service providers, content distribution service providers are growing rapidly in the commercial world, to speed distribution of content to end customers.

This sort of "server farm" approach seems like a necessary response to the information technology needs of nonprofits, which increasingly face enormous difficulties in designing and paying for their data storage and access systems and in hiring and keeping competent personnel to maintain their information technology services. A national set of server farms would not be intended to replace the local data and application storage facilities of educational institutions, but rather to offer a way for shared, open-source content of the kind envisioned in these recommendations to be jointly created and then used by a coalition of nonprofit institutions and the public at large.

ASSURING THE VALUE OF KNOWLEDGE CAPITAL

There is hardly a word powerful enough to express the magnitude of the exponential growth in online information in recent years, a trend that seems likely to continue and even accelerate. There are already billions and billions of web pages on the Internet, and the imminent arrival of digital television is going to bring another vast array of choices in sources of information. How is it going to be humanly possible to make informed judgments about the value and accuracy of individual items in this incredible plethora of data? No task generated by the information technology revolution is more daunting than answering this question. In short, we need to work to find ways to assure the value of our knowledge capital by doing what we can to vet its accuracy and reliability and to hold its creators responsible for what they create.

Jason Epstein finds "strong grounds for optimism. The critical faculty that selects meaning from chaos is part of our instinctual equipment and so is the gift for creating and re-creating civilizations and their rules without external guidance. Human beings have a genius for finding their way, for making orderly markets, distinguishing quality, and assigning value. . . . There is no reason to fear that the awesome diversity of the World Wide Web will overwhelm it."[7] It is now time for us to take practical steps to put that "genius" into practice for credentialing online information.

Traditionally, one of the functions of nonprofit educational institutions, from academic departments to university presses to museums, has been to vet, filter, and, ultimately, credential information. This tradition has various weaknesses in practice, and some critics have even questioned its desirability. In any case, however, it has only been possible because the amount of information being credentialed, while large, was nothing even remotely like what the information technology revolution is generating. Many, many more individuals and groups are going to become publishers and broadcasters in the new environment, whether by using electronic, publish-on-demand services such as Xlibris (according to its advertisement, a "strategic partner of Random House Ventures" that promises "Now your book can get published the way you hoped it would. Publish your book in no time . . . and at no cost"), or by setting up their own servers for distributing content over the Internet and through interactive television. It goes without saying that it will be physically impossible even to list, much less seriously review and credential, all the materials that are going to be available electronically in the near future, which makes it even more pressing to educate the public about the nature of proper credentialing and how to protect themselves by demanding transparent and trustworthy descriptions of the sources and method of creation of any and all information available online.

The nonprofit coalition proposed by Digital Promise could support this goal by establishing a template for the nature and depth of description of authors and sources of evidence that every online publication will need to show, if it is to be credible. When using online information, people need to become accustomed to look for and evaluate the kind of information meant to be supplied in the template. It would be a significant public service if the coalition could establish an appropriate credentialing template as customary for all online data made available by its cooperating nonprofit institutions. It also might be possible for the alliance of nonprofits to establish a mechanism for applying the template to information created by others, to help strengthen public awareness of the need to insist on transparency of sources and verification of accuracy for online materials.

As a complement to the idea of designing a template for establishing the bona fides of online information, the coalition also should create an Internet portal to attract users to the kind of projects and digital data that this position paper recommends and to help prevent the credentialed information created by nonprofits from being overwhelmed by the electronic cacophony of commercial information. The primary sources available through national open-source inventory would be one obvious destination reached through the portal.

Furthermore, it would be very useful to find a way to have a link to such a portal prominently displayed on the commercial portals that seem poised to provide the main gateway to digital television watching. The recently formed company Gemstar-TV Guide International plans to use its Interactive Programming Guide (IPG) to dominate interactive television. "In a universe of 500 or more channels, the IPG could become a portal site similar to Yahoo! or Netscape Netcenter on the Web. When the availability of digital connections and interactive services reaches critical mass, viewers flipping on the TV will likely be greeted by a welcome screen, from which viewers can program their VCR, check local weather, peruse theater listings and even buy tickets."[8] I would add that they should also, from the same screen, be able to link directly to the portal for nonprofits that I am suggesting.

The technology for constructing such a portal apparently will be freely available through the FirstGov portal project being created by Eric A. Brewer, a computer science professor at the University of California, Berkeley, and the cofounder and chief technology officer of Inktomi Corporation. FirstGov will be an ultrafast database linking and supporting queries to all the federal government's websites, which by now include some 100 million web pages. David J. Barram, administrator of the General Services Administration and a member of the board of directors overseeing the portal, has said that "universities, businesses, and individual entrepreneurs will be free to use the FirstGov database and the name 'FirstGov' to build specialized government information portals for educators, journalists, or other interest groups, provided they conform to the government's rules for the project."[9]

There may be opportunities for cooperation in building this sort of portal with nonprofits such as the Alfred P. Sloan Foundation. Sloan has in recent years put millions of dollars into creating distance-education resources, but the foundation now has begun to refocus its efforts to promote and explain to students the opportunities that they currently have, to "try to help students weed through the thicket of opportunities that already exist."[10] Therefore, Sloan is creating an Internet portal in the form of an online catalog, called the Sloan Consortium Catalog (www.sloan-c.org/catalog), to provide information on different online education programs already in operation. This is meant to be a nonprofit and informational portal differentiated from commercial ones. Sloan's goal is not necessarily to provide "credentialing" of online resources and courses, but nevertheless their project seems complementary to the one envisioned here.

The Social Dimensions of Learning

All the ideas I have so far mentioned involve online projects that users would access remotely, whether in a classroom or at home (in a distance education program or simply on one's own). I have to stress, however, that the past teaches me that the future cannot be entirely online. One of the most important lessons I have learned in the past twenty years of trying to make appropriate use of information technology in my academic field is that the more we use information technology, the more valuable and even necessary that face-to-face gatherings of people become. To speak only of student-teacher interaction, my colleagues and I using Perseus to teach in a research-based mode have found that we need to spend more time than ever talking to students to help them develop the intellectual skills necessary to formulate good research inquiries and to understand and explain the meaning of the raw data that they accumulate. While they can assimilate rather quickly the technical knowledge needed to run the hardware and software that we use, it is much more labor intensive to teach them how to be intelligent interpreters of primary sources. We use e-mail and chat rooms and every other form of technological communication to help do this, but, in my judgment, there is no adequate substitute for face-to-face communication for imparting this complex kind of knowledge based on experience.

This is so, I believe, because there is in point of fact no way that remote communication, not even video conferencing in virtual reality, can offer the same incredible richness and complexity of communication that human beings routinely experience when meeting with one another and engaging in the full range of possibilities, aural and visual, of oral communication. In the interest of saving space and not going beyond my area of expertise, as there are experts far more qualified than I on this point, I will not try to describe the specifics of what I mean by "richness and complexity" in this context. But I will report that my experience strongly tells me it is true.

My firm opinion, then, is that complex learning is a social experience in important ways and that remote or distance learning cannot completely supply that context. Learners in social groups, for example in classes and in informal conversations at colleges and universities, learn "distinct ways of judging what is interesting, valid, significant, and so on," to quote John Seely Brown and Paul Duguid in their book, *The Social Life of Information*.[11] As they also point out, employers prefer to hire students who have the social experience provided by a traditional college or university, even when distance-learning graduates have just as good scores on tests and measuring scales.

I suggest that the coalition of nonprofits should consider ways of addressing this issue in the context of the increasingly technological and decentralized environment of education today. One way in which this could perhaps be done would be to sponsor and subsidize many small-scale, face-to-face learning groups that would meet at nonprofits to provide a social experience for learning. Since face-to-face meetings require appropriate physical space to take place, nonprofits could play an invaluable role by making such space available to appropriate groups. I realize that there are many practical obstacles to such a plan, such as how to organize, perpetuate, and evaluate such gatherings. Nevertheless, it is imperative not to lose sight of the social dimension of learning even as we forge ahead with technologically based projects to create knowledge capital in the national interest. The coalition of nonprofits that Digital Promise advocates can and should be a catalyst for providing solutions to the need for maintaining the social dimensions of learning in the information technology revolution that continues to transform our educational institutions and thus our very lives. In this way, as in the ways suggested above, nonprofit education in the humanities and social sciences can play an active and needed role in creating the knowledge capital so vital to our future.

NOTES

1. Michael Jensen, "Information Technology at a Crossroads: Open-Source Computer Programming," *Chronicle of Higher Education,* October 29, 1999, p. A92.

2. Interview in the *Chronicle of Higher Education,* June 30, 2000, p. B13.

3. Jim Bodor, "Media 100 Software Introduced," *Worcester Telegram and Gazette,* July 17, 2000, p. E1.

4. Committee on Information Technology Literacy, National Research Council, *Being Fluent with Information Technology* (Washington, D.C.: National Academy Press, 1999), available at http://stills.nap.edu/html/beingfluent/ch1.html.

5. Interview in the *Chronicle of Higher Education,* May 5, 2000, p. A49.

6. Jensen, "Information Technology at a Crossroads."

7. Jason Epstein, "The Rattle of Pebbles," *New York Review of Books,* April 27, 2000, p. 59.

8. "Gemstar-TV Guide Watching Interactive TV," Associated Press, as reprinted in *Worcester Telegram and Gazette,* July 24, 2000, p. E1.

9. Florence Olsen, "Berkeley Professor Builds an Ultra-Fast Web Portal for the Government," *Chronicle of Higher Education,* August 11, 2000, p. A50.

10. Sarah Carr, "Sloan Foundation Turns Its Attention from Creating Programs to Promoting Them," *Chronicle of Higher Education,* June 2, 2000, p. A49.

11. John Seely Brown and Paul Duguid, *The Social Life of Information* (Boston: Harvard Business School Press, 2000), p. 220.

6.
THE PROMISE OF THE DIGITAL AGE FOR THE RENEWAL OF REGIONAL CIVIC CULTURE

MARY L. WALSHOK

We live in a time of unprecedented opportunity for modern communications technologies to serve the public good. The most advanced forms of technology—digital, interactive, and wireless—are capable of reaching all communities and citizens with voice, video, and text at a level of quality and affordability unprecedented in human history. We also live in a time of enormous shifts in economic and social relations driven by the new knowledge economy, globalization, and worldwide demographic trends. The challenge confronting communities across the globe is how to build social, civic, and economic institutions capable of not only reacting to but also harnessing and managing the forces of continuous change in a manner that balances local needs and capacities with global imperatives.

In such a world, geographic regions with shared economic, social, and political traditions and capabilities become increasingly important to the challenging process of understanding, managing, and integrating change into the core institutions of society. State and federal resources represent less and less the leaders or drivers of this continuous process of adapting to change. Increasingly, they are the "enablers" of regional initiatives through public policy and resource allocations that empower decision makers and implementers at the "local" level. Similarly, institutions that have been based on national networks and standards—education and training, healthcare, public utilities, and communications—are looking for ways to achieve a better balance between regional needs and capacities and national and global frameworks and decision making.

The paradox of diversity and sameness that characterizes this new knowledge-based economy represents an incredible opportunity to build a communications system to serve the public that is simultaneously rich in local culture, information, and civic affairs and still connected to globally significant intellectual and cultural resources. Models for how to achieve this are few and far between, however. This is in part because for more than five decades the broadcast media (including public and educational broadcasting) have attempted to achieve enhanced quality and economies of scale through national networks and centralized programming. In the process, they have built an infrastructure of production, distribution, and financing that is not well suited to the new challenges and opportunities of the more nimble, localized demands of a "digital" society.

Nonetheless, as has happened in many other industries over the last two decades, innovations have been occurring on the margins of the established public broadcasting institutions. Much can be learned from these innovations about how to create cost-effective, public service–focused telecommunications capacities that are deeply tied to their regions. It is possible to serve a wide array of specific community knowledge needs while simultaneously providing informational, cultural, and civic programming of global significance.

UCSD-TV, a low-power, campus-based broadcast television station (licensed to the regents of the University of California) with an annual budget of less than $1 million, whose daily programming is received by 800,000 households in the San Diego region, represents one such innovative model. UCSD-TV's mission is to provide communities and citizens access to a multitude of cultural, educational, informational, and civic issues through a mix of programs with regional significance. Of these, 40 percent are "acquired," 30 percent are produced (primarily in studio, occasionally in the field), and 30 percent are "captured" events, that is, performances, readings, debates, and lectures in community settings. The latter is accomplished through partnerships with a rich array of cultural, artistic, and civic institutions in the region. In this way, UCSD-TV produces approximately two hundred original programs annually, in contrast to a half dozen on the local public broadcasting affiliate.

The regionally focused, intellectually rich programming of UCSD-TV represents a promising example of how regions across the country might organize and fund a vibrant broadcasting capability whose mission is first and foremost local public service. How and why UCSD-TV came into being, what it takes to sustain this capability, and how its web of community relationships and high-quality, low-cost production capabilities can be leveraged for more diverse educational and civic purposes are the focus of this paper.

WHY UCSD-TV GOT STARTED

The decision to launch a television broadcast service with a broad public service mission, rather than an exclusively instructional mission, came out of a deliberative process among a diverse group of campus representatives in response to the offer by an off-campus friend and donor to assist the university in applying to the FCC lottery for one of the new, low-power television channels made available in the late 1980s. It was the chancellor's decision to participate in the lottery and to appoint a broad-based campus committee (chaired by the university's dean of extension) to come up with both a recommendation on whether or not to start a station (were we to win the lottery) and a set of recommended purposes for such a station. UCSD-TV was awarded LPTV Channel 35 in the fall of 1987, and in March of 1988 the campus committee strongly recommended moving forward with the creation of a new kind of television station that would be intellectually connected to the work of a research university and primarily focused on topics of interest for and about the region. The committee's report emphasized the need for this station to differentiate itself from PBS, whose fare was nationally produced cultural and public affairs programming for a well-educated "general audience" on the one hand, and from community access and instructional stations focused on narrowly defined audiences for highly specific purposes on the other. The exponential growth of C-SPAN at the time of the committee's deliberations had many describing the goal of UCSD-TV to be the C-SPAN of the research university in the San Diego region. In many ways, that is what it has become over a decade of planning and operations.

The committee put a strong emphasis on broadcasting campus lectures, colloquia, and performances. It also recommended public interest and outreach programs to communities not typically served by UCSD or local broadcasters: new immigrants, the large Latino community in the region, and constituencies not served or underserved by the health care establishment. Finally, the committee recommended, as an alternative to the "sound bites" on local commercial stations and the exclusively national news of the local PBS station, public affairs programs that dealt in depth with regional issues, as well as significant conversations and debates on topics of civic interest.

It took five years from the spring 1988 report to the chancellor for the station to go on the air. The small implementation committee made up of the dean of extension, the director of the University Media Center, and the director of campus telecommunications services had prepared a two-year timeline, which was extended an additional two and a half years due to: (1) the complexities of securing approval from the regents to launch the university's first broadcast station; (2) settling the licensing issues with the FCC, which were seriously delayed given the necessity of approvals from both Washington and Mexico, given UCSD's location twenty miles from the Mexican border; (3) the problems mounting a broadcast antenna on a UCSD-owned hillside contiguous to affluent residential neighborhoods; (4) the challenges of putting together a financing package for a completely new broadcast entity; (5) the process of building a core staff; and (6) developing a model program schedule in the context of the highly consultative, faculty-governance structure of the UCSD campus.

Had it not been for the continuous moral support of the chancellor and senior vice chancellor for academic affairs, the extraordinary generosity and technical problem-solving skills of the Media Center director and the director of campus telecommunications, and the broad network of faculty, community, and funding resources of the extension dean, the station would never have been launched. In addition, by early 1992 two highly experienced individuals had emerged from the documentary and public affairs television worlds who were willing to be the "start-up" team for UCSD-TV: one as director of programming and operations, the other as a full-time producer. Also, the station's start-up and momentum were inextricably tied to a group of community advisers who, between the fall of 1988 and going on the air in the winter of 1993, shared ideas and experience and provided encouragement and know-how. They also opened critical doors to influential people in the broadcast television world and in the cable industry, including the regional Time/Warner Cable general manager, the editor of the *San Diego Union-Tribune,* the general manager of the local NBC-TV affiliate, a member of PBS's national board, the director of the local science museum (and a former documentary filmmaker), and a variety of academics knowledgeable about film and media from several disciplines. There was a certain kind of esprit de corps that developed around the entire effort, much like the "hey kids, let's put on a show" spirit characterizing the Mickey Rooney/Judy Garland Hardy Boys movies of the 1940s. There was never a doubt that UCSD-TV would come into being; it just took twice as long as originally expected.

How the Station Is Structured and Programmed

At start-up, the organization and staffing of the station was much sparer than it is today. The effort required for capturing events for later television broadcast as well as the complexities of in-studio production were initially underestimated. What began as three full-time people and a large pool of freelancers has grown into a highly professional team of eight, including a managing director, four producers, programming staff, and a core pool of freelance photographers and editors. Because of its location within a large, self-funded extension and public service division, the station has been able to secure all of its human resources, purchasing, accounting, promotional, and fund-raising infrastructure from existing university staff. Because of the unique skills and contributions of the director of UCSD's Media Center, the station has unparalleled and mostly free engineering and facilities support. Because of the station's status as a non-commercial, low-power, public service television enterprise, authors such as Jane Smiley and George Plimpton, celebrities such as Danny Glover and Diana Rigg, politicians such as former governor Pete Wilson and Secretary of State Madelyn Albright, and artists such as Dale Chihuley, Ravi Shankar, and Janos Starker agree to be videotaped at no charge. Finally, because of a decision to use the most modern and flexible production and editing equipment available primarily in capturing events in auditoriums, lecture halls, and galleries, as well as conversations in offices and seminar rooms, the station has invested prudently in equipment and studio production facilities. For these reasons, the station can operate year-round on a budget of $750,000.

This budget supports the production of more than two hundred programs annually in five thematic areas, each of which are programmed one day a week: science, health and medicine, art and music, humanities, and public affairs. Programs include lecture presentations (46 percent of airtime), interviews (20 percent), documentary-style programs (15 percent), and performances (11 percent). In addition, the station acquires approximately three hundred programs from other universities, independent producers, and the public domain at little or no cost. The station's programs are presented to local cable and broadcast audiences from 4:00 P.M. to midnight every day. The university provides approximately $300,000 of annual funding to the station through various vice chancellor contributions and income from revenue generated from a UCSD-owned transmitter tower. The remaining $450,000 is generated through underwriting, grants, production funding partnerships, and private contributions (about 10 percent).

UCSD-TV's UNIQUE FORMULA: PROGRAM PARTNERSHIPS

A fundamental premise underlying the development of UCSD-TV was that it should be possible to provide challenging, interesting, and useful programs at minimal cost through a programming approach that emphasizes "capturing" events and partnering on programs with "the best and the brightest," both on campus and in the community. This turned out to be a politically inspired strategy as well as a financially sound one. The viewership and profitability needs of commercial broadcasters and the high overhead and fund-raising needs of the local PBS station had left a void into which UCSD-TV readily stepped. Librarians, museum directors, performing arts organizations, civic organizations, and even the local newspaper were eager to extend their reach through broadcast television, and UCSD-TV was eager to "capture" talent and collaboratively develop original, regionally anchored programming. In its first year, the partnerships were with allies who were nearby: the UCSD and City College music departments, the UCSD School of Medicine, and the Scripps Institution of Oceanography. But very quickly, thanks to a diverse and active community advisory board and a truly gifted collection of content–based producers and editors, creative partnerships were forged with a wide range of off–campus institutions. It helped that within the first two years of operation, UCSD-TV had secured countywide cable carriage, and within another year, its programming appeared in the daily TV grid of the local newspapers. Today, UCSD-TV regularly covers speakers and events at local institutions such as the City Club, the *San Diego Union-Tribune,* the Natural History Museum, the Fleet Science Center, the Museum of Contemporary Art, and performing arts organizations such as the La Jolla Chamber Music Society and Malashock Dance Company. In addition, the station collaboratively creates season-long series exploring stage productions at the San Diego Opera and the Old Globe Theatre.

These important partnerships are possible because of the "intellectual capital" the lead producers bring to the station and the collaborative culture shaping all of its work. By emphasizing specific sectors such as science and the arts, the producers are deeply invested in their areas of responsibility and build long-term relationships with university and community resources that result in high-quality, codeveloped, cofunded, and copromoted television programs of community value. The producers also bring a commitment to high output with contained costs and are capable of performing the multiple tasks required in production, from writing to lighting and shooting to editing. Seeking partners rather than clients allows the station to retain editorial control over the programs being produced, even with campus partners. UCSD-TV has built a reputation as a source of legitimate information rather than as a promotional mechanism for either the university or its partner institutions.

In addition to a highly competent and committed group of producers, essential to making all these quasi-autonomous production partnerships work is the station's managing director's role in integrating the diverse range of productions into one cohesive program schedule. The vision, diplomacy, and commitment of this person have been critical to ensuring the coherent sense of mission and the clear identity UCSD-TV has always enjoyed. Finally, the in-kind contributions, the access to talent, and community outreach through the newsletters, brochures, and audience programs of the partner institutions represent hundreds of thousands of dollars in marketing and communications costs UCSD-TV does not have to bear. Equally important, however, is UCSD-TV's contribution to these partnerships, which includes creative production and editing talent, a major investment in equipment and broadcasting support, as well as the access to 800,000 households UCSD-TV brings to the table. It is this ability to leverage capabilities and share unique resources in a manner that benefits both partners, but most importantly the San Diego public, that differentiates UCSD-TV from any other broadcast station in the nation.

WHAT LIES IN THE FUTURE FOR UCSD-TV

Over a seven-year period, UCSD-TV has developed a set of capabilities that can be used for many purposes beyond daily broadcast of information-rich programming. The studio equipment and production capabilities of the station are poised to move into new forms of communication at the regional level. The only thing limiting taking the next steps is budget. The budget as it now stands is sufficient to produce and capture events that are broadcast in a one-way format. However, were funding to become available from regional, state, national, or foundation sources, the station is ready to mobilize in a variety of new directions.

UCSD-TV has already been involved in some externally funded experiments that suggest there is a desire and readiness for a more activist and interactive role for the station in San Diego. For example, Alliance Healthcare Foundation provided $125,000 to produce a series of health information programs in Spanish, which were broadcast as well as distributed broadly in the community. More than 1,500 videotapes of these programs were requested by local clinics and health care providers working with Spanish-speaking populations. The station also has extensive experience in doing in-depth political coverage of state and regional candidates and expects there would be a large audience for interactivity with these sorts of programs; unfortunately, UCSD-TV simply does not have the resources to put in the phone lines and manage the telephone calls. The station also can broadcast live to a large general public, having done so when President Clinton was a graduation speaker at UCSD. The team is eager to move into more live and interactive broadcasts, particularly on public policy issues and topics of regional concern. It is also clear that in the health care area there would be a great opportunity to program interactively.

UCSD-TV also has a number of interesting collaborations with county schools to produce enrichment programming that is broadcast into classrooms subsequent to teacher preparation on the specific topic, such as music. Television stations including UCSD-TV could be much more active producers of enrichment programming that would feed into the schools and include interactivity in the form of young students asking questions of experts or performers located on a university campus, in a museum, or in a library. UCSD-TV has had extensive discussions with the regional network of branch libraries and the *San Diego Union-Tribune* about the possibility of collaborating in "electronic town halls" on topics of significance to the region, be it bilingual education, water issues, or utility rates. The network of branch libraries is increasingly tied to the Internet and the local cable companies are creating connectivity, making it possible for neighborhood groups to gather at branch libraries and interact with a series of experts or decision makers in a central studio facility.

Finally, with support from Intel and in partnership with InterVu, UCSD-TV also experimented with videostreaming programming over the Internet to the desktop with some promising results. Videostreaming represents a very exciting capability of the station in the near future that will be especially useful to provide research briefings and professional updates in scientific, technical, and professional fields where the knowledge base is changing very quickly. It can also be a valuable resource in professional continuing education. Rather than relying exclusively on the traditional model of broadcast television instruction, UCSD-TV hopes to produce informational and instructional programming that is not only useful in a broadcast mode but can also be videostreamed to computers in the office and at home.

These are but some beginning thoughts about where a station like UCSD-TV can go. The reason the station is uniquely equipped to move forward on these sorts of developments is because of (1) the network of partnerships developed throughout the region in the health care, education, high technology, cultural, and civic arenas, and (2) the tradition of partnering in the coproduction and cofunding of programs with a variety of research, cultural, and civic institutions. With a very modest infusion of capital, it would be possible to expand significantly on the ways in which UCSD-TV programs reach the citizens of the San Diego region.

7.
FATHOM:
A CASE STUDY OF A PUBLIC/PRIVATE
PARTNERSHIP IN HIGHER EDUCATION

ANN KIRSCHNER

FATHOM OVERVIEW

Fathom is the first international digital media company to market and distribute branded content and commerce from premier higher education, research, and cultural institutions. Targeting a worldwide audience of knowledge consumers, Fathom will offer a wealth of free, high-quality digital media in the form of lectures, articles, performances, and specialty websites from leading universities, museums, and libraries.

Fathom's partners are the leading universities and cultural institutions of the world, including Columbia University, the London School of Economics and Political Science, the University of Chicago, the University of Michigan, Cambridge University Press, the British Library, the New York Public Library, RAND, the American Film Institute, and Woods Hole Oceanographic Institute. These partners are among the most valuable names in the international knowledge and education markets. They are rich in intellectual capital, resources, and experts.

Fathom's high-quality content will make it an important knowledge destination and the leading marketer of online courses and other knowledge products, including emerging products such as e-books and specialized online databases. Its revenues come primarily from marketing commissions on the sales of these products. Fathom is the first for-profit company that will have comprehensive licenses from leading institutions of education and culture—precisely what is lacking in the current online knowledge/education marketplace.

WHY FATHOM WAS CREATED

Fathom was founded by Columbia University in 1999 in recognition of several factors:

- *The dominance of the knowledge economy.* Today's knowledge economy is fueled by intellectual capital. Working adults need to improve their professional skills continually, and extended years of productivity drive their need for lifetime learning. Universities are rich sources of intellectual capital through their academic community (that is, their faculty, researchers, and students), through their libraries, and through other resources devoted to learning.

- *The need to move beyond training to education.* It is important to move beyond the narrowly defined vocational training and skills acquisition. The knowledge economy demands education, not just training. These more sophisticated needs will drive professionals and lifelong learners to seek the comprehensive and fresh source of learning traditionally associated with universities.

- *The importance of authenticated knowledge.* The Internet offers unprecedented but fragmented and unauthenticated access to information. The market demand for branded, authenticated knowledge on the Internet is increasing, driven by technology as well as the increasing pace of change and specialization across all areas of knowledge. Branded and authenticated content will become even more important as the online audience becomes more mainstream and international.

- *The new market attracts new players.* The huge marketplace opportunity created by the Internet for postsecondary education is already driving well-capitalized, for-profit companies into the market. Universities face long-term strategic threats to their economic base and to their relationship with their faculty unless they can navigate the dangers and the opportunities posed by the advent of international, distributed learning.

- *The extended mission of the university.* Online learning is a positive extension of the basic mission of the university. Working directly with faculty to resolve issues of quality and intellectual property ownership, universities can use technology to extend their identity online and reach new students. This can be done without compromising their values as academic communities dedicated to the creation and preservation of knowledge

- *The need for for-profit help.* While rich in intellectual capital, universities are weakened as competitors by their internal structures. The very things that make them strong as seats of scholarship—the need for careful vetting of ideas, peer review, low risk profiles, and the academic calendar—may compromise their ability to innovate institutionally. Creating for-profit, entrepreneurial companies supports the university's need to raise capital, move quickly, and attract talented management teams to develop strategies to move the university online. These new hybrids seek to maximize the university's market share of the digital, online higher education marketplace in a way that is still consistent with the traditions and values of the university.

Recognizing that no single university could provide sufficient intellectual capital for an international audience seeking multidisciplinary knowledge, Fathom recruited a consortium of leaders in education and culture as partners in the venture. Museums and libraries were included in the consortium since they too are rich in intellectual capital and also in resources for marketing to the kind of audience that will be attracted to Fathom. Museums in particular have taken on the challenge of crafting an educational experience that is learner-centered rather than teacher-centered. Successful, modern museum exhibitions are great examples of this—meeting the standards of scholarship as well as popular appeal. The Internet will likely intensify this focus on the learner, rather than the teacher, as online education takes hold.

Fathom's Relationship with Its Partners

Fathom provides its partner institutions with:

- High-quality production resources to bring their content online. Fathom works directly with the faculty, curators, and researchers to adapt current content or develop new content. This might be based on exhibitions, lectures, colloquia, performances, or existing digital assets.

- A quality online home for their content, marketed to an international audience.

- A multidisciplinary approach to their intellectual capital, linking faculties of different institutions and academic approaches.

- A marketing platform for their courses, software, or other knowledge-related products.

- Positioning of the institution as an innovator in developing a twenty-first-century approach to scholarship and teaching.

FATHOM'S CHALLENGES

BALANCING PUBLIC AND PRIVATE SECTOR OBJECTIVES

Fathom strives for a balance between its goals of profit and public interest. There is no fundamental reason why a high-quality knowledge company cannot be a profitable enterprise, careful to protect rather than dilute the brands it represents. As Fathom moves ahead in the implementation of its business plan, it will select long-term strategic investors who will share the company's determination to maintain that balance.

REACHING K–12

Today Fathom is targeted at a postsecondary audience, but it is obvious that its high-quality educational programming should be adapted for the important K–12 audience. In the future it will develop and implement a strategy for younger students.

EXPANDING BEYOND THE ENGLISH-SPEAKING STUDENT

Fathom is initially targeting English-speaking audiences. Later it will develop and implement a strategy to expand its reach to non-English-speaking audiences, both inside and outside the American market.

SURVIVING IN THE ACADEMIC COMMUNITY

Thus far, Fathom has enjoyed unprecedented support from its institutional partners and from their faculty and staff. History would suggest, however, that challenges lie ahead as Fathom implements its unique approach to providing content previously confined to these institutions. Its success will be determined by the support it receives from its partners and its own skill at addressing the needs and concerns of the academic community.

COMPETITION

Fathom's competition will come from other institutional consortia, from for-profit learning ventures, and from current leaders in educational publishing or media that will take aggressive positions in the online learning marketplace.

FATHOM AND DIGITAL PROMISE

The Digital Promise initiative emphasizes many of Fathom's most important issues and could be an excellent partner as Fathom meets these challenges. As a start, elevating the dialogue on how digital media can offer significant benefits to the public and how it can educate and enrich a democracy would be helpful. The primary focus on the Internet today has gone from IPO fever to a postcrash referendum on fads in business models. It is critical to move ahead to consider where this most promising of all media might be headed and how best to get there.

In the meantime, use of the Internet continues to climb. With the growing numbers of individuals and businesses on the Internet, it is essential to find—and fund—ways to support the growth of worthwhile online activities.

The Digital Promise project also can help to pinpoint areas where specific companies or projects might benefit from well-timed support, either financial or conceptual. Public funding will help ensure the balance between private and public policy objectives. Dollars are not, however, the only source of support that would be helpful. The Digital Promise initiative also could be a vocal supporter for the idea of online education as a new source of an educated populace, essential to a democratic government.

Finally, the Digital Promise project should support the effort of leading American educational and cultural institutions to extend their reach digitally. Some of these institutions are already leaders in this area; others lag behind. There is a great deal of confusion and frustration, driven by the conflicting needs to "do something" but "do no harm." The Digital Promise initiative can serve as a consultative group to help nonprofits realize their goals with smart strategies for the future.

8.
BRIDGING THE DIGITAL DIVIDE:
PUBLIC SERVICE TELECOMMUNICATION
IN THE INTERNET AND DIGITAL AGE

MARTÍN GÓMEZ

Not a day goes by without reference in the media to the widening digital divide—also known as the gap between information haves and have-nots. Public policy advocates routinely deplore the growing gap between those who can afford access to the so-called information superhighway and those who cannot. Increasing numbers of voices are beginning to scream in desperation about the lack of attention being paid to this growing crisis. Ironically, at the same time, literally thousands of new websites appear daily in cyberspace. Businesses, institutions, and individuals are seeking their place in the digital sun, often with very few clues about their audience or the merits of their message. Plowing through the fields of cyberspace, nonprofit educational institutions have begun to mount individual and collaborative efforts to establish web-based outposts on Orion—hoping that when interstellar travel is affordable and efficient, coach-fare travelers and cyber hitchhikers will find them. For many nonprofit educational institutions, major obstacles inhibit their cyber outpost from being visited by those who might benefit from their services. Detours have been erected by for-profit launchpads (otherwise known as web browsers) and commercial groups, which appear to have little interest in making sure that nonprofit information way stations are easily accessible. To add insult to injury, the architects of the information superhighway and cyberspace launchpads have done very little to ensure that access to cyberspace will remain affordable, accessible, and relevant to anybody but commercial interests. E-commerce is driving the widening gap across the digital divide, not public policy.

Libraries in the United States, and increasingly globally, have been quietly making significant efforts to position themselves as public launchpads to cyberspace. Over the past decade, public, academic, school, and special libraries have spent hundreds of millions of dollars to connect library users to the information superhighway. In some cases, the cost of doing so has resulted in reduced expenditures for staff and traditional library collections.

Any librarian worth his or her weight in salt will tell you that not building the technical infrastructure to support access to these online digital information resources is the kiss of death for libraries in the twenty-first century. Standard reference books once published in multivolume sets and scholarly journal subscriptions are sometimes no longer available "in print." Instead, libraries purchase licensing agreements that grant them the "privilege" of making articles available to a discrete number of "end users"—usually defined by a specific number of library cardholders. Should these licenses lapse (not uncommon due to fluctuations in financing for public institutions), libraries may no longer be able to go to the shelves to find "back issues" of journal articles because the aforementioned licensing agreement may have expired and the back issues, available only in electronic digital format, have evaporated into cyberspace. The publishing industry's flirtation with e-books only ups the ante.

At the turn of the twentieth century, public libraries like my own, the Brooklyn Public Library, were established to provide access to knowledge and information, especially for those who could not afford to purchase books or subscribe to newspapers, magazines, or journals. In the digital age this concept is truer than ever. The Brooklyn Public Library, like many public libraries across the country, has created tools that enable public access to the information superhighway. Libraries also are creating content unencumbered by commercial advertising. In Brooklyn we are committed to ensuring that every resident in the borough has access to quality information that is increasingly becoming available only through commercial venues.

Historically and in the twenty-first century, our commitment to promoting equal access to information, in digital as well as traditional formats, is even more important. Libraries may, in fact, be the only publicly funded institution that values and promotes this role passionately. Readers may not know that the American Library Association was one of two lead plaintiffs that successfully led the challenge to overturn the Communications Decency Act (the other lead plaintiff was the American Civil Liberties Union). Slowly but steadily librarians have begun to transform themselves into public navigators in cyberspace, often providing low- and moderate-income communities with their first instruction in and ticket to cyberspace. In Brooklyn alone, for example, information seekers who visited the public library last year completed more than one million public Internet sessions. Thousands of Brooklyn residents surfed the Internet for the first time by attending our "Internet for Families" instructional programs. Thousands of residents accessed our online databases and subscriptions remotely, from home, office, or on the road, simply by entering their library card number. No other free public institution in New York City can claim the ability to provide access to more than fifty databases and a growing collection of other electronic resources twenty-four hours a day, seven days a week! All of these services, like our book-lending program, are provided free of charge.

We now have nearly eight hundred public access computer terminals available in our sixty branch libraries situated in every Brooklyn neighborhood. Each terminal is connected to the Internet by T1 lines. T3 lines connect the Central Library and Business Library. All provide incredibly quick and free Internet access for all Brooklyn residents. This level of public access is unsurpassed by any other publicly funded institution anywhere in New York City.

After four years in the making, and at a cost of more than $12 million, we now are asking how we are going to be able to maintain state-of-the-art public access to ensure that the level of access will be based on advanced telecommunications protocols and not outdated technology. We have built a significant and highly sophisticated digital infrastructure that is making it possible for us to realize our goal of becoming the "center of Brooklyn's knowledge network." The only thing holding us back is supportive public policy and adequate public funding. We have already demonstrated the axiom from the movie *Field of Dreams*: "If you build it, they will come!"

The reality is that maintaining this technology is extremely expensive. In order for us to ensure that our digital infrastructure remains sophisticated, we are going to need a steady revenue stream and a cadre of public-service-oriented professionals who are technically competent not only to keep the system running but to keep it on the cutting edge. We also will need political leadership to drive good public policy based on the principle that providing equal public access to information is a necessary element in a democracy.

However, it would be a critical mistake for librarians to think that they can erect this public policy bridge alone. The digital information age has created tremendous opportunities for libraries to establish coalitions and collaborative efforts with other nonprofit organizations to package information in new, exciting, and dynamic ways.

As digital technologies begin to merge, opportunities for creating new learning and instructional delivery systems are emerging as well. New developments in digital data compression, audio and video streaming, and mixed media presentation hold tremendous promise for creating dynamic ways for children and adults to learn and for the delivery of information. The public library of the twenty-first century must take greater initiative to bring various nonprofit organizations and institutions together to experiment with new ways to reach diverse segments of the community. For example, in 1998 the Brooklyn Public Library created the Brooklyn Expedition (www.brooklynexpedition.org), a website that provides access to the collections of the library, the Brooklyn Museum of Art, and the Brooklyn Children's Museum. Content is organized in a format that is designed for elementary school–age children and their teachers. Topics include "structures," Latin America, and the history of Brooklyn. Students and teachers can maintain electronic "diaries" about their travels in cyberspace and visit some of the most authoritative electronic sources about each of the topics mentioned above. Because of the Brooklyn Expedition, each institution involved in creating this virtual "alter ego" has found a new way to build and reach new audiences.

Efforts to develop new tools for learning in the twenty-first century require vision, a willingness to experiment, and money. Too often, projects like the Brooklyn Expedition are funded by short-term grants from foundations and governmental agencies such as the Institute for Museum and Library Services. Publicly funded agencies like museums, libraries, and schools must have a dedicated source of revenue that will enable us not only to erect the technological infrastructure to support a sophisticated telecommunications network but also to develop new content.

Fortunately, the Telecommunications Act of 1996 provides an opportunity for schools and libraries to be reimbursed for expenses related to the delivery of telecommunication services, but political game playing by some elected officials continues to erode public perception of the merits of the program. The E-Rate program does not provide support for the development of new content for schools and libraries, nor does it provide support to hospitals, public health agencies, or environmental/consumer advocacy organizations to provide telecommunication service networks.

What is at stake is who will benefit from the digital information age. How can we ensure that low- and middle-income communities can enjoy the benefits being promised to all but so far affecting only a few? As Congress continues the process of selling off high-speed bandwidth to commercial interests, we must advocate aggressively for a return on sale that will benefit libraries and other nonprofit organizations that are committed to the public good. Nonprofit organizations must be given greater opportunity to use this new technology to reach wider audiences and deliver services to those who need them. It is incumbent upon our political leaders to make sure that a portion of the new bandwidth is set aside for public benefit. Experience has shown that relying solely on commercial enterprise to behave in the public interest does not produce results.

A tremendous opportunity exists to improve access to knowledge and strengthen the educational delivery system in the United States. Libraries and other nonprofit organizations should forge strategic alliances with other public interest advocates to make sure that the opportunity to secure bandwidth for public benefit is not lost to a system that only the more privileged can afford. Our agenda is simple: we should work together to ensure

- guaranteed access through the creation of bandwidth "set-asides" for non-profit organizations that function in the public interest;

- low-cost opportunities for nonprofits to upgrade to the latest advanced telecommunications technologies from telecommunications and cable service providers;

- funding support for new collaborations among nonprofits to develop content for local and distance learning; and

- a guaranteed presence for nonprofit institutions in cyberspace.

Congress and the executive branch must provide national leadership that will bridge the digital divide. Good public policy must be established that will provide incentives for local, state, and regional authorities to build and maintain publicly accessible and affordable advanced telecommunications networks. Libraries and librarians must play a critical and necessary role to ensure that people know how to use the networks, can identify qualitative sources of information on the networks, and have access to new learning environments that bring local as well as global institutions together.

In the twentieth century, federal public policy was the spark that established a national public transportation system that led to the creation of jobs, growth of new communities, and new economies throughout the country. In the twenty-first century, good public policy is needed to spark similar economic growth through the new digital information technologies.

9.
HOW TO PUT THE WEB TO WORK FOR NONPROFITS

SUSAN A. ROGERS

In 2001, nonprofit organizations lag behind for-profit businesses in using the Internet to benefit their constituencies—clients, students, visitors, members, and users. By contrast, a decade ago, government agencies, universities, and research institutions were the earliest users of the Internet, and enjoyed the fastest and best connections to it.[1] In 1993, academics and scientists installed a new kind of software on their computers, Mosaic, a "browser" developed at the National Center for Supercomputing Applications, a unit of the University of Illinois at Urbana-Champaign. Mosaic's use of visually lucid hyperlinks and graphics was inspired by the work of Tim Berners-Lee and the World Wide Web Project. Mosaic changed the way people used the Internet to connect to remote computers. Before Mosaic you could log on to available computers anywhere on the Internet, collaborate with distant colleagues, and see text and data, but it was an environment for specialists that required knowledge of advanced computer commands.

Mosaic made it possible for its users to go places, such as the Honolulu Community College's Dinosaur Exhibit, and see and hear things, such as taking a tour of dinosaur models and listening to history instructor Rick Ziegler describe them. Many people who saw and heard the Internet using Mosaic's intuitive user interface were captivated instantly. "Cool" home pages were added to the World Wide Web daily. Regional schools like Honolulu Community College gained international exposure. Academic institutions and nonprofits embraced burgeoning web technologies early, months before many companies "discovered" the Internet.

Today, the Internet provides opportunities to communicate up-to-date information, improve the delivery of services, recruit staff, reach new audiences, and more. It has allowed profit-making organizations to move up several levels to providing services, and means of delivering them, that were literally undreamed of a decade ago. (See Figure 9.1.)

FIGURE 9.1: WAVES OF INTERNET INNOVATION

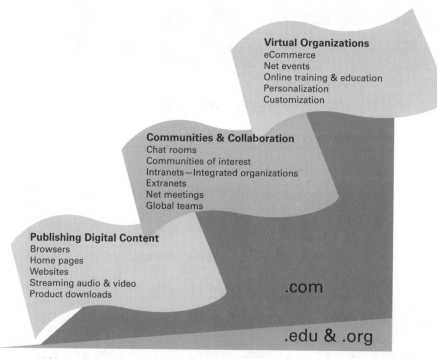

Virtual Organizations
eCommerce
Net events
Online training & education
Personalization
Customization

Communities & Collaboration
Chat rooms
Communities of interest
Intranets—Integrated organizations
Extranets
Net meetings
Global teams

Publishing Digital Content
Browsers
Home pages
Websites
Streaming audio & video
Product downloads

.com

.edu & .org

1993 - 1994 - 1995 - 1996 - 1997 - 1998 - 1999 - 2000 - 2001 - 2002 - 2003

The same array of opportunities is open to nonprofit organizations. To understand how a nonprofit might use web technologies to enhance its activities and expand its reach, the organization needs an overall web strategy aligned with its mission. Starting not with technology but with organizational goals, the purpose of a web strategy is to respond to a breathtaking array of new possibilities. It is as dramatic as if we woke up one morning and were no longer limited by gravity. In this antigravity-like state:

- we have access to information and services anytime, anywhere;

- all information products—text, graphics, sound, video—are digital;

- digital products can be delivered electronically;

- go-betweens are not needed since people can look up, book, order, study, research, and publish directly;

- we communicate with people and groups over the Internet;

- almost anyone or any group anyplace in the world can join in.

Broadly speaking, a web strategy describes how an organization's core activities, operations, and relationships can be enhanced and extended through the use of technology. (See Figure 9.2.) Technology is simply a tool that organizations or schools can use to expand their horizons or make it easier to achieve their goals—but it is that tool that makes these activities possible. An effective strategy assumes that the web is not an isolated application or a toy but the plumbing connecting all of an organization's core activities.

FIGURE 9.2: TOPICS COVERED BY A WEB STRATEGY

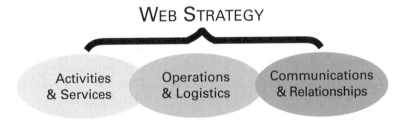

OPPORTUNITIES

It is not overstating the case to say that the majority of nonprofit organizations have not taken advantage of the Internet nearly as much, as intelligently, or as productively as the for-profit sector. This is unfortunate since the Internet offers nonprofits excellent opportunities to increase their usefulness to their constituencies. This paper will show how some innovative nonprofits (.orgs and .edus) have used new technology to enhance existing programs and services and extend their reach to new audiences.

Nearly all businesses have set up web pages and websites. These are generally classified into one of three types: public websites, intranets, and extranets. Companies use public websites to market and sell products, reach new consumers, and provide improved service in less time. Within companies, employees log on to private, web-based intranets to read company news, connect to local databases, and get training, and e-mail is the ubiquitous replacement for interoffice memos. Significant changes in business models are unfolding as companies create extranet links to their partners, suppliers, and customers, speeding up business and creating closer bonds through timely, plentiful information. Organizations of all types have been able to connect their computers and their data (or at least, the data they wish to "connect"). The result is a system that is much more valuable, and much more useful, than the sum of its parts. (See Figure 9.3.)

FIGURE 9.3: AN ORGANIZATION'S INTERNET SYSTEMS WOVEN TOGETHER USING COMMON PROTOCOLS

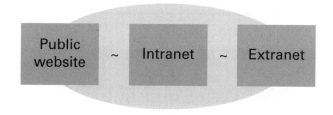

PUBLIC WEBSITES

At the most elementary level, most nonprofits and academic organizations have web addresses (also known as "uniform resource locators," or URLs), e-mail, and websites providing basic information. At this level, a simple website functions as an online brochure displaying information that does not need to be revised often, mirroring an organization's printed publications. A basic website does not "do" much—it merely broadcasts facts and contact information, with minimal need for an employee to find material requested by an outsider, put it in an envelope, and take it over to the post office.

For example, the website of the College Music Society in Missoula, Montana, "makes available a wealth of information concerning the field of music." The College Music Society "is a consortium of college, conservatory, university and independent musicians and scholars interested in all disciplines of music. Its mission is to promote music teaching and learning, musical creativity and expression, research and dialogue, and diversity and interdisciplinary interaction." This mission is supported by the website, which publishes information on participating members, upcoming conferences, colleague organizations, and online scholarly publications.

Internet technology allows organizations to do more than simply publish printed material in electronic form; websites also are used interactively. A common feature allows visitors to search a website for specific information. For example, the Smithsonian Institution's Encyclopedia Smithsonian allows users to search the entire contents of the Smithsonian's extensive website. If your questions about the Smithsonian are not answered, you can send your inquiry in an e-mail message.

Many websites have e-mail links encouraging online users to send messages. Other sites provide printed forms that can be faxed back or sent through the mail. Colleges, for example, put their applications online using these straightforward techniques. Online applications were among the first and most popular features on college and university websites.

Another interactive feature allows visitors to communicate with organizations by entering information into online forms that are sent electronically. This approach to data collection is more sophisticated than communicating via e-mail, faxes, or mailed documents because after visitors enter their data over the web, it is used to automatically update the organization's databases, eliminating the need for manual data entry. For example, instead of downloading a paper form, prospective students can choose to apply to the University of Chicago online. The university site connects to a commercial online service offered by Embark, one of several companies that have been started to process applications online. Embark's service takes advantage of the Internet's distributed nature: it does not matter where computers and services are located as long as they are secure, password-protected, and connected. Virtual organizations are defined by the logic of their connections, not their geographic locations.

Some organizations allow users to purchase products and services online using credit cards. After verifying a user's credit (performed by sending the data entered by the user to a networked credit-checking service), the transaction is completed, customer information is collected, and order information is sent directly to a fulfillment system. More advanced electronic retail operations can also check product availability while customers are online by connecting to inventory databases.

Because online retail sites are expensive to build, many nonprofits and schools have not invested in e-commerce systems. However, in addition to fundraising and membership, many nonprofit organizations have a variety of products to sell, including books, reports, educational materials, videos, tickets, and other specialized merchandise. Less expensive systems and contract services are becoming available, allowing more organizations to use e-commerce on external websites. For example, visitors to the Museum of Fine Arts in Boston (MFA) website can purchase exhibition tickets and annual memberships in the same transaction. Site visitors who might never visit the museum can order items from the museum's gift shop by linking to the MFA's online shop. Similarly, dozens of nonprofits have developed online retail sites using Yahoo Store, an inexpensive way to launch an online enterprise. Yahoo Store's software package includes database inventory, online orders, auctions, gift registries, and billing features. Using Yahoo's retail service, the Coastal Conservation Association store offers memberships and books. San Francisco's Lamplighters Music Theatre store sells tickets to performances, CDs, and videos. Human Rights Watch offers memberships and publications.

Nonprofits can use their websites as "portals," which serve as the entry point for finding a wealth of sites and information with a common theme. These sites educate users, provide basic information in their areas of expertise, and point to other experts in the field at the same time that they promote their own goals. A portal is considerably more useful than an "ordinary" website and enhances an organization's reputation and credibility. For example, the Harvard School of Public Health site includes public health information about exercise, healthy diets, and the risks of driving with cell phones. Some visitors visit the site primarily to use an interactive survey that calculates Your Cancer Risk.

A public website is working well if it:

- paints a clear picture of an organization's purpose, people, services, and products;

- provides accurate, timely information and facts for new and existing users;

- makes it easy for site visitors to join, enroll, apply, donate, or order;

- educates the public in the organization's area of expertise;

- reaches wider audiences of Internet users, expanding beyond the base of local members, visitors, and past participants.

INTRANETS

The Internet made e-mail the most common form of internal communication, rapidly replacing office memos and interoffice mail. Once staff members were networked together, businesses began building internal websites—intranets. These "internal use" networks are used to put current information and data at employees' fingertips quickly and comprehensively, with efficiency that cannot be matched by paper distribution systems. Experts speculate that eventually the use of intranets and business-to-business connections will far exceed public activity on the Internet.

An intranet is a website set up to meet the needs of an organization's employees. It uses the same software as a public website and may include public as well as private (password-protected) information. Some information on an intranet is created by employees, who place documents they have created on their own computers on the company intranet, where they can be shared by colleagues. Since most desktop documents can be saved in web format, nontechnical employees can participate in creating the information posted on a company intranet.

Today, even the smallest nonprofits have external, public websites, but a few pioneering nonprofits have transformed internal communications and processes by building comprehensive intranets that provide access to their internal information and databases—policies and procedures, schedules, project timelines, directories, and planning documents. For example, the Camp Fire Boys & Girls organization uses its intranet, "The Camp Fire Café," to link the national office in Kansas City, Missouri, to more than one hundred local councils. News and events are posted daily. The AARP (the association for Americans over fifty), in addition to an extensive external website, has developed an intranet that includes member, employee, and public information.[2] The University of Delaware's Center for Composite Materials intranet features personnel directories, laboratory safety manuals, graphics templates, purchase requisitions, travel request forms, time sheets, and vacation request forms, in addition to the center's mission statement, history, news, and publications.

Intranets that tie together all of an organization's databases are even more useful than those that simply post information for employees. Nonprofit organizations have the same need that businesses do—for the left hand to know what the right hand is doing. One way to create an integrated enterprise, close information gaps, reduce phone tag, and eliminate the need for paper reports is to provide password-protected, browser-based access to existing departmental databases. Most "old technology" systems—those designed to deal with functional areas such as finance, human resources, student records, curatorial records, and so on—can be queried from an intranet if an organization sets up web access to information in legacy computer systems. Although there is always someone around who knows how to get the information you need from each old system, intranet access can make things much easier when all authorized staff use databases as easily and conveniently as ATMs.

Examples of intranets of this type include that of the Academy of Natural Sciences in Philadelphia, which has links to the museum shop retail database and to information about its collection. Notre Dame and many other universities and large institutions have created web access to financial systems. Many colleges and universities, such as New York University, also have built intranets for their students, where they can look up their grades online. At the University of California, Irvine, Graduate School of Management, students use an intranet, dubbed Catalyst, to link to course assignments and quizzes that faculty enter into an online academic "file cabinet."

An intranet that links an organization's data systems and is the official place to post local news and announcements will become the heart of an organization's communication and information platform. A single jumping-off point for all of an organization's employees is a powerful, efficient tool. An intranet is being used well if it:

- integrates the enterprise and its people and activities;

- becomes the first place users go for internal information;

- engages the many employees who use it to communicate with each other;

- provides access to all mission-critical databases;

- presents information clearly and navigates easily; and

- replaces paper communications and documents with accurate, timely information in digital form.

EXTRANETS

All organizations have close associations with other firms and people who are practically "members of the family." Board members, for example, expect to have access to up-to-date reports and data. Extranets are another extension of the Internet idea—private ("by invitation only") networks of internal and public websites that allow organizations to share information with specific individuals and other external partners.

Companies use extranets to speed up and improve communications with their suppliers and vendors on the one hand and with customers on the other. Nonprofits manage many close external relationships with boards, trustees, foundations, donors, and so on. A website designed for members of an organization's community can improve the flow of communication and increase meaningful collaboration and partnership. For example, parents of students at Milan High School in Milan, Michigan, log on to contact school administrators and teachers, learn about sports and school events, and check out the references on the "Homework Helper." The Internet Society has a section of resources for "Members Only." Many other organizations have made web resources available as a benefit of membership. Most universities have created websites to foster continued relationships with alumni. The Idaho United Credit Union site allows members to check balances, pay bills, and make transfers twenty-four hours a day. Parents log on to see their children at Kiddie Academy in Hillsborough, New Jersey, via a web cam (a live video feed over the Internet).

An extranet may also be used to connect to services from a chain of partners and contractors. An extranet provides links to an array of other organizations that a nonprofit has established relationships with to benefit its users. When information flows smoothly and is automatically integrated with back-office databases, extranets can improve an organization's responsiveness, accuracy, and breadth of services. For example, Saint Anselm College in New Hampshire uses a large online textbook company, eFollet, to provide its online bookstore. Distance learning college Rio Salado and the libraries of scores of other institutions have licenses that allow their students to link to commercial information sources like InfoTrac and Dow Jones.

Some companies that sell exclusively to other businesses—so-called B2Bs—use the Internet to do business with each other. This improves their efficiency and productivity. For example, they can automatically reorder supplies when inventories fall below a preset point. This approach automates some manual processes and can prevent annoying situations such as running out of supplies. There are numerous areas in which such "friction-reducing" business-to-business applications can be used.

Streamlined interactions with suppliers and corporate clients will benefit nonprofits as well as companies. Organization-to-business extranets allow purchasers to enter orders directly into a vendor's order entry system, for example. Nonprofits and schools with web know-how take advantage of these developments and partners.

An extranet is a good investment if it:

- enhances relationships with close constituencies;

- improves the flow of information to the community;

- fosters cooperative partnerships;

- provides a wider range of appropriate services; and

- automatically collects data for existing organizational databases.

WEB TOOLS: TWO-WAY INTERACTIONS OVER THE WEB

One of the powerful aspects of Internet technology is its ability to support two-way communications and interactivity. A website that handles transactions as well as publishing information is interactive because it responds to specific requests from site visitors. Chat rooms, bulletin boards, and other features allow site users to participate in creating content on the website. These features may be either unregulated or closely monitored, depending upon their use. The most successful examples attract communities of interest where people share and create knowledge around specific topics. These forums are extraordinarily successful in connecting people across geographic boundaries.

In addition, real-time, interactive events can be broadcast online using web conferencing software. Events on the Internet can be directed at very small audiences and groups since it is relatively easy and inexpensive to provide the technology platform required to host web events and conferences.

WEB TOOLS: PERSONALIZATION AND CUSTOMIZATION

Internet technology allows organizations to let users provide information about their interests, activities, and requirements for products and services. When people are willing to share contact information and preferences with an organization via the web it is possible to personalize and customize news and reminders. It is also possible to build websites that create web pages dynamically, based on the specific information an individual site user supplies. These pages typically contain current information from the organization's databases, tailored to the specific user based on information previously collected about him or her. These personalized sites can provide individual feedback and assignments for students, for example. Medical practices can provide customized information for specific patients based on their medical histories and preventive medicine interests. The phenomenon of distance learning, which already has millions of participants around the world, draws upon the Internet's strengths in providing interactive and personalized experiences, as well as remote access to quality content.

HOW TO GET GOING

Every technology innovation requires a sponsor, an internal champion, and an enthusiastic, skilled implementation team. Nonprofits may need support to get from here to there. Support can come in the form of sponsorship, planning, or implementation. Given such an array of opportunities and tools, each nonprofit needs to have a vision of the path to follow in developing its response. Unlike old technology systems, web-based systems can be built in small, minimally disruptive increments, using modular units of software and improving gradually. Figure 9.4 illustrates an incremental improvement strategy that is appropriate for many nonprofits and schools. Begin by using Internet technologies to enhance existing programs and activities. Next, plan focused projects to extend existing programs to constituents that are close at hand, providing new services and interactions. Finally, pursue new audiences using skills and experiences gained previously by building integrated web systems and content.

Figure 9.5 illustrates how to align technology and goals. Guiding principles spring from an organization's mission, which defines its core activities, operations, and relationships. Technology is useful and appropriate when it supports the mission; it is superfluous and distracting when it is does not. An organization that integrates the skills of its people with its information and systems using Internet technology will find it easier to exploit the capabilities of the web. Over time, organizational content and skills developed for an intranet

FIGURE 9.4: PATH-BASED STRATEGY

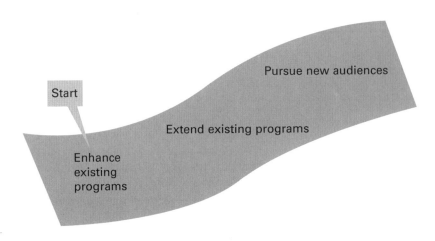

FIGURE 9.5: THE WEB, DEEPLY EMBEDDED IN THE CORE OF AN
ORGANIZATION

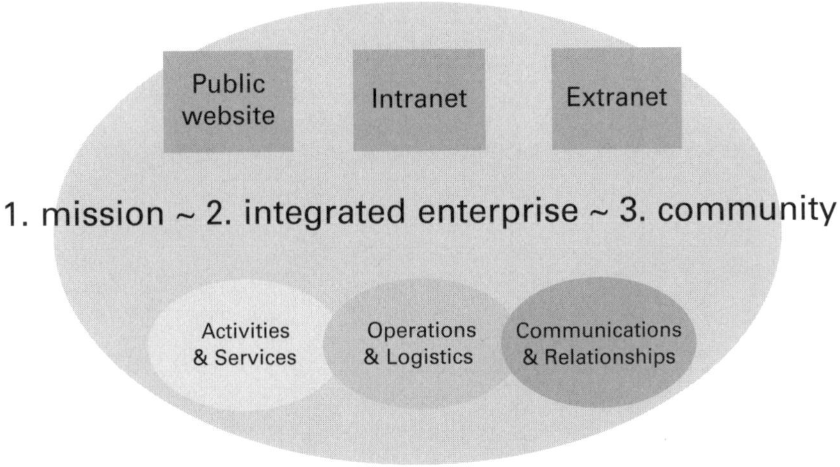

can flow easily to a public or external site. When everything works together as easily as the telephone system—so-called plug-and-play technology—and when all staff are online, innovations and improvements will develop spontaneously. The key is to focus on the needs of the community and the services an organization seeks to deliver, rather than becoming entranced with the technology. Opportunities arise from organization-wide, hands-on experience with emerging technology combined with a deep knowledge of the needs of constituents and the definition of excellence in the field.

NOTES

1. For more information, see the Internet Society's document "A Brief History of the Internet," http://www.isoc.org/internet-history/brief.html.

2. CIO Magazine's 50/50 Web Business Awards, http://www.cio.com/archive/070100_gains.html.

10.
IT'S 2001. DO YOU KNOW WHAT YOUR CHILDREN ARE WATCHING? THE CRITICAL ROLE OF CHILDREN'S TELEVISION IN THE AGE OF NEW MEDIA

RITA WEISSKOFF

This is a story I heard a few years ago: A fifth-grade science teacher asked her class, "Can someone tell me how the contributions of Thomas Edison changed the way we live our lives today?" One of the boys raised his hand, so eager to answer that he nearly jumped out of his seat. "Yes, Robert?" "Well," he said, "if Thomas Alva Edison had never been born, we would have to watch television by candlelight."

We live in a time in which our children cannot imagine there was a world without television. In fact, this story is nearly out of date because of what it omits, including video and computer games, wireless telephones, hand-held electronic organizers and, of course, the Internet, with its own games and its communities of chat rooms and e-mail buddy lists. Those of us close to the topic—which includes everybody living under the same roof with children—do not need a study to tell us that the media play a huge role in children's lives. However, I find it is always a jolt to learn one more time just how huge a role it is. For example, the Kaiser Family Foundation released a report in late 1999 entitled "Kids & Media @ the New Millennium." The report was based on in-home interviews, questionnaires, and diaries completed between November 1998 and April 1999 by a nationally representative sample of 3,155 children ages two to eighteen or their parents. The study looked at children's use of media outside of school and included television, computers, video games, movies, music, and print media. Among the findings were:

• children in the study ages two to seven spent, on average, three hours and thirty-four minutes using media each day, and for children ages eight to eighteen the number was even higher—six hours and forty-three minutes;

• many parents are not exercising much control over their children's media use: among kids eight and older, two-thirds (65 percent) have a TV in their bedroom and nearly that many (61 percent) say their parents have set no rules about TV watching; nearly one out of four in this age group (24 percent) spend more than five hours a day watching TV;

• among kids eight and older one in five (21 percent) has a computer in his or her bedroom, and nearly seven in ten (69 percent) have a computer at home; however, despite the widespread access, time with computers for fun averages less than half an hour a day (twenty-one minutes) compared to two hours and forty-six minutes a day watching TV.

Although this study did not find evidence of large numbers of children spending hours a day playing computer games or surfing the net, it seems clear that the numbers will grow. For example, according to a survey released by Grunwald Associates in June 2000, 25 million U.S. children ages two to seventeen are logging onto the Internet—three times the number of children who were online in 1997. Other smaller and/or less formal studies have found that for some children the computer is competing successfully with TV for their time.

Given the hold that the popular media have on the time and attention of our children, there has been much hand-wringing over the years about the extent to which these media support (or do not support) children's intellectual and social-emotional growth. It is as critical now as it ever has been to ask that the power of television and the new media be used responsibly to meet the needs of children. As we find ourselves propelled along in this era of rapidly expanding technological innovation, we must find ways to direct resources toward this end.

Television, I would argue, must continue to play a key role in the lives of most children in the United States. There are a number of reasons for this, including the belief of child advocates that educational programming is especially valuable to minority and low-income children because of the amount of their television viewing time and the fact that they do not have access to as many alternative sources of education, such as neighborhood libraries, museums, and so forth. Television reaches children earlier and for more hours per day than any other educational influence, except perhaps the family.

In addition, the availability of new technologies does not eradicate the need for educational programming on broadcast television since lower-income children are less likely to have access to these alternative technologies. Even as the interactive media proliferate, we need to understand the importance of television in the mix and continue to find ways to exploit its unique power to support children's learning.

What do we need to think about with respect to children's learning that could serve us as we grapple with the challenges to the public telecommunications world? Two things come to mind immediately. First, there is an assumption often made by teachers, as well as by producers of educational media for children, that school-aged children learn because we make learning happen for them. We assess the needs of our class or target audience, develop lesson plans or goals, create materials to deliver on our goals, and in many cases conduct assessments to determine whether or not we have achieved our goals. In this view, learning does not take place unless somebody designs and implements teaching materials.

On the other hand, it is almost universally understood that very young children learn from everything and everyone around them—and the knowledge they accumulate in such a short time is astounding. Think, for example, of the fact that by the age of three almost all children can use language to express themselves well enough to get what they want. By age five they are proficient speakers. Learning to talk and to master the conventions of oral language is believed by many to be a much more complex undertaking than learning to read that language, and it is done for the most part through playful interactions with family and friends. (Imagine if we believed we needed formal instruction to talk! It would probably lead, as a bemused friend of mine said, to at least three levels of Remedial Talking. But that is a story for another day.)

Why do we believe that older children always require instruction in order to learn? The fact is that they too are learning from everyone and everything around them. And that is, as they say, the good news and the bad. If children are always learning, then what they see, hear, and experience in their world is crucial to their well-being. This includes, of course, the media that absorb so much of their leisure time.

Second, it is almost universally understood that very young children learn through play, beginning in infancy and continuing through the preschool years. Their play is their work, and through play they begin to make sense of their world. Preschoolers do not distinguish work from play until they come to believe that work in school is how one learns, and one does it because it is prescribed by someone else in authority. Most schools are permeated with this concept: when you finish your work (something that has been assigned so you can learn and that must be completed to someone else's satisfaction) then you can play (something you choose to do that you think is fun). For those who buy the schoolwork/play dichotomy as children and take it into their adult lives, there is nothing more oxymoronic than the phrase "the joy of learning."

Two points of view, then, that I want to keep on the table for the purpose of this discussion are: (1) children—no matter how old—learn from everything and everyone around them, whether we intend for them to or not; and (2) to think of play and learning as diametrically opposed concepts is to think too literally of play as mindless entertainment rather than an approach that acknowledges the pleasure and personal rewards of learning.

Researchers have observed that academic achievement appears to be affected by outside-of-school involvement in learning activities. Teachers can introduce and provide practice time for skills in the classroom, but classroom time alone is not enough for real growth and development. For example, children who enjoy word games and choose to play them on their own are reinforcing language arts skills. They also are increasing the gap between themselves and children who are less adept and therefore less likely to choose to play word games. In fact, learning can be initiated and the interest in learning fostered both in school and out.

School-aged children pursue their own interests outside of school with a persistence and degree of motivation that most teachers would welcome with amazement in their classrooms. And their devotion to the popular media—television, in particular—has been impossible to miss for many years. What exactly is the proper role of the media in children's out of school learning, especially when it is clear that one institution cannot be exclusively responsible for education in its broadest sense?

On August 8, 1996, the Federal Communications Commission issued a report and order detailing new rules regarding educational television for children. It adopted the definition of educational programming as that "specifically designed" to educate and inform children. This "core" programming must be a regularly scheduled, weekly program of at least thirty minutes aired between 7:00 A.M. and 10:00 P.M. It must be identified as educational and informational for children when it is aired and must be listed in the children's programming report placed in the broadcaster's public inspection file.

How are we doing? Peggy Charren, long time champion of quality programming for children, having founded Action for Children's Television (ACT) in 1968, was quoted as saying, "We knew this didn't mean breathtakingly good TV would come out the other end, but, yes, I do think there's been an improvement. The industry no longer feels it can ignore children's TV completely." And Kathryn Montgomery, president of the Center for Media Education, said, "There's been significant improvement in overall quality."

To a certain extent, I agree. But although we can debate whether this or that show with, for example, prosocial goals is truly educational—and how do we define "educational" anyhow?—I worry about placing long-term confidence in an agreement that forces commercial broadcasters to comply with regulations that many of them find onerous. More to the point, many commercial producers (and network executives) are working against deeply felt beliefs about children and learning. They would express it something like this: I get it if we're talking about little kids. But let's face it: older kids spend a whole day in school working, studying, lugging those big backpacks around, and when they come home, they want to relax. The last thing they want to do is think some more. So you can bet they're not looking for TV that's educational/good for them/not fun!

This is the old play-versus-learning dichotomy translated as entertainment-versus-education. In this argument, entertainment implies mindlessness, and education implies boring. So the industry is too often "in compliance," a term that I have always translated as without much heart and certainly without passion. It is hard work to produce compelling children's television. It is infinitely harder to produce shows for kids that integrate learning into entertainment formats. And if you believe that learning goals will ruin the fun rather than actually make a show more appealing to your target audience, then where is the incentive to persevere?

While drafting this paper, I saw a segment on CBS Sunday Morning about the redesigned Hayden Planetarium at the American Museum of Natural History. The director, Neil deGrasse Tyson, a Ph.D. in astrophysics and the author of four books, told the story of his first visit to the planetarium. He was eleven years old, and it was love at first sight. He talked about the thrill he felt when he received a certificate for completing a course at the planetarium, and he held up his original certificate so the camera could take a good look. He told us that he still personally signs the certificates when children complete the course. (He uses a special fancy pen.) He wears a splendid vest covered, I think, with moons and stars. The man is the personification of the joy of learning.

What assumptions should we make about eleven-year-old boys and girls who have spent a hard day at school? I think it is fine if they want to chill out and stare into space for awhile or read a joke book or talk to friends or play ball or even watch some of that mindless TV. I like the idea of a wide range of media choices for older kids. But in this ironic age in which we find ourselves, how can we depend on the marketplace to respect children as people who might have important stuff on their minds? There are countless children who need support in taking themselves seriously, who are ready to be moved by the beauty of language or art or music or mathematics or the night sky—countless children who find pleasure and satisfaction in exercising their minds. It is not that we can or should transform someone else's life, but we can support kids as they think about the options that are available to them and options that might be available in the future.

The media world is rosier than it has ever been for preschoolers. For many years after *Sesame Street* came on the scene and demonstrated how to use the power of the medium to help young children learn, PBS was the whole world of quality children's television. It continues, with its Ready-to-Learn block, to be a dominant force in preschool TV, featuring other popular shows such as *Arthur* and *Dragon Tales*.

Now, for children with cable service, Nick Jr., Nickelodeon's preschool block, is a dynamic player in the arena, producing and airing curriculum-based, heavily researched series such as *Little Bill,* based on a book series by Bill Cosby, and the enormously popular *Blue's Clues*. Disney's cable channel is supporting its preschool programming, "Playhouse Disney," with a curriculum framework and educational goals. In addition, there is some good news for preschoolers on broadcast television other than PBS; in September 2000 Nick Jr. began to share six half-hour series with its new sister network, CBS.

Although in my opinion the situation for children over the age of eight is not rosy at all with respect to educational programming, there are exceptions. One promising venture is Noggin, the relatively new digital TV and online service, which is a partnership between Sesame Workshop (formerly Children's Television Workshop) and Nickelodeon. Designed as a twenty-four-hour educational environment for children from preschool through age twelve, the cable channel currently airs series from the partners' libraries, as well as newly produced programming. The online service is up and running strongly, and Noggin is working hard to develop a genuine synergy between its TV programming and online. One of Noggin's most popular series is *Ghostwriter,* a critically acclaimed mystery-adventure for school-aged children, produced by Sesame Workshop to support children's reading and writing skills. It aired on PBS in the early nineties, had high ratings, attracted a new and diverse audience to the service, and was dropped after three seasons because of the difficulties of maintaining the level of funding required. (In the interest of full disclosure, I should say that I was part of the team that conceived, developed, and produced the series, and it is not overstating the case to say that it broke our hearts to close down production, especially when we were achieving the goals we had set for ourselves.)

Why do I spend so much time focusing on the importance of television, a relatively old medium in this brave new world of interactivity and convergence? I think it has to do with promises still unfulfilled. *Sesame Street* taught us about the possibilities of television to entertain *and* educate young children, with an emphasis on reaching those who need it the most. All of us who are engaged in using popular media to support children's learning agree that it is harder to reach—and hold onto—a nine-year-old, for example, than a four-year-old. So the work is challenging. It is nothing, however, compared to trying to combat the hold the marketplace has on such a valuable commodity, especially when we are at odds about what that nine-year-old might want to see when she tunes in.

Commercial producers are fairly comfortable with shows set in the social world of kids, but they simply do not believe that "real" curriculum—school stuff such as literacy, math, or science—is viable. They think that if they made this kind of show, nobody would watch. (Actually, it is not a difficult case to make: simply run the program at a time when the audience is not yet awake or has gone to sleep, and be sure not to promote it.)

However, looking to the social world of elementary and middle school children as a compelling setting for television stories is exactly right. Here is why: The world of very young children is small; it is "me and my family." With the move outside of home and into preschool or day care settings, it expands to include other kids and their families as well as caregivers outside the family. Peers become increasingly important as children move through the early grades of elementary school, and somewhere around the end of the third grade, although family is still very important, life starts to become "me and my friends." For most children, it is, Who do I like? More important, Who likes me? Who thinks I'm cool? And if they don't, why not?

Academically, the first three grades are the years when children are expected to get their basic skills in place. The fourth grade often marks the time when children are expected to use those skills, especially reading and writing and thinking skills, to learn, understand, and be able to use information that is new to them. For children who are having difficulty and are not confident about their abilities, these new expectations are daunting. Add to this struggle the challenge of negotiating one's way through an increasingly complex social world, and you come up against a phenomenon that some teachers call "the fourth-grade wall."

This is a critical turning point for many kids who, for a number of complex reasons, may decide to adopt the position that school learning is just not for them. What *is* for them, however, is television. It is familiar, it is safe, and there are no negative cues attached to it. What a lost opportunity not to find more ways to use the medium to help children recognize the value and relevance of literacy skills or math or science or history in their own day-to-day lives, and to give them support as they develop these skills and are able to see themselves as successful learners.

Television is the popular medium, along with radio, that has the ability to tell compelling stories. It can create a world on the screen where "kids like me"—kids I want to be friends with and emulate—model the power and rewards of putting their intellectual resources to work, and viewers want to play and learn along with the characters. Making learning cool does not mean sugar-coating the lesson. Making learning clear does not mean stopping a good story to drop in the lesson. It does mean integrating the educational content so that it is critical to the drama and viewers cannot retell the story without it.

What are the critical educational content needs that are not being met on broadcast television for children? In my opinion, they have everything to do with how we should be thinking about the information explosion and the challenges and possibilities of the world of new media. Policy discussions focus on access, as well they should. The "digital divide" is what the millennium has added to the great divisions already existing in our society—divisions that many feel are becoming less rather than more amenable to change. The new technologies have given us a whole new vocabulary to describe what the have-nots do not have.

Certainly, access for all to valuable programs and services is key to the country's well-being. However, I would argue that access to more information is not the key for children, and, by itself, it is not the key for the rest of us. Go onto the web with the descriptors "children" and "educational television," and you will find 325,000 entries. That was last week; there may be more by now. It gives new meaning to the term *mind-boggling*.

Some basic thinking skills and strategies are needed to negotiate our way through these new environments. I do not think they are intrinsically different from what those fourth-graders need to negotiate their way through science, social studies, and language arts. It is all about constructing meaning for oneself, including setting goals and keeping them in mind, using what you already know (prior knowledge), understanding main ideas and details, and using resources (knowing when and why more information is needed, and being able to find it).

Television drama, mystery adventure, or even situation comedy designed for children can provide meaningful and entertaining contexts in which to model these kinds of skills so that they are both memorable and organic to the story. There is a world of subject matter to engage children's interest and curiosity. The importance of situating educational content in story is that we do not want to pretend that learning is easy. It is often very difficult, and the motivation to persist lies in believing there are satisfying and relevant rewards, the kinds that come from getting answers to questions that matter to kids. You can think of it as "content on the plotline," and television is the ideal medium in which to deliver it to kids.

I think it is safe to say that except for a few bright spots here and there, school-age children, especially those ages eight to twelve, are the most poorly served audience in broadcast television (including PBS, which continues to do an exemplary job with preschoolers but is not focusing on older kids). For all the reasons discussed in this paper, I hope that future policy discussions about the role of public service telecommunications in the digital and Internet age do not undervalue the role that television for children can play in whatever new configurations the continuing technology explosion brings us.

Unfortunately, I see no reason to believe that the brave new world of convergence will make it any easier to produce and distribute high-quality product for children that is both entertaining and useful. In addition, while it is certainly true that there are well-intentioned, talented people in the commercial world who are developing programming and materials that serve children well (especially the youngest children), we must acknowledge that the public good is of course not the first interest of the for-profit world.

It is, however, the first interest of the nonprofit world. Producers and educators in *this* world must direct their energies to creating and testing innovative formats that are entertaining and responsive to the needs of children. And we must find ways to support this work.

A colleague once characterized big challenges as "insurmountable opportunities." This is the kind of challenge we face and must meet now. It is critical to identify funding sources that will allow us to fulfill the promise made possible by the new technologies on the horizon. We need to remember, however, that we have not yet delivered on old promises of the media, particularly television, to teach, inspire, and align themselves with the bright hopes we want children to have for themselves.

11.
OLDER AMERICANS AND THE DIGITAL REVOLUTION

EVERETTE E. DENNIS

Reflecting on T. S. Eliot's lament on what has become the age of information ("Where is the wisdom we have lost in knowledge? Where is the knowledge we have lost in information?"), commentator Anthony Smith asks, "Where is the information we have lost in data?" In this formulation lurks clues about the special understanding, needs, and contributions that older persons can bring to a digital age only beginning to consider, let alone fulfill, its promise.

Older persons—those age sixty and above—lived most of their lives in the industrial age, when the big players in society were extractive and manufacturing industries, but they also have witnessed the first stirring of the age of information, including the spread and maturation of television, the explosion of multimedia technologies, and, of course, the computer as a part of everyday life. At the time of the digitization of almost everything, older persons were inculcated with knowledge, withstood the bombardment of more and more information, and know well the endless streams of data in every and all aspects of life and work. And, if anyone possesses it, they have the capacity of wisdom.

Yet, despite their great experience with the world and life, older persons are at present the least likely segments of the population to know, understand, and use effectively the complex and demanding instruments of digital and broadband communication. This is also the generation whose members cannot program a VCR and are likely to implore a grandchild to set a digital clock or, if they own one, to set up a computer. When it comes to the digital divide in America, those over sixty-five lag well behind the national average for online penetration—only 16 percent in the year 2000 but expected to rise to 48 percent by 2005, according to a report by Jupiter Research ("Assessing the Digital Divide(s)," 2000). This makes the over-sixty-five age cohort one of the fastest-growing Internet communities, but it is still behind and is apparently destined to remain so unless there is some public or private intervention. There are, of course, complex issues here and a disconnect between computer ownership on the one hand and Internet savvy on the other. Also key to online participation by older persons is the quality of available content; just having a computer and an account with an Internet provider does not presuppose that older people—or anyone else for that matter— will find intriguing, elevating, or even satisfying content, whether information, entertainment, or opinion fare.

The population of older persons, now 13 percent of the population as a whole, is anticipated to grow to 20 percent by 2030 and beyond. The splash that the baby boomers will make when they hit Golden Pond is only the beginning of a successive growth of this segment of the population—not simply persons above sixty-five but above eighty, ninety, and even one hundred, as population experts predict steady growth in each of these age cohorts. To be sure, this is not a narrow special interest but some 35 million persons in the United States alone, or one out of every eight Americans. This number is expected to grow to 70 million by 2030. Forecasters say that people will continue to live longer, retire earlier, and have distinctive new needs as citizens, consumers, and communicators. A disproportionate number of older persons are women and minorities and these representations will increase in the years ahead.

This is a group with unique and diverse living arrangements: with a spouse, family members, or in various long-term and nursing care facilities. This generation has rich and textured relationships with other population segments including their peers, children, grandchildren, and others. It is truly a group with special interests and special needs, but also a reflection of everyone's future.

More than a needy segment of the population, older persons also have considerable wealth as well as experience. And as they live longer, they are already redefining old age and retirement. While their parents retired in their mid-sixties and died in their early to mid-seventies, this generation of older persons often lives twenty to thirty years beyond the normal retirement age. They are heavy users of information and entertainment, consumers of products and services, and in search of productive activity to make the later chapters of their lives more purposeful and contributory. They can and need to become better navigators and users of the benefits of digital technologies—and at the same time they can, if given the opportunity, contribute to its development and maturation as a system of communication that is society's central nervous system.

BARRIERS TO ACCESS

At the moment, full use of the wonders, present and future, of digital technology is denied many older Americans for at least three reasons: lack of personal computer ownership and knowledge of its use, resistance to the constant change in hardware and software and a better way to keep up with the advantages of upgrading, and a lack of understanding of nonlineal thinking, a signature of the computer generation. These are technical, economic, and conceptual barriers that are, in effect, blocking access. In the first instance, people over sixty-five are less likely to own computers than are younger people, not necessarily because of inadequate financial resources but because of a lack of motivation to make purchases and a discomfort with what they are purchasing—or using in an institutional setting, such as a library, school, or long-term care facility. Some people can and will pay mightily for digital information and entertainment services, others can barely afford it, and some not at all. Here people need user-friendly instruction on the special benefits and advantages of new technologies, which do in fact outdistance the telephone, fax, or other forms. For those who cannot afford computers, both government and private philanthropy need to develop a master plan to get all persons, especially older persons and the poor, online quickly. In response to the constant change in technology, people need simpler devices and less cumbersome and demanding software (which currently gets more and more complex with each upgrade). They also need to buy low-maintenance computers.

On the issue of nonlineal thinking, people weaned on computers, attuned to television and the visual grammar of the media, simply adapt to change more readily and process this information more easily due to familiarity, if nothing else. The older generation is quick to adopt technologies that work and save time, but they also are naturally skeptical and likely to say "the emperor has no clothes" if that is the case. Older persons are more likely to compare new technologies with old ones and can be underwhelmed by bells and whistles that do little to advance the work of the telephone or the fax machine. It has been noted that an industry that does far too little market research could benefit from some focus groups or beta sites where older persons would be probed and consulted.

More difficult is learning to understand and embrace the discontinuous and nonlinear nature of computer technology, an issue for a generation that resists going to a movie midstream or leaving early. This is truly a different way of thinking that requires more than "The Internet for Dummies" or other procedural manuals, but a new cognitive mapping system wherein older persons come to experience the immersion of bombarding information their grandchildren know instinctively. This will require generational bridges for true understanding to occur. A generation embedded in the culture of print is less comfortable with the aural and visual capacity of broadband.

Less subtle is the difficulty of keeping pace with change and being able to use the Internet and its many search engines and portals to truly participate with the rest of society—whether in use of e-mail or the precision of access to the content older people need and want. This needs to be done against the backdrop of what is not changing in the world, where digital services do not yet embrace all of the information of the neighborhood library or even the daily newspaper. Clearly there is a need for better guides to use of the Internet that focus on and target specific information while maintaining a browsing function as well. Just because the information is there does not mean that it is easily retrieved. A website developed by the information sciences school at the University of California, Berkeley, for example, underscores the different search engines and portals needed for easy access to information, from the highly technical and specialized to some that can be called popular.

CONNECTIONS TO CONTENT AND UNDERSTANDING

Once the barriers mentioned above have been addressed, if not fully overcome—since that may take some time—the values older people bring to digital communication and the potential contributions they can make will become more evident. In this regard, people raised on traditional media and communication services truly understand what is different, what is not as good or effective, and what needs context and explanation. Here older persons are a great asset. The first reason for this is that, because of long experience with heavy use of other media, they almost instinctively see and understand what is truly different about digital communication—its interactivity, its reach, its ability to address specific audiences and ferret out precise details. They are the first to express excitement over these advantages. After all, they are the generation that invented conveniences of all kinds. They are also quick to spot hype, not at all bashful about offering a less than enthusiastic response to new media, and quick to say that the telephone does this too or that the online newspaper lacks the convenience of the real thing. For those not weaned on databases and online services the very real advantages of some older media forms are evident and set a standard for new developments.

INTERACTIVITY AND THE MULTICHANNEL UNIVERSE

With the coming of digital television and a great expansion of the conduits for content, enormous benefits can be anticipated for older persons. These are best set against the backdrop of the characteristics of the older population, such as their special interests and needs. At present, many of the information, opinion, and entertainment interests of older persons are being phased out by a media system driven by a desire for large audiences with a tilt toward young, upwardly mobile people. The big numbers required by network television and large urban and regional systems discriminate against older persons. Cable channels and other new television content have similarly sought out younger, upscale audiences, often ignoring those over sixty by subject matter, level of presentation, or products promoted. Television programs much loved by older persons, such as *Murder She Wrote*, have been cancelled and others proposed have not aired. That can change in a multichannel environment of five-hundred-plus venues for information, entertainment, and opinion fare tailored to the over-sixty crowd. Content might well focus on health and medicine, nutrition, recreation, and other topics that especially resonate with older audiences. Similarly, advertising and product promotion of the so-called silver industries of products aimed at older persons as well as the "boomer industries," which have depended on a population now aging, can easily generate revenue.

In addition to content that specifically serves the interest inventory of persons in the sixty-plus group, programming and information services aimed at intergenerational connections between parents and children, children and grandparents, is also an unexplored territory. Generational relationships, for better or worse, have been included in the new reality television shows where people are tested against the demands of a desert island or a house of the future. No one knows how much the youth orientation of TV programming, with its images of buff bodies and abs-strengthening machines, deflects older viewers and users. Opportunities both for new market-segmented channels and special pay-per-view programming are immense given the size of the older audience and its available income.

While the interactive advantages of the Internet and World Wide Web are now on the public agenda, the future may find that that enthusiasm shifts to include other interface developments that will merge and link the television with the personal computer and possibly add the innovation of various liquid crystal displays, which are bringing smaller and cheaper information appliances. With the comfort of new technologies, it is possible to navigate vast oceans of information. For older persons, three areas are immediately important: information about health, cognitive challenge, and purposeful work. Content interest studies have demonstrated the attention older persons pay to finance, travel, health, history and biography, cosmology, and other topics.

Already, on the information front, web services for older persons—one-stop shopping for elder care information and products—exist and are growing. But this is the tip of the iceberg; for people who grow older and anticipate twenty-five or more years after their primary career ends, the most important needs are staying healthy, being financially secure, and having a sense of life purpose. There is already a massive amount of medical, health, dietary, and fitness information online; learning to use this, compare it against other offerings, and evaluate its quality and utility proves a formidable challenge. Few Internet users realize the extensive array of search engines, navigational tools, and portals already available and growing. The universe of health information affecting all forms of physical and psychological well-being are available in this "pull" technology era when people can order up almost anything they want—if they know how to do it. Few really do and that is a challenge for digital media of all kinds: creating an interactive menu and information chain that provides information and understanding as well as problem-solving devices. With the right decision tree, it will be possible for people to get the information they need, validate it, and compare it before use. This could lead to a personal renaissance wherein physical, psychological, and spiritual options are more fully understood and realized.

In addition to conventional health needs, older persons have often been treated as though they are intellectually challenged. Theirs need not be a world of checkers and shuffleboard, but instead, continued learning and creative challenges can extend, reinforce, and even restore cognitive health. Keeping older persons intellectually and socially alive is often a great challenge when families leave home, jobs end, and other stimuli are gone. Methods of combating cognitive decline, such as critical thinking exercises, reading, and problem-solving tasks can be well served by digital technologies. Whole programs and services for this purpose can and should be developed.

No doubt there is potential commercial benefit in this, and in many instances people can and would pay to have this kind of interactive service. For those who cannot pay, a system of free, interactive information needs to be considered. People are fond of saying that the Internet is free, but Internet providers do charge fees, as do telephone companies when they are asked to install new lines. Increasingly, providers of Internet content, for example *Who's Who in America* and other reference books or the *Wall Street Journal,* charge for use. Whether the dispossessed older persons can be given free access to some paid services, especially interactive ones where feedback is important, ought to be considered by hardware manufacturers, software publishers, and other digital service providers. They have much to gain by having a truly accessible Internet.

Building good cognitive health through interactive efforts and through personal communication among people does not happen spontaneously; it needs to be planned and scheduled. Interactive software for this purpose is vital. Older persons already are discovering the benefits of e-mail for staying in regular touch with family and friends, old colleagues, and new ones in many places. There are some notable instances of senior centers in California and Indiana teaching ninety-year-olds to work online with great success.

This is, of course, fertile ground for intergenerational links between grandchildren and grandparents facilitated by e-mail and digital communication. With the various forms of visual interactivity, for example speech synthesis, the one-to-one communication of e-mail can be expanded greatly to discussion groups, chat rooms, and other group activities. This can facilitate diaries, memory jogs to other times and places, and reconnecting with old friends and acquaintances long forgotten.

Increasingly, people leave the world of work at age sixty-five or seventy or even earlier with much ambivalence. While those engaged in hard labor may face increasing frailty and lack of strength, many information workers of the white-collar class want to continue working, perhaps in a less demanding capacity, or seek new opportunities and fields as well as volunteering in their communities. The Internet and other interactive technologies as well as digital television can facilitate this. Digital head-hunting systems connect people with particular interests and expert knowledge to new ventures and experiences. The whole process of reexamining one's interests and passions as well as identifying new ones can be facilitated by new broadband channels across various media and technologies. This can enhance a sense of purpose for individuals, so vital in the older years, and it might even generate commercial and psychic benefits for society and culture.

Older persons can be assets in the new digital age, both because they have specific needs, interests, and demands and because they can contribute knowledge, information, and understanding. To make this happen, this expansive and growing segment of the population needs recognition. It is an audience to be served, a consumer group with real income and special needs. Comfortable older persons must be recognized as well as those who struggle and those in dire circumstances. Advantages are apparent for the commercial system and will unfold quickly, but there is also an obligation for philanthropy and for government to recognize fully their responsibilities to a population that can either be a contributing force or a drain on society's resources and energies.

The digital age needs the knowledge, wisdom, and information capacities of older persons. They ought to be represented in the counsels making decisions about the uses and applications of digital communication in a time of great and often perplexing change. Perhaps the flood of data now affecting almost everyone might once again be recast into information, knowledge, and even wisdom.

SOURCES AND FURTHER READING

Robert N. Butler, Lawrence K. Grossman and Mia R. Oberlink, eds., *Life in an Older America* (New York: The Century Foundation Press, 1999).

Robert N. Butler and Claude Jasmin, eds., *Longevity and Quality of Life* (New York: Kluwer Academic/Plenum Publishers, 2000).

Gene D. Cohen, *The Creative Age—Awakening Human Potential in the Second Half of Life* (New York: Avon Books, 2000).

Everette E. Dennis and John C. Merrill, *Media Debates—Great Issues in the Digital Age* (Belmont, Calif.: Wadsworth Publishing, 2001).

"Finding Information on the Internet: A Tutorial," University of California, Berkeley, Library, 2000, available at http://www.lib.berkeley.edu/teachinglib/guides/Internet/findinfo.htm.

Charlotte Muller and Marjorie Honig, *Charting the Productivity and Independence of Older Persons* (New York: International Longevity Center, 2000).

John D. Rowe and Robert L. Kahn, *Successful Aging* (New York: Pantheon Books, 1998).

Assessing the Digital Divide(s) (New York: Jupiter Communications, 2000).

Michael J. Wolf, *The Entertainment Economy: How Mega-Media Forces Are Transforming Our Lives* (New York: Random House, 1999).

12.
THE DIGITAL PROMISE
OF LINCOLN CENTER

JOHN GOBERMAN

There is no question that the performing arts fail in the marketplace. And new developments in broadcasting seem to indicate that the arts will have even less place at the table as commercial interests take advantage of remarkable advances in digital broadcasting and, most particularly, internet development. In the past, the beginning of each new medium promised the arts as one of its primary offerings, bringing the best to the many. For example, David Sarnoff, the founder of NBC, promoted radio and television broadcasting as a new way to bring the arts to the people. The NBC Symphony and the many RCA recordings by Jascha Heifetz attest to the sincerity of those intentions, which, of course, fell in face of the need for larger and larger audiences as broadcast receivers became available to more and more homes. Cable, after promising to deliver a signal to all, courted the performing arts as a primary delivery system, but abandoned them in their own search for larger viewership. Video recording devices, cassettes, and laserdiscs also initially pledged to deliver the arts. All soon recognized that the opportunity cost of the performing arts in the real world is very high.

An ominous difference now is that the newest developers of digital broadcasting and dot.com enterprises do not even pretend to be interested in the arts. Even their first flush of successful development does not include the arts or other specialized cultural interests. Their values are strictly limited to the marketplace. To some extent, this may be a result of a certain reality setting in, the sure knowledge that in this tough and fabulous new world, specialized arts interests cannot carry the freight. They simply cannot pay their way. They are organically nonprofit.

It has been the judgment of our society as a whole that the cultural institutions of this country must be supported both privately and publicly. To a certain

183

extent, one measure of the quality of a community is directly related to the excellence of its arts institutions. The artists and arts of the world represent a constant striving for excellence in its purest form, and that pursuit reflects well on all of us. Part of the mission of our great arts institutions is not only to maintain the health of the world of arts and artists, but to find ways to make sure that everyone who so wishes is entitled and able to participate in this world. It is increasingly apparent that arts institutions must find ways to use the newest developments in mass communications to further that goal. While the essential performing arts experience is being in the same room with the performer, for instance, somebody that is singing, all of the steps that lead up to that moment—background, training, and knowledge—are susceptible to dissemination by the new communications media.

What has always been missing in the scheme of new broadcast media is a means of support unrelated to revenues. How to measure degrees of support and what criteria are employed for decisionmaking are well beyond my competence, and it may be that those issues will destroy the idea of "public" support for nonprofit broadcasting. It is clear, however, that if there were a means of paying for elements of what we value to be shared universally, there would be an endless supply of great and good ideas.

Lincoln Center, as an institution, is a fine example of how limitations are placed on the fulfillment of its media mission because the only source of non-box-office funding is philanthropic. Obviously, choices must be made, and our philanthropic resources are quite rightly directed at putting operas, ballets, and concerts on the stage, with all else secondary. Of necessity, some important opportunities are necessarily forgone.

For example, the extraordinary wealth of material already amassed in our video archives, when combined with the wide-ranging written expertise of program notes from one hundred years of performances, plus the easy availability to us of great artists and teachers, is an exciting and certain basis for the richest website for the performing arts imaginable. Why don't we start tomorrow? Because there is no way to pay for it. What are the costs? First of all, for a website to live, it must be constantly tended and updated—it must keep growing. It cannot be funded by a onetime philanthropic gesture. There must be a regular source of income, most of which, we can attest, will not come from the users of the website and not from corporate sponsors.

What is so expensive? Take, for example, a single thread that an interested researcher or even casual surfer might follow on a Lincoln Center website. If someone had encountered a performance of the Cello Concerto by Antonin Dvorak on a Live from Lincoln Center telecast with the Philharmonic and Rostropovich, he or she might go to the website to find the program notes telling of <u>Dvorak's stay in Spillville, Iowa</u> (graphic link), connecting with the <u>Native American music he grew fond of</u> (audio, video, graphic link) and the <u>African-American violinist</u> (link) he knew in New York when he headed the <u>New York Conservatory of Music</u> (link), having been brought to New York by its head,

Mrs. Thurber (link), and where he wrote the American Quartet (audio link to performance by the Chamber Music Society of Lincoln Center) and *Rusalka* (link to Metropolitan Opera performances schedule and a new production in Salzburg), etc. What is expensive are the preparation of materials, the maintenance of the infrastructure, and the constant updating and refreshing of the information. Other costs would be rights associated with performances, intellectual materials, and so forth. Lincoln Center, because of its encompassing array of performing arts, could and should be, if not the world center for information and experience on the performing arts, certainly one of them. But how might we pay for it?

In addition to making the performing arts available, there is what might be called a nonpassive role in using the new communications capabilities to reach younger citizens who are, for the most part, already steeped in these online worlds. For example, in the world of games alone the performing arts could play a role—and it is not so far-fetched. Mozart himself invented a game in which bars of music were ordered by throws of the dice and resulted in a charming, if simple, minuet. This, of course, is a perfect Internet game, as is a game where you make a tune out of your phone number, or a game where you add the next note. The possibilities of development in this area are endless.

Assuming broadband capacity, the Internet offers institutions like ours an ability to offer samples, to try new things without a serious risk of time or money. New music, dance, performers, and so forth made available on a website allows those who are interested to try the new and the talked about. We must keep in mind that the challenge for the arts in the broadcast world is not a question of available airtime. And if there is available channel space in the new digital broadcast world, it is nothing new. There has always been airtime available for the performing arts, and other specialized interests. Even in the bad old days before cable, UHF was available. There has simply been no way to pay for it.

Broadcasting on the Internet has great advantages over television broadcasting because there is no competition for airtime. The problem for the arts has always been that you can get more people to watch a movie at 8 P.M. than an opera, for example. If there are no separate and controlled channels, just the widespread come-and-get-it nature of the Internet, then there will be none of the inevitable competition between an obscure opera and a special on Failed Inventions or Morris Dancing Lessons. In any case, what would be new and different in the approach digital promise is proposing is that there would be a way to pay for specialized programs in the public interest that would reach just those people who are self-selected in wanting to see it or benefit from it.

Arts organizations can only be supportive of some effort to engage with finding new and noncannibalistic means of support for media outreach programs. The performing arts are peculiarly suited to take advantage of these new media. They always have been. No one in the past has succeeded in providing a framework for ongoing, protected support of such public interest activities in the commercial marketplace. Until that support is established, many of the great and good ideas will remain just dreams.

13.
(RE)IMAGINING BAM IN THE AGE OF BROADBAND TECHNOLOGIES

WAYNE ASHLEY[1]

The widespread adoption of networked computer technology (the Internet), the coming convergence of digital TV with computer-based networks, and the increasing corporatization of access, content, and distribution all mean that the question of digital culture, and who has a stake in its production, is more important than ever. The debate is intensifying over whether or not a public space can be achieved and sustained within the digital media environment, and social and cultural organizations are asking how, with what resources, for whom, and with what efficacy they will be able to contribute to an evolving digital culture.

The Century Foundation's Digital Promise project could not come at a more opportune time. What follows is a provisional outline for how the Brooklyn Academy of Music (BAM) would use public trust fund monies from the proposed spectrum auction to widen its audiences, extend its cultural programming, and preserve its mission to be the globally acknowledged, preeminent progressive performing, cinema, and media arts center of the twenty-first century.

BAM BACKGROUND

Brooklyn Academy of Music (BAM) is America's foremost presenter of contemporary music, opera, theater, dance, and film from around the world. Every fall the renowned Next Wave Festival features innovative, often multidisciplinary new performance works, and the spring season features contemporary interpretations of classic works. Every summer BAM programs free outdoor music concerts in downtown Brooklyn and city parks across the borough. Yearlong education and humanities events range from artist dialogues to special performances for children. The four-screen BAM Rose Cinemas show daily screenings of first-run, independent films, and BAMcinematek features classic cinematic repertory as well as special festivals and retrospectives. BAMcafe offers casual or fine dining and is accompanied by live music on Thursday, Friday, and Saturday nights. The Shakespeare and Co. BAMshop features BAM-related books, CDs, and merchandise.

BAM's programming has traditionally been outside of mainstream interests, and the current executive management continues to present work that is rigorously intellectual, visually complex, and conceptually brave. Historically, media producers have discouraged BAM from telecasting its experimental programming, asserting that there were not enough viewers to sustain a lively arts segment, even when cable television emerged. The new global networked communications systems, however, are enabling different kinds of broadcast models to emerge. BAM wants to participate fully, not only by continuing the tradition of artistic creativity, but also by participating in the construction of the new communication space.

The challenge for BAM will be to deploy broadband technologies in a way that deepens its commitment to live theatrical presentation and innovation while simultaneously using the networks to expand its audience base, create new ways of experiencing and understanding art, provide new opportunities for aesthetic experimentation, create an online community of repeat visitors, and acquire new revenue streams. While some of BAM's content will be reconfigured and made specifically for distribution over the network, some of it will be designed for both physical and virtual spaces, for output to the stage and the screen.

There are no signs that information technologies will make live performance obsolete, or that they are taking over earlier forms of media. In fact, quite the opposite seems to be occurring. Artists and producers of both new and older media are remaking and incorporating one another's forms to create a variety of hybrids. Websites are looking more and more like TV, but they also draw from books, magazines, and encyclopedias; computer games incorporate cinematic techniques, perspective painting, and arcade games; graphic artists are referencing the computer interfaces of websites in their print designs; and theater and dance companies are beginning to employ video conferencing, Internet projections, computer graphics, and complex computer/body interfaces to extend, magnify, and complicate audience perceptions and experiences. Over the next three to five years, BAM will seek to position itself within these tensions—physical/virtual, screen/stage, telepresence/absence—and will explore multiple distribution platforms for disseminating its programming and interacting with its various audiences.

If given the financial, technical, and creative resources to fully participate in an information society, BAM will continue to deepen its current new media initiatives while expanding them in other ways by:

- giving access to up-to-date online information about BAM's many programs;

- developing e-commerce strategies for selling tickets online and fund-raising electronically;

- providing new aesthetic opportunities for artists whose creative process and/or final work requires the use of digital tools and electronic networks, including web-centric or hybrid creations that combine digital and network capabilities with the traditions of dance, theater, music, and graphic design;

- developing an online community engaged in dialogue about the work produced at BAM;

- creating interactive educational and humanities programming;

- beginning to digitize BAM's cultural assets and create an online archive; and

- actively seeking out strategic partnerships.

BAM's New Media Initiatives: The Challenge

BAM is actively exploring the computer's powerful computational and media processing capabilities and the rapidly expanding electronic networks to extend its artistic programming and educational, marketing, and fund-raising efforts. We are accomplishing this through a number of new media initiatives that include Arts in Multimedia, an artist-in-residency program in conjunction with Lucent Technologies; the creation of an in-house digital media lab; a series of web documentaries that chronicle the creative processes of BAM artists on our site; and an informational website about BAM's programs at http://www.bam.org.

Although we have made efforts to fulfill each of these initiatives and make them part of BAM's core mission, the ever-expanding costs of hiring new media staff and the expenses of constantly upgrading hardware and software have added an unanticipated pressure to our current fund-raising endeavors. Currently, our new media initiatives are subsidized sporadically through in-kind donations, small city-funded grants, and periodic corporate sponsorship. We will continue to cultivate these funding opportunities. However, the ability to sustain our contributions to an emerging digital culture will require sufficient seed money not only to purchase new technology and faster connectivity, but for ongoing research, design, and a cadre of new staff educated in online fund-raising, marketing, and audience development. This will not be accomplished by BAM alone. Our ability to fully realize these endeavors will depend upon strategic partnerships with other arts institutions, production facilities, research centers, and cultural foundations. Support from a public trust fund should help facilitate collaborative initiatives and partnerships.

The Digital Promise Project: Deepening BAM's New Media Initiatives

We have already implemented a number of projects involving digital technologies, and support from a public trust fund would enable us to deepen an already successful beginning.

Arts in Multimedia Project

The Arts in Multimedia (AIM) project is a two-year pilot program designed to pair artists working in new media and communications technology with scientists at Bell Labs, the research and development division of Lucent. Artists have access to new and emerging technologies being developed at Bell Labs, and scientists have the opportunity to extend ideas and research applications to new areas or to rethink old areas in novel ways. Both artists and researchers question and shape the contours of one another's work, and efforts are made to ensure that *issues* (aesthetic, social, political, and scientific) rather than "new technologies" dictate the research and exploration between them. It has been within these moments of intense hybridization that BAM has nurtured some of the most profound and influential modes of performance making, a process it hopes to continue through its relationship with Bell Labs, and future artistic development employing digital media. Currently there are three artists and five researchers working on projects in the areas of data mining and sonic representation, robotic cameras and live performance, and new forms of dramatic narrative, interactivity, and virtual reality.

Support from a public trust fund would enable BAM to continue exploring and deepening its relationships between industry and art, research, and development. Such opportunities are necessary for BAM to maintain its cultural edge and to critically interact with an increasingly global community of new artists using computers to produce, store, distribute, and view art. Creating other kinds of residencies that bring other disciplines into the art and technology mix will be important. These could include digital artists working together with anthropologists, game designers, filmmakers, and architects. The technologies we are considering have no conception of disciplinary boundaries, and sealing them off from one another will not produce the sort of larger understanding we need to inform our cultural practices, institutions, and policies in the next century.

Rethinking and Expanding BAM's Digital Media Lab

BAM's digital media lab has just been constructed above the Lepercq space, our multipurpose venue for live music, spoken word, and dining. It was built to enable artists and Bell Labs researchers to collaborate across space, using the Internet and desktop multipoint videoconferencing to exchange ideas in real time. The lab houses four workstations, a multimedia server, and T1 lines connecting BAM to an Internet service provider. The idea of the lab is to bring emergent technologies out of the controlled environments of scientific research and into the "messy," heterogeneous spaces of cultural production, where artists and other cultural workers could use it, question it, and extend it in ways it was never intended.

Currently, the lab is restricted to researchers and artists and is situated in a part of the building that is not easily accessible to BAM staff. Resident artists have begun exploring how the lab can further their artistic endeavors, but once the collaboration with Lucent Technologies has ended we will need to rethink and expand the lab's function. Trust fund monies would enable BAM to integrate the lab more fully into the institution's larger cultural mission, opening it up to the needs of our education and humanities department and our computer training, programming, and marketing endeavors. The lab would function as a production facility for creating online curricula, producing video dialogues with artists about their work, and documenting our various humanities symposia for online consumption. We also would explore ways of extending the lab to an increasingly sophisticated and technologically savvy artistic community.

Documentaries for the Web

As part of BAM's increasing activities in New Media, BAM's website has begun hosting a series of web documentaries about some of its featured artists. These documentaries simultaneously educate new audiences about BAM's Next Wave programming, create new ways of understanding the art-making process, and further define BAM as an institution consciously and critically invested in new media. We have produced a documentary on artist David Roussève and have licensed another on director Robert Wilson. The most recent project, an online interactive work based on choreographer Ralph Lemon, transforms Lemon's travel journals, dramaturgical notes, musings, and rehearsal videos into a compelling new piece for the Internet with its own aesthetics, viewing practices, and audiences. Users can view the site at http://www.bam.org/tree.

Currently these are web-based and low bandwidth. They employ rudimentary programming and mark-up language, digitized images, and highly compressed video segments. Artists, archivists, and educators want to explore newer and more sophisticated technologies for documenting, analyzing, and creating deeper insights in performance making. For example, real-time visual information systems that are currently being used to archive sports actions could be deployed to document and understand theater and dance events. One such system, being developed by Lucent Technologies, processes video from multiple cameras that are poised to record the specific actions of tennis players, including their motions on the court, the position of the ball, and the geometry of the environment. Once this data is archived and processed, users can access the information from a computer database in multiple forms—animated visualization of court coverage and virtual replay of action from arbitrary viewpoints. Applied to theatrical events, visitors to the BAM website could glean insight into how various choreographers use space differently, how they deploy props and theatrical objects, or how specific directors orchestrate bodies in space and time to create emotional and narrative effects.

Two other emerging technologies would move our documentation efforts to another level. The first is video analysis technology, which integrates video processing, coding, graphics, and animation to offer new forms of visual communication that are very low in bit rate and would stream easily over current networks. This technology offers new ways of automatically transforming video into potentially compelling animation. The second is video database management software systems, which would allow users to browse and query video documentation of rehearsal footage on demand.

Transforming an Informational Website into a Rich Media Site with E-Commerce Capabilities

Originally designed and built by one of our corporate sponsors, the BAM website contains information about BAM's various programs, descriptions of performances, directions to the facilities, and basic ticketing. It primarily contains text and static images. New funds would help us transform the site into a richly produced multimedia platform with sound, music, video, and animation. This would significantly help market and communicate our main-stage programming, which is often visually and aurally complex. Further software development would allow us to automate and customize a more robust online ticketing service with detailed seating options and tie-ins to our financial and patron databases.

The Digital Promise Project: Expanding New Media at BAM

Digitizing BAM's Cultural Assets: Creating an Online Archive

BAM has become a full-time, innovative arts destination—a place that attracts audiences 365 days a year with live performances on stage; informal music events, poetry readings, and story-telling; movies; and an expanding educational and humanities program that presents dialogues with directors, filmmakers, and choreographers as well as international symposia, workshops, and teacher training. Additionally, we keep an ongoing repository of historical documents, including thirty years of analog video recordings, representing some of the major artistic achievements of late-twentieth-century European and American performance, photographs, documents, letters, programs, newspaper clippings, sound recordings, and posters dating back to 1891.

We are prolific content makers. Unfortunately, this plethora of content disappears soon after we bring it to stage, and rarely is there the opportunity for repeat viewing or putting it to new uses. For BAM to become an important contributor of digital content, it will need to begin digitizing its cultural assets. Exploring the extent to which these digital streams can be captured, cleaned up, tagged, described, stored, archived, and put into an accessible database is one of the first challenges BAM would face if given the technical, financial, and creative resources for deploying broadband technologies.

Users would be able to search, browse, and view thirty years of BAM programming, with new and up-to-date content uploaded every month. Users could access an entire video production, a single scene, or a single frame of Peter Brook's *Hamlet*, for example, on-demand. A teacher could create customized programming of selected workshops, discussions, dance, theater, and music by African American artists or pertaining to African American issues; access all BAM workshops and educational material on Shakespeare; or view digital videos of women artists who performed at BAM between the years of 1980 and 1990.

Digital technologies would enable BAM to broadcast its varied music programming live from the BAMcafe—a newly renovated space above BAM's lobby that is designed to be free and open to the public—and archive it on our server for later listening. We could produce and sell CD compilations of the music in our BAMshop, featuring musicians ranging from emerging artists drawn from the diverse and vibrant local Brooklyn and greater New York community to performers who have garnered national acclaim.

At stake here are not only issues of storage, automation, preservation, and updating hardware and software but also of intellectual property rights and union issues that continue to challenge making our assets available to a desiring public. Subsequent use of broadband technologies must go hand in hand with negotiating the best compromises for artists, cultural institutions, and union workers alike. This is not for BAM alone to resolve. Ultimately, a consortium of cultural institutions will need to face these questions collectively.

INTERACTIVE EDUCATION AND HUMANITIES PROGRAMMING THROUGH VIDEO CONFERENCING AND INTERNET-BASED RESOURCES

The number of educational and humanities programs at BAM has multiplied over the past three years to include (as of the 1999–2000 season) a total of four presenting programs, ten in-school and after school arts education programs for students, and a variety of humanities programs for adults. These programs provide New York City students and adults opportunities to enhance and enrich their knowledge and experience of the work on our stages, as well as engage in discussions, guided by thinkers and artists, about issues and ideas in society. Such programs as *Dancing into the Future*, *Folk and Protest Music Program*, *Young Critics Institute*, *Shakespeare Teaches Teachers* and *Shakespeare Teaches Students*, and *New Europe* provide multiple opportunities for participants to gain insights into artistic processes through both hands-on practice and critical thinking. Many of our programs provide study guides and classroom visits through our Pre-Show Preparation program. And there are multisession residencies with artists and BAM staff members that also include study guides and training in art forms that young people may never have had access to before.

Trust fund monies would enable BAM to extend and remake these educational opportunities for an increasingly eager local and international online audience of knowledge seekers. Schools are drawing more and more upon Internet-based resources, and distance learning is increasing dramatically. Arts education is significantly absent from the roster of the online curriculum.

Broadband-enabled Collaborative Learning. Funds for purchasing video conferencing equipment would enable us to broadcast educational programming in real time, permitting audiences from other cultural institutions the opportunity to interact directly with featured artists and educators at BAM. For example, high school students in a suburban area of Illinois and students from rural West Virginia could join Manhattan inner-city students from Martin Luther King Jr. High School in BAM's latest film program, *Screening Prejudice*. After viewing the same American films dealing with the theme of prejudice in twentieth-century America, video conferencing would allow students from spatially dispersed areas to participate in panel discussions with leading commentators from such diverse fields as sociology, history, cinema, journalism, and psychology. At BAM, film critic J. Hoberman, directors Spike Lee and Melvin van Peebles, actor Sidney Poitier, attorney Elizabeth Holtzman, and professor of history and political science Manning Marable would use the films to engage the networked students in probing discussions about the historical and shifting attitudes toward prejudice, stereotyping, and racial interactions. Students would be invited to ask questions and debate issues with their geographically dispersed counterparts. BAM would not only be extending its programming to learning centers unable to mobilize the resources for producing such an event; it would use the network to intensify dialogue and connections among students across geographies, classes, ethnicities, and belief systems.

Actor Training, Multimedia, and Telepresence: Shakespeare Teaches. Through video conferencing and streaming multimedia, New York City students and teachers in our *Shakespeare Teaches* program could study and rehearse scenes from A *Midsummer Night's Dream* with students in England in connection with the Royal Shakespeare Company's engagement at BAM. Its director, Michael Boyd, could coach the students from his theater in England. Additionally, BAM teaching artists would have access to a rich computer database of digitized footage of rare films showing famous actors doing the same scene from the play, exceptional theater archives from the Royal British Museum, and three-dimensional, computer-generated spaces of the Old Globe Theater that students could navigate through. This streaming multimedia curriculum would provide a rich layer of information and experience unparalleled by books alone.

NEW AESTHETIC OPPORTUNITIES: EXPANDING BAM's ARTISTIC PROGRAMMING

Access to broadband technologies would enable us to coproduce and support works that expand how we create, view, and distribute art in the twenty-first century. An essential part of BAM's mission is to confront assumed ideas about performance in the context of rapidly changing information and interactive technologies. How will technology change our ideas about theatricality, and accompanying notions regarding roles, narrative, presence, the physicality of the body, mise-en-scène, space, time, stage, authorship, and audience? In what ways will performance seek to refashion itself to answer the challenges of new media? The number of international artists deploying faster computers and more sophisticated ways of processing data is increasing. Displaying their work requires special plasma screens, high-resolution video projection systems, kiosks, DVD players, motion sensors, and other complex ways of inputting and outputting data in real time.

BAM does not have the technical infrastructure to exhibit emerging artists who use digital technologies to augment, transform, and intervene into social and performance spaces. Access to public trust monies would enable us to present the following kinds of programming.

Real-Time Collaborative Cinema. Adrift is an evolving improvisational networked performance event. Three artists and programmers who live in separate locations—Helen Thorington, Marak Walczak, and Jesse Gilbert—stream computer information back and forth, creating an interplay between their environments and the various geographies, scales, and narratives represented in their work. Thorington creates the text and sound in New York, Walczak creates the VRML and three-dimensional computer environments in London, and Gilbert composes music in Boston. All of the various data streams are sent to a centralized server where they are mixed together and rebroadcast to a projection system in a New York venue. At any given moment the artists can make changes, capture sounds and pictures in real time, and integrate those into the work. Simultaneously, individuals who have adequate broadband can view the work from their own computer terminals at home.

Electronic Narratives and Hypermedia. David Blair uses broadband technologies to create very elaborate, online multimedia narratives by providing individual users the means to navigate, explore, and "orchestrate" stories from previously digitized video, thousands of stills, and three-dimensional environments. While interacting with the narrative the user can change the scale of representation, moving from an image-based outline of the video to a complete script, or a particular shot to a three-dimensional scene based on this shot.

Digital Video and Sound Installation. Bell Labs multimedia communications researcher Jakub Segen, audio scientist Nicolas Tsingos, and digital artist Paul Kaiser are creating an installation combining projected digital video, computer-generated 3-D objects, and a complex acoustical environment that will pick up the sounds of audience members and remix them back into the installation's soundscape. Using a motion-tracking system and infrared cameras, viewers will be able to affect the screen narrative by their movement and position in space. The work, entitled *Trace,* explores Kaiser's memories of growing up abroad in the repressive regimes of Eastern Europe and South Africa, and the surveillance constantly trained by the governments on their subjects and alien nationals.

DEVELOPING ONLINE COMMUNITIES

The Internet has emerged as an important social context with extra-aesthetic possibilities: prolonged social interaction, user feedback, and the establishment of virtual communities. Some of the most powerful experiences being created for the Internet incorporate ongoing opportunities for social transaction and iterative dialogues. Regardless of the distribution platforms available to BAM over the next three to five years, we hope to maintain the network's interactive, two-way communication capabilities to enhance public understanding of contemporary performance and participation in the issues of our times.

Provide Scheduled Online Chat Forums. Currently we have no opportunity for our theatergoing public to interact with BAM's artists or partake in dynamically monitored real-time chat forums about issues pertaining to the creation of the work. Trust fund monies would help us develop ways of combining streaming audio, text, and e-mail discussion to involve focused interest groups in dialogues about contemporary art, intercultural performance, Asian experimental performance, new European choreographers, and other topics pertinent to BAM's programming.

CONCLUSION

BAM has grown considerably in the past several years, from a venue primarily dedicated to the presentation of live performance to a cultural institution with four cinemas, a growing education and outreach program, an ongoing music series, dining facilities, and a store. This has consumed every grant-writing, fund-raising, and sponsorship effort. Taking on the full ramifications of information technologies and integrating them creatively into BAM's programming, market-ing, and administrative activities will require a concerted effort, far greater than the isolated project-by-project approach we have been able to manage thus far. And while we have learned much from collaborating with Lucent Technologies, producing two interactive web documentaries and creating an informational website, most of the institution remains peripheral to the technology's creative potentials. Without the collaboration and assistance from such initiatives as the Digital Promise project, BAM's participation in the emerging digital culture will be relegated to web design and online ticketing, at least for the foreseeable future.

NOTES

1. For their lively engagement of the issues addressed here, I acknowledge my colleagues Lane Czaplinski, BAM's program manager; Neil Sieling; and Edith Bjornson. For encouraging me to write this paper, I owe special gratitude to Karen Brooks Hopkins, president of BAM, and Alice Bernstein, executive vice president and general manager. Finally, this paper draws on the imaginative pro-gramming of BAM's curatorial staff, including Joseph V. Melillo, executive pro-ducer; Jayme Koszyn, director of education and humanities; and Limor Tomer, BAMcafe programming; as well as internal documents written by Matthew Bregman, director of development and institutional giving; Anna Kalbitzer, grants coordinator; Robert Boyd; Sherry Hunter; and Sharon Lehrer. I dedicate this paper to my father and mentor, Joseph Ashley.

14.
YOU WILL FIND NO PROFIT IN WINNING, BUT IF YOU LOSE, YOU LOSE IT ALL

RICHARD KIMBALL

Susan Brandis, a Project Vote Smart board member, once advised, "Some issues are endlessly fought and must be won every single time; if you lose just once, you lose it all." The struggle to govern ourselves is just such a fight, and its success has always been anchored in one simple, painful, and expensive notion—that we somehow must ensure the people's access to independent, abundant, accurate information about those who govern or those who wish to replace those that do. A loss of that key to our political stability—voter education—is a loss of all we depend upon in our democratic society.

A longtime supporter of Project Vote Smart and foundation executive expressed this point of view: everything that is good and needed in our society is not necessarily profitable. Even to expect self-sufficiency may be antithetical to the aim of the mission of some fundamentally essential activities. Markets are highly efficient. What they do, they do better than any form of regulation. However in a civilized society, there are critical and valuable things markets cannot do—and should not be expected to do. Our present admiration of the market as the measure and arbiter of all things puts at risk some of the most fundamental and irreplaceable underpinnings of our democracy and our culture.

Project Vote Smart was inaugurated in 1992 by Presidents Jimmy Carter and Gerald Ford, Senators George McGovern and Barry Goldwater, and thirty-six other prominent political leaders. These leaders put their differences aside for the purpose of creating a national library of political information to which all Americans could turn. The strict principles by which Project Vote Smart is governed ensure both conservative and liberal citizens alike that there is at least this one institution to which they can turn in absolute confidence of receiving independent, abundant, accurate information relevant to their own unique concerns— the kind of information source that is essential in our historic struggle to self-govern. Those principles and many others like them have been the reason for the unusual and perhaps unique growth of Project Vote Smart since 1992.

An academic explanation of Project Vote Smart is that the project researches the background and positions of political candidates and issues, from local city races through the presidency. Project Vote Smart is a library of factual information covering biographical data, voting records, campaign finances, and candidate performance evaluations done by a variety of special interest organizations on more than 48,000 holders and seekers of public office in every state of the Union. The project also has provided various services to more than six thousand political journalists, four thousand libraries, and countless schoolteachers and students, and has published a variety of research tools covering all political websites, issue experts, voting histories, and other data, translated into languages from Mandarin to Vietnamese to Spanish. This information collected by Project Vote Smart is distributed free to any citizen who asks for it through our toll-free Voter's Research Hotline (888-Vote Smart), the Vote Smart Web (www.vote-smart.org), and millions of printed manuals distributed in a variety of ways.

All of this has been accomplished through the collective efforts of tens of thousands of citizens who have given millions of dollars and worked endless hours over the ten years of our existence. These people are not paid. They work solely to help inform themselves and to protect themselves and their fellow citizens from the intentionally confusing, manipulative, insubstantial "stuff" of campaigns that citizens are now subjected to and apparently required to tolerate in modern American politics.

It seems that it has become commonly accepted that the American people have changed, that they no longer care about politics, and that they no longer vote. Particularly, this is accepted wisdom about the young. Why is it we accept that we are much more aware, educated, and sophisticated—about sex, guns, or drugs—but that when it comes to politics we are a bunch of unconcerned idiots who will not vote?

The problem may be that we are *not* unconcerned, and *not* stupid. The citizens and the young care very deeply. Project Vote Smart has shown that again and again, in every way it can be shown: in our research, in the millions of people using our virtually unknown services, in our contributions, in the two hundred people a week who ask us about coming to help. We have grown from 211,000 citizen inquiries during our inaugural 1992 election year to over a million a day in 2000, and from 1,850 contributing citizens to 45,430. Voters want untainted information.

Our political system was conceived to strip away advantage, but factions seeking advantage are threatening our struggle to self-govern. Participants in the project have three rules that ensure the organization's independence and nonpartisanship:

1. No prominent political leader may join the founding board without a political enemy joining as well.

2. No contribution may be accepted from any corporation, union, PAC, or any organization that lobbies at any level of government or supports or opposes any candidate.

3. The organization operates much like the Peace Corps: 90 percent of its full-time staff must be volunteer, and those that are paid are paid minimal wages. The first priority has to be commitment to the organization's goals.

These rules ensure that the information gathered is absolutely clean, unbiased, and reliable. This is not a profitable venture, nor can it be. Nor should it be. Its independence is too important to the political health of our nation to risk being tied to the marketplace.

It is, however, very expensive. How should the existence of such an important institution, founded on these difficult principles of independent information for citizens' use, be guaranteed?

COMMERCIALIZING DEMOCRACY

The commercialization of this kind of information is upon us. It is part of the frenzy to set up profitable dot-coms. Project Vote Smart has proved that there is an audience, but we have scrupulously declined to call it a market or to think of it that way. Even the League of Women Voters, formerly a bastion of "good government" information resources, has recently decided to commercialize. The commercial political dot-com's objective, as the league points out, is to "create the leading website for voters interested in local, state and federal electoral and candidate information." That is the desire of all for-profit political dot-coms.

As "good government" groups, for-profit or nonprofit, find an audience, they also will have found commercial value. The successful groups will be approached and tempted by businesses whose understandable and expected interest is money and/or the promotion of their own concerns. Where better for a corporation to do that than as gatekeeper to a citizen's access to information about candidates and issues, information upon which the public makes up its mind, information essential to the people's ability to make wise and prudent decisions in the voting booth? In the best case, competitive systems will require each citizen to purchase this crucial information either directly or indirectly, for example, through receiving commercials. In the equally likely worst case, the information will inevitably be sanitized to the commercial interests of the supplier. To be successful, to be commercially viable, these dot-coms will need Project Vote Smart's customers—they need our audience of 1.5 million inquiries a day!

The train is pulling out of the station, and Project Vote Smart, and other organizations like it, are tied to the tracks without any power to stop commercialization from arriving at its natural destination.

Enormous amounts of money are in the offing. Either Project Vote Smart can sell out, or these corporate interests will find it necessary to duplicate us. As the political dot-coms become commercially viable, the dot-orgs struggling to remain untainted and independent of special interests will fail, either because they cannot get funding or because their information, which is free, will be cherry-picked by the commercial interests and resold.

Most important, and basic to my purpose for writing this paper, the vast majority of citizens (94 percent) have no idea that Project Vote Smart exists, even though it was unanimously selected by the American Political Science Association as the best political website in existence and government and news organizations almost universally refer to the project as the ultimate source for accurate, comprehensive information on elected officials and political candidates. We do not have the resources to continue some of our data collection, and we certainly lack the resources to make the general public aware of the service and its uniqueness.

In spite of its clear success and essential contributions, Project Vote Smart now staggers under the load of competition from special interests, the changing character of political candidates, and private foundations' "election fatigue" and declining interest in this most exposed and fragile of human arenas—governance, the source on which all other human endeavor has been nurtured or has so agonizingly suffocated. Governance, in the terms we know it today—self-rule, independence, freedom—historically has existed in but one of every two thousand years of human existence.

The enormously powerful new communications technologies have certainly provided those who would seek advantage a tool with which to achieve it. Can we afford to let that technology ignore another and contradictory need in our society—for support of those fundamental requirements of an informed, educated, and cultured modern society?

As the commercialization of democracy, or the information essential to it, comes to pass in America, I have no doubt that it will be credible in the short run—many involved are sensible, honorable people, and, after all, we are all watching now. We will be vigilant—they will be vigilant. In fact, I think during the few years just ahead, it may be hard or impossible to make a case to those making Project Vote Smart possible—its users, members, volunteers, students, and contributors—that the facts on political dot-com sites are any different than our facts. The only apparent difference, in the short run, may be in the more colorful, more entertaining presentation they can and are already affording.

But in a slightly longer time frame, do we think the for-profit intent will suddenly have no interest in influencing legislation or the candidates who will make the laws that they must live and benefit by? Is it reasonable, despite the best initial intentions, to expect such a system always to remain untainted, unfettered, undiluted, unused by interests representing less than the common good? Will it remain abundant, accurate, comprehensive, and fair? Will there be choice and relevance to all? Will it be there at all if the market gets tight?

Or will there be emphasis, inevitable if subtle emphasis, on certain issues of particular concern and certain kinds of candidates? Will selections of information be made based on commercial interest, driven by what the market will bear and by return on investment? Will they further homogenize and center attention on the more lucrative middle, limit the extremes, and marginalize innovation and difference from their preferences? Will they promote the safest, richest roads, where little progress is made in human events? I believe the answer to be: absolutely!

If we can have an impact on the future of the Internet, with its wondrous potential to serve a free people, and we fail to find a way to protect the information essential in this one area, we make a mistake—perhaps the biggest mistake. To put such power exclusively in the hands of commercial interests in this crucial area we call governance and expect everlasting benevolence and service to the public interest is to expect something that never has been nor likely ever will be.

A commercial enterprise in the free marketplace is a good and practical thing, but it is not a fair thing. To make AOL, insurance companies, drug companies, and the others who have invested in political dot-coms the gatekeepers of information essential to successful self-governance—the information that molds the public mind—is not a move into the future but a step back into the darker ages of human history, when few made a distinction between special interest and the public's interest.

Funding Dilemma: Can't Foundations Do It?

This section indicates why current philanthropy is not the answer for mission-driven public interest activities. Foundations quite properly have particular interests, which change and evolve. They respond to their leadership and to their boards, as properly they should. They must make bets on grants and move on to other projects and people. Governance grantees understand this, but for their part they must find funding to survive to pursue their missions.

For a time, Project Vote Smart was able to anchor its rather unique achievements to supportive foundations. However, the project's success with foundations was unusual and often not married to the merits of the enterprise. We learned some things that are instructive to those who will design the system of distribution for the Digital Opportunity Investment Trust. I point out our experiences not to criticize foundations but in the hope that some of the unintended consequences that public interest organizations suffer can be avoided in the digital future.

The most important element is the most difficult: if an enterprise should not appropriately be expected to support itself, then sustained support must somehow be achieved when the goal is deemed long-term and valuable.

What Project Vote Smart cares about is that we develop for the public the ability to make choices, and the tools with which to do so wisely, regardless of one's political views. Our purpose for being is to develop at least one easily accessed, sustained source of independent, abundant, accurate, relevant information to which any citizen can turn in absolute confidence. When the citizens care enough, we must be here.

Our mission is not the same as changing foundations' interests, and our time frame is longer. We are not in the business of "get out the vote," or campaign finance reform, or controlling special interests. Yet, in order to get the money that we desperately need to do what we do, we have often had to bend ourselves into someone else's mold.

As an example, if a foundation thinks the public is interested or should be interested in campaign finance information, we may have evidence to the contrary but fail to convince the foundation. They will give us funds for personnel or equipment that will be underutilized. While we wait for them to be needed for the foundation's purpose, those people and that equipment can be put to use for our primary task. One foundation may want us to print publications in various foreign languages—we have done them in Mandarin, Vietnamese, and more. When they pay for these additional versions, our overall printing costs go down because of the increased volume. Or perhaps another foundation thinks it is a terrific idea to have bilingual hotline researchers. We may know that bilingual researchers are rarely needed—virtually every Spanish-speaking immigrant interested in voting can work in English—but when we do what the foundation wants we get funds for a couple of Spanish-speaking researchers who rarely have anything to do. We can then put them on other tasks while they are waiting for the two non-English-speaking calls we will get during the average election year.

Illogically, when you ask for help with real, mission-critical needs you will hear: "We do not fund existing efforts," or "we do not provide general support. What do you have that is new?" (meaning cutting edge). "Our board is interested in this or that, do you have anything going there?" And so on.

Another harsh lesson all governance grantees learn, which we must hope will not be true in an effective trust fund, is that no foundation wants to build on another's success. Add to that the lesson that all new foundation leaders demand their own dance in the sun—they will not build a reputation on the turned earth of their predecessors no matter how fertile the land. Of course, for us that makes building something substantial in this crucial area all but impossible.

Generally, foundations are unwilling to invest significant resources (no brick and mortar, no endowment, nothing lasting) in the "hazardous arena of elections." No program, no matter how promising, is nurtured for long. Harsher than banks, governance grantors want their investment to be proved unnecessary—instantly.

Government did not mutate into this morass of money, manipulation, and obfuscation overnight. Both citizens and candidates alike are trapped in its demands and habits. Like a lifetime of fast food, it now eats its way into the heart of our democracy. The cure will not be easy and certainly not quick. But we must sustain the nourishment of those programs that hold real promise, for what else could possibly win the day? To date, governance foundations play for a while, get discouraged, lose interest, or change leadership and quit the field.

The practical impact and damage of this approach is seen easily at Project Vote Smart. Foundations have funded a lot of good programs here. We have a Reporter's Resource Center, a K–12 Education Program, Inclusion Programs for Minorities, Youth Inclusion Programs, and Congressional Snapshot programs for newspapers and radio. We have had publications for journalists, schoolteachers, and new immigrants, and some publications that we have translated into half a dozen different languages—all programs undertaken at the behest and with the money of a foundation. What is left unsaid, however, is this: all the foundations that funded those programs knew at the outset that they had no chance of becoming self-supporting, but eventually they stopped funding them anyway.

Today, you could walk through our offices and see volunteer after volunteer struggling to keep those programs going, programs that various groups of needy citizens learned to expect from us and in some cases are dependent upon. Those efforts now eat up substantial portions of our own funds and enormous amounts of staff and volunteer time. It is disheartening to a volunteer-based nonprofit like Project Vote Smart to see so many of our tenuous resources consumed because foundations abandon their funding.

The unkindest cut of all: it isn't the voters who have changed, it is the candidates. When it comes to voting, the public simply has no choice. We choose our candidates only from among those who can be managed by their parties or, at a minimum, are willing to be in debt to commercial interests, measure what the public wants to hear, and then sound as much like that as they can. The new, the innovative, the cutting edge no longer survives or is taken seriously in politics. The stimulation, the excitement, the adventure—all of the reasons to get crackin' and go vote have quietly disappeared. The candidates have all become very much the same. It isn't that the public has changed; it is the candidates who have changed. Adlai Stevenson may have put it best when he refused to do a television commercial in his campaign for president, saying, "If we are to advertise ourselves like boxes of cereal democracy will die, for you could not win the Presidency without proving you were unworthy of the job."

People are not disinterested, certainly the young are not; there just does not seem to be much point in voting.

Over the past fifty years the concerns Adlai Stevenson first warned of have reached unimaginable dimensions. Major political parties now conduct candidate recruitment classes and training sessions on how to avoid issue information and citizen inquiries, trash opponents and aggrandize oneself, and control information access through commercials, brochures, and stump speeches. In fact, we now select our candidates only from that portion of society that is willing to twist the arms of strangers for money, measure what the public wants to purchase in the political marketplace, tailor an image to fit, and then bombard us with the meaningless, issueless, expensive emotionalism that we have all grown both to expect and detest.

The real leadership in our society exists among those people in our Vote Smart community. They would never consider behaving the way our politicians do; they consider such activity distasteful and dishonorable. The maturity, self-esteem, respect, and compassion that would make these citizens great leaders also prohibits them from participating in a process that would require them to be less honorable than their natures allow them to be. All of this is known by citizens, young and old alike; in fact, the problem is that they *do* know, not that they do not.

Over the past ten years, Project Vote Smart has constructed a highly sophisticated, detailed, candidate-by-candidate study of this dilemma, involving some of the country's most prominent political scientists, political leaders, and 365 news organizations. The project repeatedly confronts each of more than 13,000 candidates over a six-month period with questions regarding the concerns facing society. In early 2000, for the first time in the ten years the study has been conducted, the project discovered that a majority of the candidates running for public office were refusing to make a good-faith effort to provide information on issue intentions, no matter who asked them, when they are asked, or how they are asked. That represents a complete breakdown in the most essential component in the citizens' struggle to self-govern.

The single most important fight, the one that must be won every single time, is the fight for an educated citizenry. A people that cannot win the battle to maintain their access to independent, abundant, accurate information cannot expect to remain their own governors.

15.
WHOSE VOICES COUNT:
A PROPOSAL TO STRENGTHEN THE COMMUNICATIONS CAPABILITY OF COMMUNITY GROUPS

MARK LLOYD

A teenager is forced out of a broken home. Her parents are alcoholic and abusive and usually out of work. She looks for ways to support herself from one day to the next while attempting to stay in school. Sasha Bruce Youthwork, a teen shelter and counseling service in Washington, D.C., has case workers and volunteers who go to schools and community centers and even roam the streets to hand out information to teens who may be in trouble or may know someone in trouble. They provide straightforward information about living on the street. They also provide counseling about drug abuse, unprotected sex, and prostitution. They serve as a trusted link between teens and those with whom they are most often in conflict—school administrators, police and the courts, and, perhaps most important, the young person's family. Teens who have gone through Sasha Bruce's programs, and the counselors who have helped them, also have worked with business and government leaders to address the problems they face.

A middle-aged son knows that his ailing mother needs more constant care than he can provide. He wants information about nursing homes, and maybe even counseling and support to help him cope with the anticipated loss of his last living parent. Iona Senior Services works with two dozen churches in Washington, D.C., and local universities to provide a wide range of services to the elderly. In addition to home delivery of meals, fitness classes, and access to the Internet, Iona provides a reliable, nonbiased referral service anchored by a regularly updated database on local nursing homes and home care providers. Senior citizens who have gone through Iona's programs and the counselors who have helped them have also worked with business and government leaders to address the problems they face.

Both Sasha Bruce and Iona would love to advertise the work they do and advocate for policies on behalf of the teens and seniors they serve, but they cannot afford to buy time on commercial broadcast stations or cable operations, nor can they afford providing underwriting support to public broadcasters. In short, because their resources are severely limited, they cannot participate effectively in the local public dialogue. These are but two examples of local community groups struggling to do the essential work of informing both those who are in real need and others who have the power to help.

To point out that a fundamental part of the work that community groups do is to communicate seems too obvious to dwell on. It is much like saying that a fundamental part of being a parent is communicating with your darling child, or that a fundamental part of being a child is communicating with your stubborn parent. This paper focuses on the simple fact that, not unlike parents, community groups are also important political communicators. Although they often are applauded for the direct services they provide, they are much more than places where the well-off can gather to hand out bread to the poor. Community groups often are unheralded incubators for reform, informing the practices and policies of government and business. In addition, whether directed toward eradicating sweatshops, improving the health of pregnant women, or bringing the nation's attention to the problem of drunk drivers, community groups bring much more than theory to our deliberation over public policy. They bring urgent, hard knocks experience to their advocacy. The power held by community groups is mostly the power derived from hard-won truths and the ability to communicate those truths in the public square.

To the extent that our means of communication with each other and with policymakers requires money, to the degree that participation in the public square depends on the ability to buy or rent the soapbox, democracy is poorer because community groups usually do not have the funds to participate effectively in the "marketplace of ideas." I have worked for corporations who have paid a great deal of money for political insiders to lobby for them. And I have worked with dozens of community groups that, by and large, cannot afford such essential support. I have worked for corporations that either control the airwaves and/or have substantial media budgets to advertise their message on television and radio. And while a few national nonprofit organizations I have worked with have budgets for media outreach, it is rare for such a group to have an advertising budget sufficient to tell their story on television or radio. While enterprising business and government leaders and media sometimes seek out these groups, sole reliance upon the kindness of strangers (who are sometimes adversaries) is no assurance that community groups will be in a position to contribute to the public debate.

The major argument of this paper is threefold: (1) that our democracy was founded on the notion that community groups would be an important actor in the public arena; (2) that the public arena has moved from the physical space of taverns and town squares to an electronic space of broadcasting and cyberspace, but federal policy did not move to protect the role of community groups; and (3) that our democracy would be strengthened by protecting and promoting the communications capability of community groups.

As a lawyer with an education in political philosophy, I will, as a habit of training, ground my value choices in both historical context and law, asking, in other words, what would the nation's founders do and what does the Constitution permit? As a journalist with extensive experience with various community groups, I will also base this essay on what I have witnessed. I believe we are, yet again, at an important crossroads between communications policy and democracy, and that the current ahistorical focus on consumer markets and government power distorts our ability to confront our true choices. I propose that we can reject both an overbearing government and a laissez-faire market, and choose instead democracy. I propose that we return to our true course and support the role of community groups in the public square.

What Are Community Groups?

The community groups mentioned above, Sasha Bruce Youthwork and Iona Senior Services, are only one type of local organization that is neither private industry nor government. In addition to local direct-service organizations, other community groups or associations included in our considerations here are local chapters of well-known, national civic organizations, such as the Parent-Teachers Association or the National Organization for Women. I am avoiding the term "charitable organizations" because I want to focus the attention here on political activity (particularly political speech), rather than charitable services. Because other papers submitted as part of this project will focus on other important community institutions such as schools, libraries, and museums, I will not attend to the communicating work of those groups per se, though I recognize that many civic organizations are affiliated with those institutions.

Community groups, for the most part, tend not to fall into neat categories. For example, Sasha Bruce is a member of a variety of other national organizations that focus on the problems of teenagers. They provide charitable services, such as a free bed for the night. They receive funding from state and federal agencies to provide professional counseling. They work closely with schools to provide educational services and materials. They direct their attention to both long-term problems and immediate crises. What local associations, in all their complexity, have in common is a mission to address needs unmet by either the market or the government, including the need to communicate messages either the market or the government is unaware of, or is ill-suited to communicate.

What follows derives not only from my volunteer work with groups like Sasha Bruce and Iona, but from a rich body of literature regarding civic associations. And as many before me have done, I put roots in the work of Alexis de Tocqueville. Tocqueville is useful as both a political theorist and as someone who could describe the society, not as debated by the founders, but as created by the founders. In addition, I lean heavily on the modern political philosopher Benjamin Barber.

Barber suggests a social world of "at least three cells": the state, the private individual, and civil society. In this latter, and less familiar, cell, "individuals encounter one another neither as voters or politicians . . . nor as producers or consumers . . . rather, they encounter one another as neighbors, friends, and collaborators." In the third cell Barber "sees individuals taking responsibility for their local communities, working in local block associations or participating in local charities or *organizing neighborhood social movements, say in protest against redlining or a toxic waste site.*"[1]

Though much debated, the work of Robert Putnam, depicting an increasing civic disconnectedness in America, is also well worth noting by anyone concerned about the health of communities and democracy. However, the observation that there is a relatively recent decline in participation in bowling leagues or in formal associations informs, but is not central to, my thesis. Nor does the relative increase in soccer leagues have any bearing on what I argue is a need to support the communications capability of community associations.

However, understanding that the communication of these groups is an important form of "social capital" (in Putnam's terms) is essential. As Putnam writes, "when people associate in neighborhood groups . . . their individual and otherwise quiet voices multiply and are amplified." More important, voluntary associations can serve as both "schools for democracy [where] civic skills are learned" and as "forums for thoughtful deliberation over vital public issues."[2] I have seen such thoughtful discussion among volunteers and teens at Sasha Bruce, and among volunteers and seniors at Iona Senior Services. But these voices, so vital to understanding and resolving our common problems, are not heard by the public. Instead they are overwhelmed by the much more amplified voices of government officials and commercial advertisements.

In his book *Jihad vs. McWorld*, Barber writes that around the time of the nation's founding, the social conditions of the United States led to an active civil society: "a modest governmental sphere and an unassuming private sector were *overshadowed by an extensive civic network* tied together by schools, granges, churches, town halls, village greens, country stores, and voluntary associations of every sort." Today, "civil society has been eclipsed by government/market bipolarities, and its mediating strengths have been eliminated."[3] Again, what I mean to clarify is that the principal "mediating strength" of past and present voluntary associations is to communicate, and the power of associations to communicate effectively in the public square has been eclipsed not by technologies per se, but by short-sighted government policies that allowed private commercial interests to dominate our electronic public square.

TOCQUEVILLE AND THE HISTORIC
ROLE OF COMMUNITY GROUPS

> In no country in the world has the principle of association been more
> successfully used or applied to a greater multitude of objects than in
> America. . . . The citizen of the United States is taught from infancy to
> rely upon his own exertions in order to resist the evils and the diffi-
> culties of life; he looks upon the social authority with an eye of mistrust
> and anxiety, and he claims its assistance only when he is unable to do
> without it.[4]

This famous passage from the notes of Alexis de Tocqueville circa 1831 is
particularly remarkable because the young French aristocrat found this "principle of association" remarkable in a newly United States.[5] While we think of
associations as being rather harmless today, Tocqueville reminds us that the regular assembly of common folk to address civic issues was not only uncommon in
the nineteenth-century aristocracies of Europe, but such associations were
thought to be a danger to stable societies. The founders chafed under colonial
rule, which feared civic assemblies, and thus they established one of the now
more overlooked clauses of the First Amendment to the U.S. Constitution: "the
right of the people peaceably to assemble."[6] Tocqueville understood these assembled groups, these associations, to be a powerful force, and a necessary part of
what seemed to be successful about the American experiment in democracy.

Tocqueville's appreciation for "associations" was due to their power in the
political realm. "If men living in democratic countries had no right and no incli-
nation to associate for political purposes, their independence would be in great
jeopardy. "[7] Tocqueville saw associations as a vital pillar in the U.S. system. As
Benjamin Barber argues, part of the "genius" of the U.S. system was not only
creating adversaries within the government (the much touted three-part system of
government with its checks and balances) but "encouraging the growth of an
unofficial representative system (of lobbyists, interest groups, voluntary associations) to challenge, balance, and complement the official representative system."[8]

Conservative commentators are quick to point out Tocqueville's reliance
upon associations rather than government to solve problems, while ignoring his
focus on associations not as charities but as political actors. They also ignore
Tocqueville's advice to limit the political power of financial interests: "It must be
admitted that these collective beings, which are called companies, are stronger
and more formidable than a private individual can ever be, and that they have
less of the responsibility for their own actions; whence it seems reasonable that
*they should not be allowed to retain so great an independence of the supreme
government as might be conceded to a private individual.*"[9]

Tocqueville was preceded in his concerns about business in the political
realm by another misunderstood conservative icon, Adam Smith. Smith, that
supreme analyzer of the market, was also critically observant of human behavior.

He was particularly distrustful of political power exercised by economic interests, and frequently insisted that legislation proposed by business

> ought always to be listened to with great precaution, and ought never to be adopted till after having been long and carefully examined, not only with the most scrupulous, but with the most suspicious attention. It comes from an order of men, whose interest is never exactly the same with that of the public, who have generally an interest to deceive and even to oppress the public, and who accordingly have, upon many occasions, both deceived and oppressed it.[10]

The concerns of Smith were not unfamiliar to the founders, particularly Thomas Jefferson, whose ideal citizen was the economically independent farmer.[11]

Our circumstances have changed dramatically since the time of Smith and Tocqueville. We have largely ignored their cautions regarding limiting the influence of financial interests over government, and we have failed to fully appreciate and protect the important role played by associations in our political system. In addition, as Richard Reeves pointed out in 1982, "the miracles that were invented after Tocqueville—in communications there was the telegraph, the rotary press, radio and then television—inevitably changed the techniques of the political process he observed."[12] Indeed, the very "system" (in Barber's terms) Tocqueville found so remarkable has changed. The meliorating power of communicating associations has been dwarfed by business and government. However, the simple fact that we have more and different techniques of communication is only one factor and, I argue, not even the most important factor explaining why the communication of associations too often has been marginalized.

The primary factor is that federal policies have allowed a level of control over media by financial interests that is corrosive to democracy. And control over these technologies shapes the very nature of speech in politics. As Reeves goes on to write: "Information is power; control over the flow of information in a democracy is essential to the exercise of political power. What we know, and when we know it inevitably determines our actions as individuals, citizens, officials—as a nation."[13] Reeves's principal concern is television (and for good reason as I will discuss later); however, the problem is not simply the mesmerizing effects of television, but also the altered environment of the public square. It is the way citizens become informed.

In the early days of the nation people depended upon newspapers, pamphlets, public notices, and, most important, public meetings to learn and to deliberate over events in their community.[14] There was less attention paid to federal action (of which there was little) and more focus and engagement over local issues. The face-to-face, neighbor-to-neighbor nature of communication helped to steer this focus. Print publication helped to inform local action so that it could work in concert with national concerns, but it was not so powerful as to alter the local nature of the concern.

Not even two decades have passed since Richard Reeves retraced Tocqueville's journey, and his concerns about media now seem quaint. Besides radio and television we now have cable, the Internet, and satellite and digital television. Modern communication is not only faster and more engaging, it is dominated by national concerns. People learn from their local radio and television more about the president's arguments with Congress than about what the mayor and city council are arguing about in their community. And they tend not to get their information face to face, but face to machine, isolated in their homes, away from any possibility of a neighbor shouting, "Well, what are we going to do about it?"[15] Moreover, in part because politics is largely conducted over television, big business has taken a firm hold on the political process, resulting in more concentrated power over politics and political information than ever before. Let me be clear, however, that the thrust of my argument is not about limiting the speech rights of financial interests but promoting and protecting the speech of community groups.

GOVERNMENT SUPPORT AND THE FIRST AMENDMENT

No one questions the right of community groups to speak. The problem, however, is nicely caught in the nervous laughter provoked by A. J. Liebling's famous remark, "freedom of the press is guaranteed only to those who own one." To solve this problem and to nourish democracy, the federal government needs to return to the position of the founders and support the speech of community groups.

Returning to Tocqueville, there is a direct connection between the power of association and the power to communicate effectively:

In order that an association among some democratic people should have any power, it must be a numerous body. The persons of whom it is composed are therefore scattered over a wide extent, and each of them is detained in the place of his domicile by the narrowness of his income or by the small unremitting exertions by which he earns it. Means must then be found to converse every day without seeing one another, and to take steps in common without having met. Thus hardly any democratic association can do without newspapers.[16]

Tocqueville draws our attention here not to newspapers as tools for individual rants, but as tools necessary to associations for purposes of political power. And while he did not draw the direct connection between government support of newspaper distribution and the power of associations, he did note that:

the post, that great instrument of intercourse, now reaches into the backwoods. . . . In 1832, the district of Michigan, which . . . was hardly more than a wilderness, had developed 940 miles of post roads. The almost entirely unsettled territory of Arkansas was already covered by 1,938 miles of post roads. . . . There is not a province in France which the natives are so well known to one another as the thirteen millions of men who cover the territory of the United States.[17]

Little wonder that U.S. federal investment in postal service had well eclipsed that of France by 1832. The 8,764 federal postmasters made up over three-quarters of the entire federal civilian workforce, delivering 16 million newspapers. By contrast, the federal army consisted of 6,332 men.[18] Though historians often ignore it, the federal investment in postal service made possible a democracy thought by many to be a ridiculous notion over so great a geographic area.[19] As Richard John argues, in Tocqueville's time, "for the vast majority of Americans, the postal system *was* the central government."[20] It was the largest single employer in the country. No "financial interest" came close to its size and reach. The founding fathers did not subsidize printing presses, but they did subsidize the distribution mechanism so that the ink-stained paper spilling from those presses could be read beyond the next block.

They also allowed postal service for newspapers on unusually favorable terms (those subsidies continue). "Who paid for the newspaper subsidy? Not the central government . . . to reduce the cost of securing political information for citizen-farmers. . . . Congress increased the cost of doing business for merchants."[21] Indeed, even while they raised an army and organized a bank, the founders spent most of their resources and established additional taxes on private commercial interests to make political communications possible throughout the territory. Because they saw political communications as necessary to a democracy, they limited the federal government's ability to restrict speech and saw nothing inconsistent in establishing policies and spending money to promote speech.

Admittedly, the founders present a very complicated picture regarding the involvement of the general public in politics. Michael Schudson notes that elitist "notions of consensus, property, virtue, and deference came naturally to them."[22] Alexander Hamilton harbored strong concerns about the power of mobs,[23] and Madison's warnings against factions in the Federalist Papers are well known.[24] Nevertheless, there were few advocates of the distribution of newspapers more stalwart than Madison, who urged (one year after the adoption of the Bill of Rights) passage of the Post Office Act of 1792 for the "circulation of newspapers through the entire body of the people."[25] It is important to note that in Tocqueville's time, the vast majority of newspapers were concerned with national and international affairs, not local news. Madison and others saw newspapers as a way to build an informed national citizenry, to bind a fractious populace.[26]

Does federal funding of speech tread on First Amendment grounds? Unfortunately, today, as former FCC commissioner Newton Minow argues regarding children's programming, the First Amendment is too often cited to end discussions about public policy rather than to begin them.[27] Nothing in First Amendment jurisprudence suggests a barrier to this proposal to support the speech of associations. Indeed, much of First Amendment law suggests a priority should be set for the political speech (regardless of content) of citizens as balanced against the commercial speech of private business interests.[28] The First Amendment values of diverse, even contentious political speech are not threatened by government support for the Corporation for Public Broadcasting, or the access granted C-SPAN. The underlying goal of the First Amendment is the promotion of diverse political communication.[29] Perhaps because our political debate, including discussions regarding the interpretation of the First Amendment, has been so dominated by the financial interests feared by both Adam Smith and Alexis de Tocqueville, we have lost sight of the democratic goals of the First Amendment and the shared will to promote those goals.

COMMUNITY GROUPS AS COMMUNICATORS AND MODERN PUBLIC POLICY

Community groups struggle under severe limitations to remain relevant political actors in the debate over national policies. Organizations as diverse as the AARP, the Sierra Club, Planned Parenthood, and Common Cause use their own publications through the federally subsidized postal service to engage millions of members in political discussions. And while groups such as the Coalition for America's Children, the United Negro College Fund, and Partnership for a Drug Free America work with the Advertising Council to produce public service announcements (PSAs), which are broadcast on radio, television, and cable, their speech is only indirectly political.

Spokespersons from the National Organization for Women and the National Urban League sometimes find themselves in local and network news stories and often have editorials published in the comparatively few newspapers left in the United States. In addition to very skillful public relations officers, some of these groups have their own television programs airing on local broadcast stations or local cable operations. And every now and then, demonstrators are able to organize marches and other protests to get some part of their message before a United States far vaster than the country Tocqueville explored. While some groups are well funded and represent themselves fairly effectively in the public arena, to suggest that they have a voice comparable to the insurance industry lobby cannot be supported. More important, to suggest that the situation of the NAACP or Planned Parenthood is comparable to that faced by community groups such as Sasha Bruce Youthwork and Iona Senior Services, even when limited to local policy issues, would be hopelessly naive. Associations are not nearly the powerful voice they were in the eighteenth and early nineteenth centuries. In order to get their message out they must rely not upon newspapers (of which there are fewer, and to which fewer Americans turn for political information), but broadcast media.

Again, that this is so is not due to the intrinsic technological nature of broadcast media, or the inherent limitations of the electromagnetic spectrum through which their signals are carried. The relative lack of communicative power of community groups is the result of policy choices our government officials have made, largely influenced by corporate interests. In the late 1920s, government officials decided not to follow the successful precedent of the postal service and put broadcasting in federal hands (as would be done in England and other industrial nations). Instead, the U.S. system relied upon federally licensed private broadcasters to operate "in the public interest." Not only were community groups now at the mercy of commercial broadcasters, those community groups that established their own stations were gradually forced off the air based on the rationale that they spoke to their particular interests rather than what the Federal Radio Commission called the "general interests."[30] It would be another forty years before a community group (the Jackson, Mississippi, chapter of the NAACP) working with church leaders (the United Church of Christ) would win a court battle against both the Federal Communications Commission (FCC) and a local Jackson television station, establishing the right of citizens, as distinct from broadcasters, to challenge a broadcast license on the grounds that the public interest was not being served.[31]

COMMUNITY GROUPS, PBS, AND PSAS

In 1967, President Johnson helped push through federal support for "educational" broadcasters with the creation of the Corporation for Public Broadcasting (CPB), thus establishing some possibility that noncommercial interests would be able to speak to mass audiences.[32] But in comparison to the founders' communications policies resulting in extensive federal support of the postal system (and in comparison to the policies of other industrial nations), the congressionally funded CPB would make a painfully small contribution to a fractious and underfinanced "system" of public broadcasters.[33] (That system includes the Public Broadcasting Service [PBS], National Public Radio [NPR], the Independent Television Service [ITVS], the local public broadcasting stations, and other entities.)

Moreover, while public broadcasting stations provide many good programs, particularly those devoted to science and children, they are an inconsistent partner to community groups seeking to express political opinion. For example, PBS guidelines state that it applies three "tests" to every proposed funding arrangement in order to determine its acceptability: "Editorial Control Test: Has the underwriter exercised editorial control? Could it? Perception Test: Might the public perceive that the underwriter has exercised editorial control? Commercialism Test: Might the public conclude the program is on public television principally because it promotes the underwriter's products, services or other business interests?"[34]

These guidelines rarely seem to limit sponsorship by Mobil or General Electric in connection with a program on the environment or energy (though how those sponsors could pass the second two tests is a mystery). However, rarely, if ever, will you see a local or national PBS program on labor sponsored by a union. Not only are there few, if any, programs directly reflecting the views of public interest groups, PBS programs tend to ignore speakers from the public interest community. In a 1998 study conducted by sociologist William Hoynes of experts on the PBS flagship program NewsHour, of 75 programs, including 276 stories and 651 on-camera sources over a two-week period, Hoynes found that 75 to 90 percent of the sources that appeared on camera were "elite voices," that is, corporate representatives, government officials, and professional journalists and academics; the same voices one hears on commercial television. Citizen activists accounted for only 4.5 percent of all sources.[35]

If not to public broadcasting, perhaps community groups can go to the commercial broadcasters? Community groups have had some success with certain network programs willing to write their issues into a show's story line; if they are sufficiently entertaining they may be able to get the attention of one of the news or magazine programs, and, as mentioned earlier, some are working with the advertisers to present polished public service announcements to local stations and the networks. Unfortunately, there seems to have been a decline in local and nonpromotional public service announcements. In comments before the FCC, Gail Parson, a consumer associate with Illinois Public Interest Research Group, writes, "Public service announcements are a way for stations to give back to the community in which they broadcast. If public service announcements are aired at all, they are aired when most viewers are asleep."[36] According to Susan Grover of the Prevention Coalition of Southeast Michigan, "Over the past years we have seen a dramatic decrease in the actual amount of airtime that is devoted to PSA's. In the past, we were able to consecutively air :60 spots. Currently, we are confined to :30 or :15 spots. The seriousness of these community health issues has not decreased. Unfortunately, the available airtime has decreased by up to 50%."[37]

I must confess that I have spent part of my career working with groups such as these to help them become smarter about getting coverage or putting mass media tools into their own hands. These efforts almost never break into the public dialogue, and they will continue to be marginal as long as our national policies fail to promote the speech of community groups on television.

TELEVISION AND MARKET FAILURES

Why focus on television? Ninety-eight percent of American households have one television; 67 percent have two or more. According to the National Association of Broadcasters, the average American watches nearly nine hours of television every day.[38] The average American child spends more time in front of the television set than any other activity of his or her waking life.[39] Neither tragedy nor triumph registers with most Americans if it is not reported on television. Even the most important issues, events, and entertainments become marginal if they are not advertised or reported on television. In perhaps too many ways, American culture is defined by television.[40] Americans rely upon television to keep entertained and informed about local, national, and international events more than any other media.[41] When people watch cable, they are most likely watching a retransmission of a television broadcast signal. Neither newspapers, nor radio, and certainly not the Internet have the mass audience of broadcast television. Television is not only the most pervasive entertainer, television news and public affairs programming is the most powerful determinant of what issues we debate in our communities and what we hold our political representatives responsible for.[42] But how television shows cover or ignore issues and politicians is not the only influence TV has over our political life. Television is the single reason our political campaigns cost so much money.[43]

It is clear to most Americans that the vast wasteland described by President Kennedy's FCC chairman, Newton Minow, nearly forty years ago has only become more vast. When flipping channels, it is difficult to take seriously the National Association of Broadcasters' report bragging of billions of dollars of local service (which includes the public's charitable donations to hurricane victims).[44] I participate in a national coalition of community groups called People for Better TV, which is attempting to bring meaning to the term "public interest" as it applies to broadcasters. In the winter of 1999–2000, People for Better TV members in chapters across the country monitored and inspected the public files of local television stations. What we found is a retreat from "the discussion of local issues" by too many broadcasters, and a destruction of community affairs departments justified by "deregulation."

"There are not enough local programs dealing with important local issues. Local elections had very little public programming, [there is also little attention paid to] local transportation or initiative issues or information about what is happening in our state legislature," writes Phyllis Rowe, president of the Arizona Consumers Council.[45] In cities across the country, members of People for Better TV reviewed quarterly reports that demonstrated little or no attention to the needs and interests of the diverse members of their communities. Helen Grieco, president of California NOW, writes, "Earlier this month I visited two stations, KTVU-TV and KRON-TV. While these stations provide a standard list of community issues, it is clear from the program reports to the FCC that this list isn't worth the paper it's printed on. Not only are their lists so generic as to be unhelpful, it's clear that they don't change from quarter to quarter (quite unlike the challenges in our very diverse community)."[46] Paul Schlaver of the Massachusetts Consumer Coalition writes, "I simply cannot recall one decent local [station] offering some in-depth coverage of these complex issues. Such stories [state privacy legislation and broadband access] cry out for more time and attention."[47]

These comments reinforce research commissioned by the Benton Foundation. Professor Philip Napoli of the Graduate School of Business at Fordham University studied 142 commercial broadcast stations over a two-week period in January 2000. He found that of the 47,712 broadcast hours, only 156.5, or 0.3 percent, were devoted to local public affairs programming. To say that there has been a decline in public affairs programming would be an understatement. Between 1973 and 1979, public affairs programming averaged 4.6 percent of total broadcast hours.[48] In January 2000, over fifteen years after deregulation, local plus national public affairs programs reached 1.09 percent of total broadcast hours studied.[49]

Napoli's findings undermine the core rationale of the FCC's 1984 *Revision of Programming* decision that "licensees will continue to supply informational, local and non-entertainment programming in response to existing as well as future marketplace incentives."[50] Republican FCC commissioner Harold Furchtgott-Roth repeats well the arguments of financial interests used to eliminate the meliorating power of community groups vis-à-vis local broadcasters: "Broadcasters have every reason to serve their local communities and, if they do not meet that challenge, they will go out of business."[51]

The broadcast market did not, does not, and will not ensure that local communities will be served. The broadcast market dictates meeting the short-term desires of its potential paying customers. Those customers, of course, are advertisers. Advertisers, and the broadcasters who serve them, may determine, as they have in the past (rightly or wrongly), that ignoring certain minority groups, or women, or the elderly, or the disabled, may be the most efficient market action.[52] Thus, broadcasters certainly need not go out of business if they ignore the needs of certain groups. Indeed, broadcasters may see ignoring those needs as protecting their ability to best serve both their core customers and the audience that those advertisers seek. However efficient it may be to ignore the needs of certain groups, it is certainly not in the best interests of either the ignored community segment or the community at large. Community needs and interests cannot intelligently be confused with short-term market dictates.[53]

Broadcasters will argue that the market has worked to put more local news programs on the air than ever before. While current news programming may be more entertaining than ever, broadcasters should be shamefaced to claim that local news serves the public interest. A Kaiser Family Foundation/Center for Media and Public Affairs report shows that crime and accidents make up roughly 30 percent of local newscasts. Sports and entertainment combined for 10 percent. Reporting on local city or state government was only 2 percent combined.[54] These findings are in line with the comments of Professor Xandra Kayden, Los Angeles chapter president of the League of Women Voters (LA-LWV): "If 70 percent of Americans get their news from television—and local television is devoted to personal tragedies, natural disasters and consumer news—it is not difficult to explain the decline in affiliation with our political system." Kayden cites as evidence the LA-LWV study of local news, "Media Watch."[55]

Public interest programming may not be responsive to the market, but its disappearance seems closely tied to the disappearance of FCC public interest regulation. In various cities, People for Better TV members found cutbacks in community affairs departments justified not by the market, but by the perception of recent deregulation. Jason McInnes and Gordon Quinn of Kartemquin Films write that one Chicago station executive explained the cutback in public affairs programs as follows: "With the FCC de-regulation things have changed."[56] Cher McIntyre of Consumer Action in Los Angeles writes, "local Los Angeles stations (ex. CBS-KNXT-LA) have elected to eliminate Community Relations Departments altogether."[57]

In the early 1980s, the Federal Communications Commission embarked on a bold experiment eliminating requirements won by community groups little more than a decade before. Using the rhetoric of getting the government off our backs, Reagan policymakers swept away limits on commercials during children's programs, requirements that broadcasters seek out a wide range of community leaders to discover issues of importance to various neighborhoods in their license area, and "Fairness Doctrine" requirements to provide balanced political discussion. Instead of the heavy hand of government guidelines, they argued, the market would address these needs.[58] That commission's "free market" experiment has worked only to undermine the sense of responsibility of broadcaster to community. This experiment has failed citizens hungry for the discussion of important local issues. Combined with deregulation of previous limitations on ownership,[59] recent public policies have eliminated all but the fig leaf of the original deal of free licenses to local broadcasters in exchange for local "general public service." Television, as currently regulated, provides little hope for community groups.

NEW TECHNOLOGIES: PANGLOSS OR PANDORA

Benjamin Barber writes,

> Anyone who reads good-time pop-futurology knows the penchant of the future mongers for Panglossian parody. Their view of the future is relentlessly upbeat and ahistorical, mindlessly naive about power and corruption as conditioners of all human politics. . . . [This view suggests that] without either having consciously to plan to utilize technology to improve our lives, or having to worry about the insidious consequences of such usage, we can rely on market forces to realize the perfect technological society.[60]

The failure to set rules to preserve the active participation of associations in our society applies not only to television. The rules regulating television were largely derived from radio, a medium that, since the 1996 Telecommunications

Act, has undergone a massive concentration of ownership and resultant limits on diverse speech.[61] The hope for a "wired society" through cable has been largely impeded by federal law focused on the preemption of local franchise agreements to support the cable industry's commercial vitality as a competitor to television networks, rather than spur their public interest duties (yes, they have them as well) to serve local communities. While there are great examples of how community cable systems can promote local speech, especially Chicago Access Network Television, the Manhattan Neighborhood Network, and the efforts of Bill Rosendahl at Adelphia Cable in Los Angeles, Professor Patricia Aufderheide has well documented the failure of the cable access movement.[62] Until recently, for reasons which can be attributed mainly to the power of the cable lobby, satellite has been prevented from carrying locally originated programming. And while regulations have been put in place requiring satellite companies to provide 4 percent of their channel capacity (which may translate into twenty or more channels) to educational nonprofit purposes, there is no evidence that this will serve the communications needs of local community groups.

What about the Internet? Despite the distortion by some who describe the Internet as unregulated,[63] the Internet is made accessible to the vast majority of Americans because of local telephone access regulation that keeps it affordable. A development of government-funded research, largely for military purposes,[64] the Internet offers expansive opportunities for organizing like-minded citizens, and accessing information (some of it useful and accurate) from government and private sources. Its very ease of use, however, may blunt its effectiveness as a means of petitioning government. Half a million e-mail messages were sent to Congress through the "Censure and Move On" website. Still, the e-mail generated by that site (combined with national polls calling for an end to the Clinton impeachment hearings) had little effect on the pursuit of the president. Perhaps congressional staff were simply too overwhelmed by messages. As Daniel Bennett and Pam Fielding point out, "sending millions of messages to Congress is not . . . the same thing as Congress receiving millions of messages."[65] There is little evidence to support the proposition that sending an e-mail message to Congress demonstrates the same sort of clout as buying television time in either a congressional district or the nation's capital to communicate with members of Congress. Others fear that the dominance of financial interests (and the lack of interest by foundations to provide support) will severely marginalize civic associations on the Internet.[66] Neither radio, cable, satellite, nor the Internet provides the instruments to amplify the voice of community associations so they might meliorate the communicative power of either business or government.

In addition, the proliferation of new media, particularly cable, satellite, and the Internet, creates what Barber calls "the new tower of Babel."

In place of broadcasting comes the new ideal of "narrowcasting," in which each special audience is systematically typed, located, and supplied with its own programming. The critical communication between

groups that is essential to the forging of a national culture and public vision will vanish, in its place will come a new form of communication within groups, where people need talk only to themselves
and their clones.[67]

Cable and satellite add the additional problem of being dominated by a
few commercial interests, each one supplying dozens of "consumer" choices.
There are certainly potential problems along this line with the Internet, suggested by the concerns over the merger of telecommunications companies, the growth
and dominance of America Online (AOL), and the limitations AT&T seeks to
place on Internet providers over its cable system.

I would disagree with Barber here only slightly, but the distinction is important to understanding the problem. The Internet and other multichannel media
do not replace broadcasting, they simply complicate a media environment in
which television remains the dominant mass force. Broadcast radio did not
replace newspapers, broadcast television did not replace radio, cable and satellite did not replace television, and neither will the Internet.

And while "narrowcasting" limits audience exposure to diverse and oppos-
ing views, newspapers in Tocqueville's time tended to be narrow as well.[68] The
major difference between that time and now is not that the technology of electronic communication replaced the technology of print communication, but that
electronic technology displaced the public square because of government policies
that did not preserve the public square in the broadcasting environment.

Our communications environment is much more complex than it was in the
late eighteenth century. Isolating the different media limits our understanding of
the interconnection among them. The fact of this interconnection is so apparent
that it is invisible to most Americans. For example, radio programs and newspaper text can be found on Internet websites, websites in turn are promoted on
broadcast television, which is transmitted via cable systems and direct broadcast
satellite (DBS). Because commercial interests dominate what goes on television,
they have the ability to draw attention to other messages on other media. It is this
complex, interrelated combination of media sources, dominated by television,
which has replaced that public square, where associations were once most powerful. The very fact that abundant media and entertainment sources exist in the
home begs the question, why go to the public square to get information?[69]

NOW COMES DIGITAL TELEVISION

Digital television presents us with yet another set of challenges and opportunities.
As Mark Cooper of the Consumer Federation of America argues, the revolutionary technology combining broadcast television with the interactivity of the
personal computer and the Internet is being developed in a manner to create
not a super town hall but a super advertiser, "direct mail on steroids."[70]

Moreover, the ability to send multiple signals seems to be leading to business plans based on pay-per-view models of programming, leaving the least attractive fare for free, over-the-air television.

Digital television could provide deeper information about local issues by allowing viewers to see what the editors cut out from the city council meeting. Digital television could provide "click through" direct access to community websites providing solutions to the problems reported on the news shows. Digital television could make programs accessible to the hearing or sight impaired, or to those who speak languages other than English.

However, empowered by Congress to set rules but cowed by the broadcast industry, the Federal Communications Commission has since 1998 issued more than one hundred licenses to broadcast digital television, and yet two years later it has yet to suggest a single rule regarding how digital broadcasters are to operate in the public interest. In the winter of 1999, prodded by People for Better TV and others, the FCC opened an inquiry into the public interest obligations of broadcasters, but who would know?[71] Controlling the public square creates the advantage that not even a government-sponsored debate need be given any attention. What better example could be found of the censorship power of financial interests? What better example of the importance of access to television: the inquiry was reported in newspapers, and over radio, cable, and the Internet, and still the voices of associations as vital as the American Academy of Pediatrics, the Communications Workers of America, and the League of Women Voters were marginalized.

It is not argued here that new technologies present us with Pandora's Box; quite the opposite. Without being Panglossian, the new multimedia, interactive communications environment, merging all media through digital technologies, provides exciting opportunities both to be better entertained and to be better consumers and producers. They also provide opportunities to be better citizens, better informed about common problems, and better engaged in solving them at both the local and the national level. The technologies promise much. Our policies, however, narrow those possibilities considerably.

Despite the rhetoric of competition over the past ten years, policymakers have allowed unprecedented media concentration and have relied upon "market-based"solutions to determine how communications technology is to be developed. This course may indeed support a robust economic environment and provide a multitude of consumer choice (Barber's vision of "McWorld"). It does not protect the First Amendment values of the discussion of diverse political views. And, as Barber suggests, there is nothing inherent in the technology to suggest it will guarantee that civil society will flourish. The technology makes possible a communications environment where the majority of Americans have access to, may indeed be inundated by, newspapers, magazines, radio, television programs, websites, and interactive communications over the Internet, and these media will be available to us over air and via cable and high capacity telephone lines. And while the technology does not limit us to a grand shopping mall of media and distribution mechanisms, neither does it guarantee a true public square where common problems can be solved in common, where citizens in associations are once again as powerful communicators as corporations or government.

A MODEST PROPOSAL

What I propose here is only a general outline of a plan, the details of which should be subject to intense public debate. It would be inconsistent to argue that our democracy needs the active participation of community groups without proposing first that community groups participate in the formation of any plan to promote our common interest in their engagement. Government and corporate interests should also participate in this debate, though neither should be given a veto over its enactment.

Simply stated, the proposal is that public broadcasting should be well funded and reformed to allow the active participation of local and national nonprofit associations to express political opinions. The basic elements of this plan should include the following: (1) the local public airwaves should be set aside, on the range of that which has been allocated to at least one analog and one digital broadcaster in the community combined—12 MHz; (2) the local public broadcasting station should serve as the local trustee of the use of this spectrum, with a board appointed by local representatives; (3) every channel broadcast, carrying video, audio, data, or text, should be required carriage by the cable systems, telephone companies, and satellite systems; (4) the funding level for both the national program sources and the local stations should be comparable to the levels spent by local stations and a national network, with funds from the federal sale of spectrum rights to all commercial operators, fees derived through the ancillary or supplementary use of broadcast spectrum by commercial operators, a tax on all communications equipment sales, and a tax on all nonprint advertisements now deducted as a business expense; and (5) coverage of all local, state, and federal government meetings should be required, along with daily news and public affairs programming, and diverse, independent political and cultural expression should be encouraged.

If such a system were in place, imagine the possibilities for civic debate. The current wrangling over what to do about the future security of the Social Security system might be informed by the AARP working in conjunction with community groups such as Iona. Working through the national and District of Columbia CPB, AARP and Iona could produce reports, or mini-documentaries, or even mini-dramas examining certain proposals on strengthening Social Security and the potential human impact of these proposals. Full-length interviews derived from these programs could be made accessible in text or video form on the Internet. The documentaries could be followed by town hall meetings conducted in communities across the country and broadcast around the nation. Experts might be asked to attempt to meld the different approaches together and then present them to the public. Where common ground cannot be found, debates could be held, and designated citizens could vote on which proposal seemed best. All programs and Internet activity would be available in all languages spoken in the broadcast area, and made accessible to the disabled. All of these programs and the related Internet activity could be promoted across all media platforms, including commercial and print media. Imagine political candidates talking about Social Security in front of citizens exposed to such programming.

None of these ideas are new. Barber points to many examples of media being used to spur civic discussion, most notably a project sponsored by the federal government (through the National Science Foundation) and developed by New York University to use the cable system in Reading, Pennsylvania, to establish an interactive communications network for senior citizens, featuring public meetings on interactive cable. The results were increased political participation.[72] The Benton Foundation has an exciting project called Debate America, featuring the opportunity to conduct moderated debates on the Internet. Debates have been conducted in cities such as Pittsburgh and Seattle.[73] And, many years ago, Norman Lear produced a public affairs program for local television called "The Baxters." A typically squabbling Lear family (think: a younger, more middle-class version of Archie Bunker's family) would confront, but not resolve, issues as diverse as marital rape and nuclear power. I, and hundreds of other talk show hosts and producers across the country, would conduct a discussion program following the drama. The discussion was usually held with a studio audience, or with a group of local "experts," and then edited into a half-hour program. Occasionally the program was followed by live town meetings; several of my "The Baxters" programs in Toledo, Ohio, featured not only live studio audiences (with elected representatives present), but audiences gathered in local malls, and people who called in questions.

Again, let me stress that the goal should be to allow community groups the same opportunity as major corporations or the government to communicate their messages and concerns *across* electronic media platforms. The above proposal to support an independent public broadcasting system could also support the work of groups like Iona and Sasha Bruce by producing and distributing educational programs and public service announcements over the designated spectrum. For example, instead of limiting educational sessions on exercise or nutrition or new pharmaceutical products to the few people able to attend Iona classes, these classes could be recorded and provided on demand through videostreaming via the Internet. Sasha Bruce might be able to produce programs on drug abuse or the dangers of unprotected sex, which could be used by counselors in local schools or community centers, and accessed via the Internet.

Community groups also could be encouraged to use their new communications capability in partnership with others, to strengthen community across narrow interests. For example, Iona and Sasha Bruce might work together to address the problems of elderly shut-ins or teens who might benefit from mentoring programs with seniors, perhaps via wireless communications systems over a local station's datacasting service. Indeed, teens might be able to use broadband communications systems to communicate voice, picture, and data regularly to seniors about the conditions of the local schools and why their support is necessary for a school bond initiative. Perhaps most important, if community groups such as Iona and Sasha Bruce come to develop close working relationships with local public broadcasters, broadcaster and association become partners helping to bind a strong community through the preservation and promotion of a true public square. The exciting merging technologies of computer and television provide a chance to restore community associations to a prominent place in our civil system, but only if they have the funds to participate effectively.

The media tools are available to create a true public square across communications platforms and technologies. An electronic commons is possible—open to the government, corporate interests, and community associations, closed to no one on the grounds that they cannot afford to participate effectively in the public debate. What is missing is the political will.

Conclusion

I have tried to show that we have three vital pillars in our civil society: government, private industry, and public associations. I have argued that our democracy was established and nurtured in its infancy with a deep appreciation for the importance of, and public support for, communications and associations. The crucial balance of powers among the government, financial interests, and associations has been distorted by policy that allowed financial interests to dominate broadcast technologies. Our democracy would be improved if we would create policies to restore that balance.

If I have been hard on private industry, it is not because I do not appreciate the great benefits they bring to society. If I have not been hard enough on government, it is because one of the benefits of private industry is its effective blunting of government efficacy. I believe that we can have, indeed that we need, a largely unrestricted commercial media. I argue here that what we most need is a vital and competitive alternative, driven by neither business interests nor government. We have the former. We do not have the latter. Our democracy suffers as a result.

There are still those in the United States who value the economic independence of individuals (even corporate "persons") over democracy. They might tolerate taxes for national defense, but little else. I must acknowledge little patience with this. Absent government support for public roads, or schools, or scientific research, or the development of standards that make everything from electricity to food safe, we would be a much poorer people and these theoretical "individuals" would have far less money in their pockets to hoard.

Amartya Sen, the Nobel-winning economist, is barely heard above the clamor of more popular economists who believe in markets as if in a holy war. In a recent series of essays on *Development as Freedom*, Sen argues for the importance of democracy and for the need to continually find ways to make it work well, including encouraging the participation of "organized opposition groups." Among the freedoms he cites as necessary to development, even development in the United States, is "the liberty of acting as citizens who matter and whose voices count, rather than living as well-fed, well-clothed, and well-entertained vassals."[74]

We are leaving the industrial world, embarked on an exciting voyage of scientific discovery. We are powered on this voyage by the engine of global interactive digital communications advances. This new journey makes possible better medicines and environments, vigorous markets, more accountable governments, and informed and engaged citizens. If we do not put the technology to the purpose of revitalizing our democracy, the fault lies not in our machines.

Notes

1. Benjamin R. Barber, *A Passion for Democracy: American Essays* (Princeton: Princeton University Press, 1998), p. 147, emphasis added.

2. Robert D. Putnam, *Bowling Alone: The Collapse and Revival of American Community* (New York: Simon and Schuster, 2000), pp. 338–39.

3. Benjamin R. Barber, *Jihad versus McWorld* (New York: Random House, 1995), p. 281, emphasis added.

4. Alexis de Tocqueville, *Democracy in America*, vol. 1 (New York: Vintage Classics, 1990), p. 191.

5. As an example of this "principle of association" he offers the following: "If a stoppage occurs in a thoroughfare and the circulation of vehicles is hindered, the neighbors immediately form themselves into a deliberative body; and this extemporaneous assembly gives rise to an executive power which remedies the inconvenience before anybody has thought of recurring to a pre-existing authority superior to that of the persons immediately concerned" (Tocqueville, *Democracy in America*, vol. 1, p. 191). The preceding is an example of a public problem solved in concert by those members of the public most immediately concerned, without recourse to government. While Tocqueville does not raise the issue, it is useful to note that the assembly does not wait for the "invisible hand" of the market to move the cart out of the road. Surely an enterprising man would come along to solve the problem for a negotiated fee? Tocqueville's example is also useful because the now blocked "public road" (drawing from George Lawrence's translation of the same text) was more than likely created by the government for public purposes, as we shall discuss later.

6. Americans were well aware of the danger of even Tocqueville's "extemporaneous" assemblies. For a hundred years before the passage of the Bill of Rights,

states such as New York and Virginia had laws preventing the assembly of blacks. A. Leon Higginbotham, Jr., *In the Matter of Color: Race and the American Legal Process: The Colonial Period* (New York: Oxford University Press, 1978), pp. 39–40, 117.

7. Tocqueville, *Democracy in America,* vol. 2, p. 107. Tocqueville notes that while their freedom may be in danger, "they might long preserve their wealth."

8. Barber, *A Passion for Democracy,* p. 47.

9. Tocqueville, *Democracy in America,* vol. 2, p. 311, emphasis added.

10. Adam Smith, *The Wealth of Nations* (London: Penguin Classics, 1986), p. 80. See also, Amartya Sen, *Development as Freedom* (New York: Knopf, 1999), pp. 123, 255, for an excellent discussion of Smith on private commercial interests.

11. Jean M. Yarbrough, *American Virtues: Thomas Jefferson on the Character of a Free People* (Lawrence: University Press of Kansas, 1998), pp. 55–101.

12. Richard Reeves, *American Journey: Traveling with Tocqueville in Search of Democracy in America* (New York: Simon & Schuster, 1982), p. 244.

13. Ibid.

14. As documented in Edwin Burrows and Mike Wallace's tome on the history of New York, *Gotham*, while the petitions of aristocrat merchants to the British government for repeal of the Stamp Act were ignored, others from different classes gathered in taverns and coffee houses, posted notices for meetings, and gathered in public commons to share information and exhort each other to boycotts of British goods. Often looked down upon as a common mob, these different classes ranged from the middle-class privateers (government-sanctioned pirates who plundered the ships of enemy nations), artisans, apprentices, and laborers who made up the Sons of Liberty, to the more destitute poor, including tenant farmers and slaves. These associations of the working class and the poor demanded far more radical remedies than those pursued by the merchant/aristocrats of early New York, remedies that led eventually to revolution and the nation's founding. Edwin G. Burrows and Mike Wallace, *Gotham: A History of New York City to 1898* (New York: Oxford University Press, 1999), p. 191.

15. Putnam argues that it is not simply TV that encourages a decline in community activity, it is TV entertainment programs. TV news and public affairs, on the other hand, encourage civic engagement. Putnam, *Bowling Alone*, pp. 220–46.

16. Tocqueville, *Democracy in America,* vol. 2, p. 112.

17. Ibid., p. 404.

18. Richard R. John, *Spreading the News: The American Postal System from Franklin to Morse* (Cambridge, Mass.: Harvard University Press, 1995), pp. 3–5.

19. Barber, *A Passion for Democracy,* p. 43.

20. John, *Spreading the News,* p. 4.

21. Ibid., pp. 39–40.

22. Michael Schudson, *The Good Citizen: A History of American Civic Life* (New York: Free Press, 1998), p. 55.

23. Burrows and Wallace, *Gotham*, p. 224.

24. Alexander Hamilton, John Jay, and James Madison, *The Federalist Papers* (New York: Mentor Books, 1961), pp. 77–84.

25. John, *Spreading the News*, p. 61.

26. Ibid., p. 41.

27. Newton N. Minow and Craig L. LaMay, *Abandoned in the Wasteland: Children, Television, and the First Amendment* (New York: Hill and Wang, 1995), p. 107.

28. Cass R. Sunstein, *Democracy and the Problem of Free Speech* (New York: Free Press, 1995), p. 121.

29. Ibid., pp. 241–52.

30. Robert W. McChesney, *Telecommunications, Mass Media, and Democracy: The Battle for Control of U.S. Broadcasting, 1928–1935* (New York: Oxford University Press, 1994), p. 28.

31. *Office of Communications, United Church of Christ* v. *Federal Communications Commission*, 359 F.2d 994 (D.C. Cir. 1966).

32. Erik Barnouw, *Tube of Plenty: The Evolution of American Television*, 2d rev. ed. (New York: Oxford University Press, 1990), p. 398.

33. James Day, *The Vanishing Vision: The Inside Story of Public Television* (Los Angeles: University of California Press, 1995), p. 360.

34. "The Indie Scene," available at http://www.pbs.org/independents/resources/under/index.html.

35. Jerold M. Starr, *Air Wars: The Fight to Reclaim Public Broadcasting* (New York: Beacon Press, 2000), pp. 40–43.

36. "The Illinois Campaign for Political Reform," available at http://www.bettertv.org/ 360d3a.pdf.

37. Ibid.

38. "TV Basics," available at http://www.tvb.org/tvfacs/tvbasics/index.html.

39. National Institute on Media and the Family, http://www.mediafamily.org.

40. "Television, by most accounts, is the most powerful source of socialization in society. Silber describes it as the most 'important educational institution in the United States.' It has replaced other formative institutions like church, family, and schools, 'thoroughly eroding the sense of individual obedience to the unenforceable on which manners and morals and ultimately the law depend.'" Don E. Eberly, *America's Promise: Civil Society and the Renewal of American Culture* (Latham, Md.: Rowman & Littlefield, 1998), p. 116.

41. According to a Roper poll published in May 1998, chances are that you watched a television program at home this week, like the vast majority of Americans (93 percent). About two-thirds watched cable, less than a quarter of Americans watched premium cable, and about 15 percent went online. In its annual report on media use, Roper cited TV as the first choice of most Americans for entertainment and the most trusted source for news; 69 percent of Americans cite TV as the most trusted source compared to 37 percent for newspapers, 14 percent for radio, 5 percent for magazines, and 2 percent for the Internet. Available at http://www.roper.com/news/content/news10.htm.

42. See, generally, Shanto Iyengar, *Is Anyone Responsible? How Television Frames Political Issues* (Chicago: University of Chicago Press, 1991); Shanto Iyengar and Richard Reeves, eds., *Do the Media Govern? Politicians, Voters, and Reporters in America* (New York: Sage Publications, 1997).

43. "Channeling Influence: The Broadcast Lobby and the $70-Billion Free Ride," available at http://www.commoncause.org/publications/040297_rpt7.htm.

44. *A National Report on the Broadcast Industry's Community Service*, National Association of Broadcasters (April 1998), claimed $6.8 billion of service to community. However, as demonstrated by *A Methodological Evaluation of the NAB Report*, Project on Media Ownership (January 2000), the NAB's report cannot be taken seriously.

45. "The Illinois Campaign for Political Reform."

46. Ibid.

47. Ibid.

48. *Revision of Programming and Commercialization Policies, Ascertainment Requirements, and Program Log Requirements for Commercial Television Stations*, 98 FCC 2d 1076, 1080 (1984).

49. Philip Napoli, *Market Conditions and Public Affairs Programming: Implications for Digital Television Policy*, Benton Foundation, March 2000. Napoli used the same definition of public affairs as the commission in its *Revision of Programming and Commercialization Policies, Ascertainment Requirements, and Program Log Requirements for Commercial Television Stations*.

50. Ibid.

51. Notice of Inquiry, *In the Matter of Public Interest Obligations of TV Broadcast Licensees*, MM Docket No. 99-360, December 20, 1999, Separate Statement of Commissioner Harold Furchtgott-Roth.

52. See, generally, Kofi Ofori, *When Being One Is Not Enough*, Civil Rights Forum on Communications Policy, 1999.

53. Andrew Graham, *Broadcasting Policy in the Digital Age: Evidence to the Advisory Committee on Public Interest Obligations of Digital Television Broadcasters*, submitted to the Public Interest Advisory Committee, July 1998, pp. 10–15.

54. *Assessing Local Television News Coverage of Health Issues*, Kaiser Family Foundation/Center for Media and Public Affairs Report, 1998.

55. "The Illinois Campaign for Political Reform."

56. Ibid.

57. Ibid.

58. *Revision of Programming and Commercialization Policies, Ascertainment Requirements, and Program Log Requirements for Commercial Television Stations*, p. 1116.

59. Robert W. McChesney, *Rich Media, Poor Democracy: Communications Politics in Dubious Times* (Urbana: University of Illinois Press, 1999), pp. 75–76.

60. Barber, *A Passion for Democracy*, p. 248.

61. See, generally, Kofi Ofori et al., *Blackout: Media Ownership Concentration and the Future of Black Radio* (New York: DuBois Bunche Center for Public Policy, City University of New York, 1997).

62. Patricia Aufderheide, "Cable Television and the Public Interest," *Journal of Communications* (Winter 1992): 52.

63. See, generally, Lawrence Lessig, *Code and Other Laws of Cyberspace* (New York: Basic Books, 1999). Lessig explodes the myth that the very nature of the Internet is such that it cannot be regulated.

64. See, generally, Katie Hafner and Matthew Lyon, *Where Wizards Stay Up Late: The Origins of the Internet* (New York: Simon & Schuster, 1996).

65. Daniel Bennett and Pam Fielding, *The Net Effect: How Cyberadvocacy is Changing the Political Landscape* (Merrifield, Va.: E-Advocates Press, 1999), p. 130.

66. Richard Kimball, *The New Gatekeepers*, comments before George Washington University's Democracy Online Project, April 17, 2000.

67. Barber, *A Passion for Democracy*, p. 241.

68. George N. Gordon, *The Communications Revolution: A History of Mass Media in the United States* (New York: Hastings House Publishers, 1977), pp. 21–22.

69. "Nothing—not low education, not full-time work, not long commutes in urban agglomerations, not poverty or financial distress—is more broadly associated with civic disengagement and social disconnection than is dependence on television for entertainment." However, "[e]xperimental research has shown that pro-social programming can have pro-social effects, such as encouraging altruism. Moreover, television (especially, but not only, public affairs programming) can sometimes reinforce a wider sense of community by communicating a common experience to the entire nation." Putnam, *Bowling Alone*, pp. 231–43.

70. Mark Cooper, *A Consumer Perspective on Economic, Social and Public Policy Issues in the Transition to Digital Television*, Consumer Federation of America, October 1999.

71. Notice of Inquiry, *In the Matter of Public Interest Obligations of TV Broadcast Licensees*.

72. Barber, *A Passion for Democracy*, p. 243.

73. Debate America Home Page, http://www.debateamerica.org.

74. Sen, *Development as Freedom*, pp. 287–88.

16.
THE PUBLIC RADIO STATION
OF THE FUTURE

LAURA WALKER

As we enter the twenty-first century, the Internet and satellite radio offer a dramatic increase in audio programming. However, at the same time, the digital divide is rapidly growing and our population is becoming increasingly diverse. As a result, we must examine the role of the local public radio station to see how this institution can best serve the digital future. I believe that we must enhance the fundamental mission of public radio in five ways:

ONE: BECOME INDISPENSABLE LOCALLY

First and foremost, I believe that public radio stations of the future have an opportunity and a responsibility to become stronger, recognized and distinctive voices in the cultural, political, and intellectual life of their local communities— to become indispensable locally. By creating high-quality local radio and interactive experiences, we can play an increasingly critical role for our listeners in helping them be informed, engaged, and active members of their own communities. This will pay dividends: experience has shown that when a station covers local news and issues well, it attracts large audiences, and funding.

There is evidence from both public radio and commercial broadcasting that local focus draws and retains listeners. Consider WNYC's local show *New York and Company*, featuring Leonard Lopate who interviews high-profile authors, actors, politicians, and so on. It is the highest rated weekday program between 9:00 A.M. and midnight on WNYC-AM. Consider Howard Stern's unsuccessful attempt to challenge the Twin Cities dominant talk show host, Tom Barnard, in his own hometown. After a two-year onslaught from Stern, Barnard had suffered only marginal losses in market share. While it is true that Barnard had the backing of Disney and was willing to take program content to the lowest common denominator, another compelling reason for his ability to fend off a national challenger was his in-depth knowledge of the local scene and his daily commentary on local events: he was there, while Stern was not.

In order to serve a local audience that has more and more ways to find high-quality audio programming, we will need to bring more creativity, better quality, and more resources to local news, talk, music, and documentary programming. As chroniclers of our local communities and people, we also must work in new ways with museums, orchestras, artists, community organizations, journalists, and others in our own communities to create new content that is locally oriented. We should see radio as a catalyst for listeners to tell their own stories, playing an expanded role in our neighborhoods. To do this well in New York and in many communities across the country means exploring ways to create programming that serves and mirrors a more diverse audience. Only then will we become an indispensable source of local programming.

TWO: EXPLORE A DYNAMIC NATIONAL/LOCAL MIX WITHIN PROGRAMS

I believe that there is a very exciting opportunity to create an even stronger, more vital national/local programming mix for radio and the Internet. By strengthening local reporting efforts, creating new ways to reach and listen to local communities, and combining these efforts with focused national efforts, we can better meet our mission to foster discussion about important issues, to educate our listeners, and, as the WNYC mission states, "to make the mind more curious, the heart more tolerant, and the soul more joyful." CNN, public television, and the networks cannot mix the national and local. They do not have local news efforts. No other media organization has the reporters and personnel in communities around the country that public radio does. It is time to redefine this opportunity.

One example is *Morning Edition*. This daily morning news program produced by National Public Radio (NPR) in conjunction with local stations is probably the most successful program in public radio today, and I believe that a large part of its success is due to the fact that it combines strong national and local components. This approach of weaving local and national elements together can be taken much further by creating programs and web activities that explore critically important issues of our time on neighborhood, local, regional, and national levels. For example, during the course of one month, NPR and all local stations might choose a major topic of national interest, such as race or how families juggle work and family obligations. NPR as well as public radio stations across the country would produce features, host local and national online discussion groups, ask for user-generated content, and hold community forums. The result: listeners could explore an issue with members of their own neighborhood, city, state, or nation, seeking solutions and common ground.

THREE: BUILD LOCAL COMMUNITY THROUGH A MULTIPRONGED APPROACH TYING RADIO, INTERNET, AND PROMOTION TO BECOME MULTIMEDIA BUSINESSES, OFFERING BOTH ON-AIR BROADCASTS AND PERSONALIZED ONLINE EXPERIENCES FOR LISTENERS

At the public radio station of the future, our on-air offerings will be just the tip of the iceberg. Say, for example, we have Frank McCourt, author of *Angela's Ashes*, for a live interview. That interview could be supported on our website with four other web-streamed or print versions of interviews done at other stations or on television, the opportunity to buy *Angela's Ashes* and *'Tis* online, plus a chat-room in which listeners could discuss McCourt's work. Or if NPR or Marketplace does a special series, or reports breaking news, our station websites would have deep and interactive content, providing a local angle where appropriate.

It is essential that stations develop active websites that extend all the programming on our radio stations—national and local. Just as the Internet poses a threat to individual stations because national producers will bypass stations and provide audio directly to our audiences, it also provides an opportunity for us to deepen our mission by extending on-air programming through our own websites and providing a forum for dynamic local/national discussion. Successful websites also will increase listener loyalty and membership.

We must learn to cross-market—from radio to Internet to satellite radio to downloadable audio. Each venue offers targeted ways of reaching people. At WNYC, we start with a great asset—two broadcast frequencies from which to drive traffic. Our challenge is to use the air to drive radio listeners to our web-casts and other offerings and then to create opportunity for user-generated content that extends the information and discussion.

FOUR: BY THINKING LOCALLY, WE WILL SUCCEED NATIONALLY, OFFERING DISCRETE STREAMS OF PROGRAMMING AND UNIQUE BRANDS FOR NATIONAL AUDIENCES

Major new distribution technologies, including the Internet, handheld devices, and satellite radio outlets, provide dramatic new demand for proprietary programming, both traditional and new. Public radio stations can provide this programming. The station of the future—with a heavy emphasis on very high quality, local programming, and a strong Internet site—can create and develop streams of programming and program brands designed to reach "obsessed communities of interest" (for example, news and information junkies, media fanatics, opera buffs, and so on) nationwide. Programs and personalities with a distinctly local flavor will become national brands. The station will become the laboratory for new ideas.

This distinct content must be targeted, easy-to-use, and sharp enough to cut through the clutter. It can be syndicated on radio and to the many Internet sites that will carry audio. We need to become better inventors and managers of brands that embody the missions and values long associated with our core programming and learn to speak to multiple audiences with new and more targeted programs.

In order to assure that public radio will continue to produce relevant and high-quality content, and meet the challenge for innovative ideas, we need to bring new talent to public radio, to find new ways of attracting and discovering those who have their fingers on the pulse of our communities, who can tell stories of the human condition with distinction and innovation. At WNYC we are drawing from the New York talent pool—finding new voices, talented journalists from TV and print newsrooms, producers, and aggressive partners in the production and new media worlds. Currently, we have five national programs that we are producing and developing: *Selected Shorts, On the Media, Studio 360, Satellite Sisters,* and *The Next Big Thing.* We plan more.

To find new talent, we plan to actively employ talent scouts. But we also need to find new ways to invest in new voices and attract young, talented people who are currently being lured to Internet companies by stock options and sizzle. Most importantly, we need to experiment by investing in individuals, production companies, and pilots and by pairing radio producers with talented individuals to create radio. This approach will only work if we recognize that production is an inherently risky business, and that not every experiment will be a success. So we need to dare to fail, and in doing so, we will succeed much of the time.

In the end, it will come down to content. We need to invest in innovative personalities and concepts and execute with distinction. The integrity and quality of our content is paramount to our growth. It would be less than useless to employ new and better strategies to reach new audiences if our content did not remain relevant and superior.

FIVE: INVENT NEW FUNDING MODELS AND PARTNERSHIPS

This investment in programming will require deep pockets, deeper than those that exist at stations today. Building a strong local news effort requires funds. The station of the future will need to find new funds from foundations and major donors and explore ways to share the potentially greater financial risk of developing programs that can be leveraged across several audiences and platforms. This will mean finding partners and funding models that are new to public radio. At WNYC, we are currently partnering with Women.com, PRI, and Oregon Public Radio to produce *Satellite Sisters*, a radio program and Internet site featuring five real sisters. We are sharing the risk and the production responsibilities.

Importantly, we also will need to explore partnerships with cultural and community organizations as well as other local news providers who can contribute community-based programming, ideas, and cross-promotional opportunities. At WNYC, we have such partnerships with the Brooklyn Children's Museum, the Lincoln Center Festival, Salon.com, and Celebrate Brooklyn.

If we act now, we can join the revolution. But we need to think locally, build our local community, and invest in the creation of new programs. If we do so, the dot.coms will not overwhelm us. Rather than dwindling away, we can become indispensable and most importantly, we can redefine and strengthen our mission to educate, inform, and foster dialogue about important local, national, and international issues.

17.
PUBLIC TELEVISION
IN THE DIGITAL AGE

RICHARD SOMERSET-WARD

A COMMUNITY PARTNER

The Carnegie Commission report of 1967 provided the vision and impetus for what very quickly became the public broadcasting system in this country. The commissioners believed that public television should be "a civilized voice":

> As we have pursued our study, all that has come before us strengthens our conviction that the American people have a great instrument within their grasp which they can turn to great purposes. Through the diversified uses of television, Americans will know themselves, their communities, and their world in richer ways . . . Public Television is capable of becoming the clearest expression of American diversity, and of excellence within diversity.

The vision has hardly become reality—but that is not to say never. Indeed, there is good reason to believe that public broadcasting might finally be able to fulfill its original mission, and more. The great instrument is in place, and the digital transition is about to make it a much more powerful instrument than the Carnegie Commission could possibly have foreseen. Maybe this is the time when it can finally be harnessed to great purposes.

To make such a statement might seem to fly in the face of history. How can an underfunded, underperforming, and somewhat dysfunctional system play any meaningful role in a marketplace that is already overcrowded with aggressive and profitable media? Between satellite, cable, commercial broadcasting, and the Internet, are not all the bases covered?

That would be true if all we are entitled to expect from our media is that which makes money. In such a universe, where does education stand? Or public health? Or civic democracy? Are e-commerce and the availability of advertising revenues to be the only criteria for using the new technologies to provide media coverage and services within our local communities?

If we are entitled to more than that, then public broadcasting stations, which are present in every community in America, are surely a resource that can help to provide it. Already, the best of them are beginning to develop into multi-platform, multimedia organizations in which radio, television, datacasting, and online services are converging to create a powerful new form of local communications for, and with, their communities.

What it will take is energy, imagination, and purpose within public broadcasting, but also some visionary help from outside. As Justin Morrill did for public education, and Andrew Carnegie did for public libraries, so we need to do for public broadcasting if it is to be the miraculous instrument the Carnegie Commission declared it should be.

A SYSTEM MADE FOR LOCALISM

The single greatest strength of the public television system is localism. It consists of 179 licensees, representing about 350 stations. They are dotted around the country in such a way that there is no community that does not have access to a station—and unlike most of their commercial equivalents, these stations are all locally owned and operated, whether by a community nonprofit organization, a statewide system, or an educational institution. That is what makes it unique.

However local their roots, very few of these stations have been able to deliver much in the way of local service. That is largely because they have never found sufficient funding to do so—but it is also because very few of them have sought partnerships within their communities. They have concentrated instead on trying to reinforce their own station "brand" on the back of national programming supplied by PBS. This worked quite well when public stations were one of three or four broadcasters in any given community; it works less well (indeed, it is almost drowned out) when they are one of sixty or seventy channels on the local cable or satellite system.

Why should we think it will be any different in the future? Firstly, because public television stations are now being forced to turn to their local roots. If you look at it from their point of view, they have nowhere else to go. The Congress has given them powerful new digital frequencies capable of multicasting four or five separate channels simultaneously. Up to now, maintaining just one channel has been a bit of a stretch; four or five will only be feasible if they are operated in partnership with the community. That means more than just giving local institutions occasional access to airtime. It means sharing—their frequencies, their distribution systems, their content, and their funding—and that is what the most far-seeing stations are now preparing to do.

Secondly, there is good reason for communities to want to share the stations' resources. Whether they are rural or urban, rich or poor, communities need to make use of the new technologies for purposes that are not necessarily commercial. These technologies have enormous potential for education, for public health, for the furtherance of local democracy, for providing social services, for promoting cultural identity, and for creating a better-informed and more involved citizenry. That is why communities should be thinking about creating their own portals, their own gateways to local services and information. It is a way of reinforcing their identities at a time when "community" has less meaning than it used to. It is also a way of making the most important services a community supplies (education, health, civic and social amenities) more efficient and more widely used.

These portals, or gateways, could certainly be created without public television, but it would be a waste of available assets if they were. Public broadcasting (radio and television) is uniquely positioned to provide the local infrastructure for these portals—the multi-platform distribution systems, the production center, the hub of the community network. Why reinvent the wheel when it is already there?

Public broadcasting stations may be there, but they will still have to rethink themselves radically if they are to fulfill this new role:

- They have to become as adept in online communications as they are in broadcasting.

- They have to become distributors and enablers of other people's content, not just producers of their own in-house programming.

- Above all, they have to become genuine community partners—and that may often mean subsuming their own identities (or brands) in the identities of their communities.

It is this last requirement that will be hardest. Many of them think it will be unnecessary—why shouldn't the community simply adopt the station's brand? The answer is obvious, however hard to admit. The station is not the community; it is simply one of many institutions that reflect the community. It can play a vital role as a catalyst, an enabler, and a hub—but if it tries to preempt the community, or dominate it, it will be rejected.

The equation is quite simple, and like most good equations it can be expressed in terms of profit and loss:

- By becoming a genuine community partner, a public television station can give itself access to funding it has never managed to tap before—public and private funding that is earmarked for education, public health, community services, and much more (very few, if any, budget lines are specifically designated to public broadcasting).

- By failing to become a community partner, by trying to go it alone, a station will condemn itself to the same hand-to-mouth existence most of them have experienced for thirty years—a modicum of public funding supplemented by whatever the begging bowl brings forth. That was barely sufficient for analog broadcasting; it will be woefully inadequate for digital multicasting and the development of an online capacity.

This kind of logic is beginning to be understood within public television. More and more stations are developing long-term strategies that revolve around the idea of community partnership. They are beginning to form alliances with institutions and organizations which, like themselves, seek to use the new technologies for community purposes—schools and colleges, museums and libraries, hospitals and health institutes, local governments and social services, minority associations, and voluntary groups. Nor are such partnerships confined to the nonprofit world: increasingly, they encompass any organization that has a stake in the community—a newspaper, a local employer, and even a commercial broadcaster.

MODELING THE FUTURE

One of the more impressive features of public television in the year 2000 is the amount, and quality, of new leadership. PBS itself is now led by a highly regarded program-maker; many of the stations are led by people who are new to public broadcasting; several of the older, more established station leaders have surrounded themselves with young talent in tune with the age of the Internet. A number of interesting experiments have been initiated.

- *Network Chicago* is the statement of purpose of WTTW, Chicago's principal public broadcaster. It is designed as a community portal operating on five separate but related platforms—radio, television, print, the Internet, and special events staged around *Network Chicago* coverage. Already, it has greatly increased the amount of local programming WTTW originates (five out of fifteen hours of primetime programming on weekdays are now local in origin and content); it has launched *CityTalk*, its own advertising-supported newspaper; it has entered into a separate alliance with the *Chicago Sun-Times*; and it has created a gateway through a powerful new web site, *networkchicago.com*. This is just the beginning—a commitment entered into well in advance of digital broadcasting, as evidence to the Chicago community that WTTW is serious about partnership. The station has a $55 million capital campaign under way, and it is prepared to contemplate deficit funding of up to $25 million in order to ensure that it is fully prepared and equipped to supply Chicago with an efficient and fully tested community portal within the next year or two.

No other public station is as advanced as WTTW, nor are they taking the same risks, but several of them are heading toward the same goal by different routes.

• Connecticut Public Broadcasting has undertaken a two-year process of "mapping the assets" during which it has surveyed and explored partnerships with other Connecticut institutions in five areas—Lifelong Learning, Arts & Culture, Health & Well-being, Civic Engagement, and Science & Technology. Now, with the help of IBM and the *Digital Studio* concept IBM has developed, it is embarking on the next stage—"connecting the assets"— in which it will test the partnership model by linking a number of institutions through a high-speed fiber network. These institutions include Yale University, Mystic Seaport, Mystic Aquarium, the Connecticut secretary of state's office, Trinity College, Connecticut Children's Medical Center, the Discovery Museum, the Connecticut Public Affairs Network, the Connecticut Library Network, and the Learning Corridor. They will use the network to build digital assets of their own and to share each other's assets. In addition, the Minority Consortium has been invited to participate as adviser and content contributor, and the Hartford Spanish language television channel will become a distribution partner.

Connecticut was, and is, the pioneer in this process. Its $23 million budget includes a grant of $10 million from the state government. It is now exploring additional partnerships with Maryland Public Television and the New Jersey Network with a view to extending the network beyond Connecticut.

• The MoKan Kids Network, originated by KCPT, Kansas City, is an independent, nonprofit organization that serves 342 school districts (about 350,000 students) in Missouri and Kansas. It is jointly governed by school board supervisors, teachers, and public broadcasters (KCPT's head of education not only reports to his station manager; on some matters he reports directly to the local superintendent of schools). MoKan provides a wide variety of services to teachers and students, ranging from traditional instructional television to online access to educational databases, newsgroups, forums, e-mail, and Internet connections. It partners with educational and social service agencies and businesses to provide programming and outreach so that all students will arrive at school ready and able to learn. It provides compressed video conferencing facilities to enable teachers to participate in update and training classes. Most famously, it has pioneered a process known as America's Instructional Television Online (AITOL) which uses video servers and high-speed T-1 connections to enable teachers to access individual segments from instructional programs and have them delivered "on demand" to the desktop in their own classrooms. Teachers are playing a formative role in the design and development of these new tools.

- Philadelphia and the Delaware Valley is the community served by WHYY, Philadelphia. It has built a handsome new digital facility on Independence Mall and declared it "civic space." Civic space is both an actual and a virtual concept—"a space in which people can articulate the life of the community by 'being there,' by participating as well as observing, by producing as well as consuming." It represents the promise that WHYY's resources and facilities are to be shared with the community. Content strands have been established for Education, Regional & Public Affairs, Arts & Culture, Workforce Training, and Wider Horizons (mainly serving older people). WHYY is now involved in the process of developing partnerships with community institutions to contribute to all these strands. At the same time, it is adding a Learning Center to its facility, to be the focal point of the community's educational services.

- The Great Plains portal is being developed by Nebraska ETV, the nation's most advanced institution of public telecommunications. Its Interactive Media Group, staffed by as many as seventy software programmers and designers, is completing a project to put the entire Nebraska high school curriculum online. It is also undertaking a multi-platform project known as *Grassroots* to aid rural and agricultural groups to improve efficiencies and develop communal partnerships among people living on the plains. Like Connecticut, Nebraska is engaged in the process of "mapping the assets" as a preliminary step in the creation of a portal to serve the entire Great Plains region.

- Oregon Public Broadcasting (OPB) has established working partnerships with technology companies with major facilities in the state—Intel, Sharp Labs, Tektronix, and Enron. Together, they have spent three years studying the available and soon-to-be-available technologies as preparation for developing platforms and content suitable for community, regional, and maybe even international portals. Among the content in development is a remarkable design for a transmedia tool for eight- to fourteen-year-olds—*Rock The World*. Beginning as a website, it will develop into all kinds of ancillary products in different media—print, video, television, radio, data, and unique consumer electronic devices (one such prototype is already in development at Sharp Labs).

- SmART-tv is the name of a cultural collaborative being developed by Detroit Public Television and a group of cultural and educational institutions in southeastern Michigan. With the support and funding of Wayne County's Regional Education Service Agency, it brings together fifteen of the region's major cultural institutions (from Detroit's Institute of Arts, Public Library, Zoo, and Symphony Orchestra to the Charles H. Wright Museum of African-American History and the Institute for Science in Cranbrook) to align their content with the Michigan Curriculum Frameworks and deliver their programming directly into the classrooms of Wayne County. A pilot scheme in early 2000 used interactive technologies (online and teleconferencing) and will lead to a more extensive scheme in the next school year, possibly extending the system into northern Michigan and the Upper Peninsula.

• Central Indiana has a concept for a community alliance that may prove to be the most powerful catalyst available—the combination of a high-tech university and a community-minded public broadcaster. Indiana University-Purdue University at Indianapolis (IUPUI) is the home of the Abilene Network, which is the backbone of Internet2—the highest of high-tech. The university is building a Communications Technology Complex on its campus close to the downtown area of Indianapolis, and it is possible that the public broadcaster, WFYI, might relocate to the complex and become the hub of a community alliance that will include Indianapolis for certain, maybe all of central Indiana, and just possibly the entire state. The partnership of a university, with its technology know-how, and a public broadcaster, with its reach and community roots, would be an ideal combination for creating a multi-platform community portal. Without the broadcaster, an essential platform will be missing.

• Northeastern Ohio has begun by uniting Cleveland's public television station, WVIZ-TV, and its public radio station, WCPN-FM, into a single newly-formed organization. This is not just a radio and television organization: it is designed as "a digitally based public service media organization that will focus on content delivered through video, voice and data—over the air, online, and in the community." It will build interactive media platforms so that "teachers, students and curious citizens will be able to click through and sign up to bring the learning experience of their choice to their broadband system, desktop, kitchen counter or the palm of their hand."

These are just a sampling of the experiments now in progress. What they have in common is that they are all based on the idea that communities can, and should, develop their own portals through which all the citizens and institutions of a community can be served in the public interest (rather than the commercial interest). In all these examples, public broadcasters are central: they have made the decision to share their resources with their communities—some completely, some partially. And they are now in the process of creating models or pilot schemes that will prove to their communities that they are worthy partners, capable of being the hubs of fully developed community portals. The idea remains to be proved, but the available evidence suggests that it is an idea whose time has come.

THE PUBLIC TELEVISION STATION IN THE DIGITAL AGE

A national PBS service will remain an important dimension of public television in the digital age. Hopefully, this will be as a service that makes more use of the system's strength in localism, but if the local station is to become either a hub or an important contributor to a community portal, then its nature and structure will be radically changed.

It probably won't be called a public television station. It might be the Community Portal, or the Community Gateway, or the Community Connection, but its title will certainly proclaim more than just television.

It will be the headquarters, or hub, of the digital community alliance. Its most basic feature will be a portal—a gateway, or entrance point—to a multitude of services and programs that are produced and delivered by the alliance partners. What they have in common is that they serve the needs of the community. Sometimes this means the whole community, sometimes it means particular interests within the community.

No station will look exactly like any other, but a basic template might look something like this:

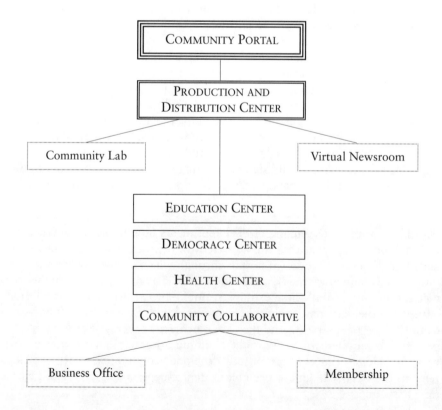

THE COMMUNITY PORTAL

The portal has two manifestations, one actual, the other virtual. In its actual form, it is the station—a building that houses the staff and plant that are necessary for the day-to-day upkeep of the portal, and the services and programs within it. The actual presence is important, but it is not as powerful as the virtual presence.

In its virtual form, it is a portal in the same sense that America Online (AOL) is a portal (except that it is free, whereas AOL is not). It is a gateway to the community's websites and its varied digital services, most of them powered by broadband. It can be used as an entrance point to both radio and television programs (though they can also be accessed without going through the portal). It will have its own browser, or search engine, enabling users to locate the particular services or programs they want.

Both actually and virtually, the portal is therefore a gateway. It will provide access to as many different services and programs as the community wishes to supply (and for which it can find the funding).

PRODUCTION AND DISTRIBUTION CENTER

To the extent that there is control of what goes on within the portal, it is exercised here. For all its democratic pretensions, there is actually quite a lot of control. The public television licensee is legally responsible for everything that is transmitted on its frequencies (or by any other means under its control). The web may be anarchic and unregulated in its totality, but individual segments of it, whether they are sites or portals, are carefully, often intricately, designed to provide the pathways through which we navigate. In other words, the architecture is supplied. It is the interior design and furnishing of the architecture (the provision of content) that is more flexible, and the principles of interactivity and participation make it certain that no one has final or absolute control over what goes on within the portal. That is the nature of the community alliance. It will doubtless raise legal and regulatory issues concerning governance and copyright that will have to be confronted sooner rather than later.

Production will be multimedia (audio, video, data, graphics, and text) and multiplatform (websites, radio, television, broadband streaming, interactive software, and print and electronic publishing of all kinds).

- The defining characteristic of this production will be broadband digital programming (BDP). "Digital television" is not a phrase that will have much meaning—but "broadband" will. Broadband programming is platform agnostic.

- The size of the production facility will vary from community to community. It will include radio and television studios (they may be the only such studios at the disposal of the alliance); but it will also include an online and web site production unit, as well as a DVD software unit, and print facilities, if possible.

Production facilities will be important, but not as important as they are at the moment. The vast majority of broadband programming will be originated without ever going near a TV studio—and it won't be long before PCs incorporate the equivalent of an AVID system for highly sophisticated home editing. But the need for studios and editing suites will not disappear, and the place for them will be at the portal's headquarters building—the station. Virtual scenery will make them cheaper to run (no need for huge scene docks); cameras will often be unmanned robo-cams. Cost overheads in general will be lower.

Distribution in this context means distribution of content between platforms and delivery systems. It might be best summed up in the word *Connectivity*.

- The broadband network will extend throughout the community on at least five different kinds of carrier—cable, telephone lines, wireless, satellite, and digital frequencies. It is not yet clear how, or to what extent, the frequencies will be able to feed broadband, but it is beginning to look as though they may become significant for datacasting (see current experiments by Geocast, iBlast, and others). Some communities may also have fiber connections (such as Lucent's GeoVideo network, which is a partnership with a group of the largest public television stations).

- The center's most important pieces of apparatus will be video servers. Broadcasting has traditionally been a one-way system, pushing content from transmitters to receivers. The new digital technologies require it to become two-way and interactive, so that it can be used for pulling as well as pushing. Servers provide this facility. They store huge amounts of programming and data and deliver them on demand whenever and wherever the user requires. Each video server will have its own Digital Handbook— an index to its contents at any one time.

- Routing of interactive pathways will be a constant activity of the center, as will scheduling of multicasting, high-compression video conferencing, and distance communications of all kinds.

THE COMMUNITY LAB

Production expertise made a few people very powerful in the analog age. They generally worked in broadcasting stations or well-equipped private facilities. Now, however, production is becoming increasingly a home-based activity—almost anyone with a computer can do it. The more valuable expertise is design—software design, the design of interactive pathways, and the design of enhanced television programming.

Every community alliance will need its own designers, and they will be housed in a digital lab. Anyone who is a potential user or producer can come to them and ask for a template or a model for a particular purpose.

- A group of high school math teachers might describe a problem. They need a way of teaching the laws of perspective to tenth graders: they think this might be done by showing them how Masaccio, Brunelleschi, and Leonardo da Vinci discovered perspective and used it in their paintings: could the designers take some of their pictures and use orthogonals, radiated across the screen, to enable the students themselves to establish the vanishing points that determine the pictures' perspectives? (This is an actual project being developed by the National Gallery of Art and Nebraska ETV.)

- On a simpler level, the local children's hospital might approach the lab with a request for a HealthTalkNet—a way in which parents of young children can get immediate and reliable information about symptoms and treatments of common childhood diseases.

The new technologies are infinitely flexible. They can be harnessed to almost any purpose, and because they are compatible they can generally be made interactive across several different platforms. It takes skilled designers to do this. The lab will be an important community resource, and one to which all alliance members should have access (teachers, doctors, librarians, and so on).

THE VIRTUAL NEWSROOM

The portal must supply the community with a constant stream of local news. Any user can access the newsroom at any time and be able to wander around within it, locating specific news desks, calling up audio, video, or data streams, referencing feature material, or scanning headlines.

Editorial control is an issue here. The newsroom must be reliable and authoritative, so input will be severely limited—in the same way that a newspaper or broadcasting station allows only authorized journalists and editors to contribute.

Quite separate from the newsroom, but linked to it, will be opportunities for users to comment on the news, or post their own news. Thus, there might be the equivalent of a letters page—a community bulletin board. It is made clear that this is a participatory space—it is not reliable or sourced in the way that the newsroom is.

THE EDUCATION CENTER

This is the largest single enterprise within the portal. As well as its virtual firepower, it will have a substantial actual presence within the station, or as an annex to it. It will be a place where performances, screenings, meetings, seminars, workshops, focus groups, and lectures take place.

But its defining resource will be its technology. Through it, and through access to other people's technology, it will be a major content provider. Some of the content it will generate itself, but much of it will come from central sources (such as PBS) and from other community institutions—such as museums, libraries, colleges, and universities. The Education Center will impact all parts of the education universe, both formal and informal, from pre-school to lifelong learning.

- Ready to Learn programming will continue on a daily basis, but the availability of multicast channels will make it easier to repeat programs several times during the day, enabling working parents to watch some of the output with their children. Outreach activities will be expanded, with more events staged within the community. New forms of interactive software will be developed for children, caregivers, and parents (DVD-ROMs, for instance).

- K–12 schools will see the greatest impact, especially as broadband connections become the rule rather than the exception. The Education Center will be a content resource in many different ways:

  - as a gateway to safe websites;

  - as a storage center for audio, video, and data material that can be streamed to classroom desktops on demand;

  - as a distance learning connection and provider;

  - as a connection for teachers to websites and other tools that will keep them up-to-date on teaching methods and content development in their subject areas;

  - as an online source for the entire high school curriculum (this has already been achieved in Nebraska, and is soon to be initiated by Kentucky and Kansas); and

  - as a link to local cultural institutions (museums, zoos, libraries, historical societies, and so forth) that can provide enrichment content for curriculum courses—electronic field trips, virtual exhibits, visits with curators and librarians.

These are just a few examples. Properly used, the Education Center will be a massive resource for K–12 schools, and especially for teachers.

• GED can be made much more widely available, with many more qualified testers working online from home, enabling adults to gain a high school diploma, often their passport to employment. This is one of many of PBS's Ready to Earn services that can be made available through the Education Center.

• Three- or four-year college degree courses can be made available through online and broadcast delivery systems to anyone in the community. Working in collaboration with local colleges and universities, the Education Center can provide not only the necessary technology, but also, if required, a central location for students and teachers to meet (actually or virtually) for discussion and tutorials.

• Workforce training is a prime area for collaboration with local business and industry. Few people now enjoy just one career, and even those who do require constant updating in the skills and qualifications required of them.

  ◦ Certification programs can provide individuals with new skills that will enable them to advance in their careers;

  ◦ Many occupations require licensed professionals to take a specified number of hours of continuing education each year in order to retain their licenses;

  ◦ Every organization needs to train its workers in soft skills, such as leadership, customer service, sales, and human resource/compliance areas (sexual harassment, diversity, and so on).

The Education Center can help to provide all these services—physically within the Center, and by providing video streaming, interactive software, online programs, and video conferencing facilities.

• Welfare-to-Work (Workfare) needs to develop cost-effective ways to train individuals with limited existing skills and/or to include them in educational programs that will satisfy welfare requirements. At the same time, it has to overcome major obstacles of child-care during training and transportation to and from training bases. By developing interactive television programming and other adaptable software, the Education Center can be a major resource in this area.

• Lifetime Learning is in ever-increasing demand, from the formal (degree and diploma courses) to the informal ("how to," travel programs, and so on). The Education Center can provide these in many different formats—direct into the home, to associations or groups at their meeting locations, or within the Education Center itself.

- Horizons—a "Web-SPAN" service that will provide online transmission of unedited "raw" material from local educational and cultural institutions, such as lectures, seminars, workshops, and so on—is a sort of cultural and educational C-SPAN, except that it will be generated online rather than by a cable producer (though WNET, New York, has already established its own MetroArts cable channel to do just this). An efficient server and indexing system will enable it to establish its own library, hopefully cross-indexed to equivalent libraries in other community portals.

As a visible, tangible entity, the Education Center will focus attention on the central purpose of public broadcasting—education. As a concentration of new technologies, it will have enormous potential for the community as a whole and will be the embodiment of all that the community alliance idea represents.

THE DEMOCRACY CENTER

The Democracy Center is about participatory democracy. It is "to keep the governors informed and the governed involved." It is not just about elections. It is about all kinds of local issues that impact the daily lives of citizens, from environmental and political issues to urban planning, agricultural policy, provision of public facilities, and the spending of public money.

Coverage of the legislature, council meetings, and press conferences will be routinely streamed on the Web. But the major part of the Center's activity will concentrate on participatory democracy—enabling citizens to discuss issues, to interact with each other and with officialdom. Some of this will be unplanned and anarchic. Pressure groups will have ways of making themselves heard, and of confronting politicians and officials. The balance between libel and First Amendment freedoms will be in constant jeopardy.

It is all the more important, therefore, that the Democracy Center should provide a framework of order and structured debate. Radio and television licensees will need it for their own protection (they are responsible, and therefore liable, for whatever content they distribute). But the Democracy Center is not like the Newsroom, where there is free access but where only a few accredited journalists and editors can contribute content. The Democracy Center has to be an entirely open area, a place where people can both listen and be heard.

The Center therefore needs the same sort of programming and scheduling that will be provided for the Education Center. Overall, it should resemble the radio chat show more than the television documentary. In other words, it will have a loose structure and be controlled but accessible. And like the Education Center, it is probably important that it has an actual existence as well as a virtual one. In WHYY's new facility in Philadelphia, the ground floor area, including the main studios, is designated civic space. Public events are held there; it is a gathering place for the community. It also gives credibility to WHYY's declaration that it is sharing its resources with the community.

Public debate is obviously a major part of the Democracy Center's mandate. But the debate must be informed by fact. That means that the Center must have the resources to produce audio, video, and data that can be used both for streaming and for broadcast programs. It will provide focus groups, voter and candidate forums, and continuing analysis of issues.

Above all, as a community resource it must partner with other community institutions. It should have close links to commercial broadcasters, as well as to local newspapers (WTTW has already formed a partnership with the *Chicago Sun-Times* for the publication of regular supplements on issues featured by WTTW's *Network Chicago*, and it is hoped that the partnership will eventually produce a daily page in the *Sun-Times*). University faculties must be closely involved with it (journalism, communications, politics, and government), and it must have a special mission to schools and students—probably linked through the Education Center.

THE HEALTH CENTER

A 1997 survey found that more than one-third of all Internet users go on line for health-related information (*Find/SVP: Emerging Technologies Group Report*). Medline alone handles 300,000 searches per day. The Virtual Hospital Web Site, run by the University of Iowa, records more than four million hits per month. Yet only 26 percent of households earning less than $35,000 a year have online access at home, according to a 1999 Commerce Department report (*Falling Through The Net II*).

The health care crisis in this country—particularly the backlash against managed care—will not be solved in individual communities, or by new technologies, but they can contribute to a solution. Health education, leading to prevention of disease, and timely treatment when it does occur, is one of the keys, and it is most effective when entire communities are engaged in it.

The purpose of the Health Center is not to be a clinic, a diagnostic agent, or a prescriber of treatment. It would better be called the Health Communications Center because its two principal roles will be:

- Health education in general; and

- Putting people in touch with health care professionals.

Many other activities and services will follow from these. For instance:

- creating health-enhancing projects;

• promoting an ongoing dialogue between citizens and health professionals; and

• providing support groups and informal networks for those in need.

The Center is not a health agency. It will not provide immunizations and pap smears, or track communicable diseases, or enforce environmental health standards, or inspect public establishments (such as restaurants). But it will promote all these things. It will employ health professionals as educators, but it will not employ them as doctors and nurses. It will have no patients of its own. No one using the Center will ever be required to give private or sensitive information about themselves, because there will be no need. Electronic privacy is not an issue the Center should ever have to deal with. If it does, it has gone dangerously beyond its mandate.

One of the Center's most basic services will be a HealthTalkNet—an interactive facility against which people can check the symptoms of about twenty of the most common diseases/complaints in the community. Places that have such a facility generally conclude that, short of a visit to a doctor's office, it is as good a way as any of separating the genuinely ill from those who think they might be ill. But the HealthTalkNet, like every other service, program, or facility distributed by the Center, will not be produced by the Center. It will be the work of some of the leading medical professionals in the community, and every page of it will be signed by at least two such professionals.

Health is an important area—important enough to merit a center of its own within the portal—but it is also a dangerous area. Public broadcasters and others who run the portal will have no part in deciding on, or providing, the content. They will merely provide the mechanisms, the pathways, through which the services and programming can reach the community.

The Community Collaborative

There may be other content areas besides education, democracy, and health that deserve their own centers within the portal; particular communities will have particular specializations. But every portal will need a Collaborative—a forum in which community institutions can interact and provide their own services. They will include:

• the Chamber of Commerce and other business associations;

• museums, libraries, historical societies, theater groups, and other cultural institutions;

• faiths and religions, as well as ethnic and minority groups;

- rural and agricultural interests;

- the philanthropic community;

- voluntary associations of all kinds.

Very often, these institutions will play a part in the activities of a particular center—probably education or democracy—but they must also have a space in which they can operate more independently.

An example in development is the Indiana Cultural Collaborative. Based on a partnership between the Children's Museum of Indianapolis and Indiana University-Purdue University at Indianapolis (IUPUI), it is designed to make the content and resources of cultural institutions available to the whole community. Part of this (programs specifically for the classroom) may be directed through the Education Center, but a great deal more of it can be directed to homes. The Indiana Collaborative has membership ranging from the Indianapolis Zoo to the Humanities Council (and it includes a vital funding source, the state Department of Education).

- The Kronos Quartet is rehearsing at Clewes Memorial Hall on the Butler University campus, for instance. It is transmitted live on a WFYI multicast, with interactive facilities enabling members of the Quartet to answer questions. It is also streamed to the desktop, with line-by-line copies of the score enabling viewers to follow the music. The television relay has enhancements—background about composers and so on. An Internet chat room in which the members of the Quartet will all take part follows the live rehearsal.

FUNDING THE PORTAL

Raising money for public television is not easy—yet APTS, public television's lobbying arm in Washington, has estimated that as much as $17 billion is potentially available to public broadcasting in the federal budget each year. Almost all of this $17 billion is to be found under the rubrics of education, welfare, or science, not public broadcasting. In smaller (but still impressive) numbers, the same can be said of local funding.

The community portal may be run by, or through, the public television station, but it will represent a great many more activities than just a television service. If its partnerships with community institutions are genuine partnerships—a sharing of content and distribution resources, not just the granting of occasional access to airwaves and facilities—then it seems likely that these partnerships will be fundable.

The role of the portal's business office will be crucial, and it, too, must be a partnership. The station's development department may form the core of it, but it will not attract sufficient funding unless it is seen to be working closely with community institutions. The portal has to be more than public television—it has to be the agent through which education, public health, civic engagement, and many other community activities are promoted and empowered. That requires a new way of thinking for fund-raisers—less mendicant, much more involved on the community's behalf—and that, in turn, requires that the content and services supplied by the portal are based on demand.

There is, of course, a chicken-and-egg situation here. Demand will only be created when the portals have begun to demonstrate what they are capable of. That is why the experiments now being undertaken in Chicago, Philadelphia, Connecticut, and other places are so important. They are beginning to reveal the potential of the community portal idea, and they are beginning to attract funding.

Public broadcasting's most prolific source of revenue is membership. It accounts for 24 percent of total revenue, and it has nearly doubled since 1990 (though it has been flat during the past three years). Each year 4.6 million members give an average of $71 to public television stations. And 2.1 million members give an average of $66 to public radio stations. In this way, about $475 million is raised each year.

Almost seven million subscribers is a good base, though it is less impressive when it is divided by the number of individual communities it comes from. Nevertheless, there is reason to believe that a membership scheme designed for a community portal (rather than just for a public television station) might provide a substantial amount of revenue. It will depend on whether the scheme is seen to deliver real benefits to its subscribers, and whether it is distanced from the begging bowl scenario that has dogged public television.

THE NATIONAL DIMENSION

If public television's future is so bound up in its local mission, then why bother with a national service?

There are only two reasons for providing a national service. One is to make money. That is the case with the commercial networks and the principal cable channels. It might also be an argument in favor of PBS, since much of the money raised in the form of donations, pledges, and subscriptions is undoubtedly prompted by the quality of national rather than local programming. But it is not a convincing argument. The other reason (and this has to be public television's rationale) is if the service provided is unique and distinctive, and cannot be found elsewhere. Quality is an important consideration, of course, but it is not sufficient by itself. Moreover, in the words of PBS's new president, Pat Mitchell, "being non-commercial is not enough."

The primetime schedule inherited by Pat Mitchell when she took up her new duties in March 2000 was very much the same schedule as that inherited by her predecessor, Ervin Duggan, in 1993. Much of it was still recognizable from the era of Larry Grossman in the late 1970s. In Grossman's time, it could be claimed with justice that it represented a distinctive voice in American life, because it contained programming unique to American television (*Great Performances*, *Masterpiece Theatre*, *NOVA*) and because it tackled conventional subject matter in ways that were alien to commercial television (the *NewsHour*, *Austin City Limits*, in-depth documentaries). The arrival of niche cable channels, largely inspired by the success of public television, blurred these differences. The voice was no longer so distinctive, and PBS failed to react.

True, there were shining hours—many of them. One could cite Ken Burns' *The Civil War*, Henry Hampton's *Eyes on the Prize*, Bill Moyers' *On Our Own Terms*, and other fine documentary achievements like *The Farmer's Wife* and *An American Love Story*. One could also cite many individual episodes of long-running series (*Nature*, *NOVA*, *American Masters*, *Frontline)*, but a part of the trouble is that many of these series have been running for so long that the prime-time schedule looks repetitive and old, even when individual programs within the series are striking and innovative. Conversely, the Ready to Learn slate of preschool programming has been fairly regularly refreshed over the years, and it remains the most outstanding achievement.

BARRIERS TO CHANGE

Changing a twenty-year-old schedule is not as easy as it sounds. The bulk of it (maybe as much as two-thirds) is provided by three stations on the East Coast (WGBH, Boston; WNET, New York; and WETA in Washington, D.C.). These stations have developed themselves around major national series, and they have sometimes taken considerable financial risks to support those series. They will not willingly see them cancelled—unless, perhaps, they provide the replacements themselves.

Nor will it be easy to get the other stations to agree on how primetime programming should be changed. PBS is, first and foremost, the stations' membership organization—a private nonprofit corporation jointly owned by the 179 licensees. Supplying programming happens to be its principal activity—but Membership (rife with the politics of the system) is not necessarily a good bedfellow for Programming (which needs a creative atmosphere responsive to the needs of the stations, certainly, but not so responsive that it becomes bland and unwilling to take risks or make changes).

All these are pressures in favor of the status quo, but there are countervailing trends. One of them is the new leadership that public broadcasting has coincidentally acquired, including a distinguished program maker at the helm of PBS, and a large number of new CEOs in the stations, some of them from the commercial world, some of them from outside broadcasting altogether. They are forces for change, and they are joined by a number of more senior station managers who have surrounded themselves with young and forward-thinking program executives. The community of independent producers, on which public television's national programming has always been dependent, is another force for change; it is abuzz with ideas, and already thinking digital.

Making space in the primetime schedule for some of these new ideas is Job One. It would be easier to accomplish if there was new money available, but that is unlikely to be the case. The budget for PBS's National Program Service in the year 2000 is $172.6 million (that includes the daytime preschool programming as well as primetime). Compared to commercial network budgets, it is a derisory amount, nor does it compare well with many cable channels.

Meanwhile, in the fall and winter of 2000–2001, PBS is conducting an experiment with seven stations to reschedule the existing primetime programming and see how it plays with their audiences. This is merely an exercise in moving around the existing blocks, but if it is a prelude to the much more difficult process of deciding what series and genres of programming need to be changed or abandoned, then it will be a worthwhile experiment. At the same time, Pat Mitchell has moved quickly to appoint regional program executives—one in the South, one in the Midwest, one in California—and that may help to move the emphasis away from the East Coast and reflect more accurately the diversity of the nation.

A LOCAL > NATIONAL AXIS

So what is it that could make public television's national voice truly distinctive amid the increasing cacophony of the media? It must surely be the system's local roots—the fact that 350 stations, locally owned and operated, all of them linked by a superb satellite system, are available to provide coverage of every community in this country, to reflect the American mosaic in a way that no one else can.

It is true, of course, that many of these stations are small and ill-funded and incapable of producing programming of the necessary quality. But there are a great many more that have the potential, if not the experience. It is also true that some of the stations have specifically educational missions, but that is no reason to disqualify them as occasional contributors to national programming. If the premise is correct—that many stations (if not the majority) will use their new digital capacity and access to online technologies to build partnerships with and within their communities—then there is surely a vast resource here that can be parlayed into national programming that is truly reflective of the nation.

It is this local > national axis that public television has to develop as a central part of its programming. It is the key that will unlock the nascent power of public television—its ability to use its local roots to enrich its national programming (and vice versa). Pat Mitchell is already thinking about initiating what she calls "big national conversations," or programming that will involve many diverse communities in examinations of problems that underlie American society (public education, race relations, the culture of violence, healthcare, immigration, and many more). All these are issues that occasionally become headline news, but what happens between the headlines? The issues do not go away, the emotional temperature is lowered. It is the proper time for constructive dialogue.

Conversation does not mean just talk. Television's ultimate power is as a storyteller in its ability to illustrate both problems and solutions in ways that are graphic and memorable, by reporting stories of how individual communities are confronting these issues. This is not pundit television (there's more than enough of that); it is the real lives of real people. The format will allow for interaction between communities, and for individual stations to stage their own local dialogues. It will also allow communities to speak to the nation, and the nation to speak to itself. As a first step in this direction, Pat Mitchell has announced that a new weekly program, *Public Square,* is being developed specifically to take advantage of the local > national axis.

Big national conversations are a dramatic way of demonstrating public television's potential, but they are by no means the only way the local > national axis can be developed. Oregon Public Broadcasting's *Rock The World* project for eight- to fourteen-year-olds may be another. The issue is not whether local stations can provide facilities for national programs (in the way that the *NewsHour,* for instance, might use a local studio to record an interview between Jim Lehrer, in Washington, and a local personality): it is whether local stations can produce their own segments for inclusion in national programs, or whole programs for inclusion in the national schedule. These stations have long bemoaned the dominance of the "big three" on the East Coast. Now is their chance to prove that they, too, can play a role on the national stage.

In 1854, ten years after the invention of the telegraph, Henry David Thoreau wrote: "We are in haste to construct a magnetic telegraph from Maine to Texas; but Maine and Texas, it may be, have nothing important to communicate." That is no longer the case, and Thoreau himself lived just long enough to witness the whirlwind that a lack of communication can bring (he died in the first year of the Civil War). No such apocalypse can be seen on the horizon today, but federalism and democracy are fragile flowers, constantly in need of nurturing. Public broadcasting can provide some of that nourishment—through dialogue, through interaction, and yes, sometimes through gentle provocation.

LOCAL > LOCAL

Within the last decade, Dr. Robert Larson, who was then the CEO of WTVS, the Detroit public television station, organized a group of fifteen urban stations into an association called the Nitty Gritty City Group. Its purpose was to pool the resources of the stations to prove the hypothesis that public television stations could contribute, through joint programming and outreach, to problem solving in the inner cities. One of the group's most successful series, *Street Watch,* compared ways in which the fifteen cities confronted problems of gangs, drugs, and homelessness. The Nitty Gritty City Group, as it turned out, was ahead of its time. It died too quickly because its vision was not shared, locally or nationally, by those who might have sustained and encouraged it; but it is a model for how public television can develop another important axis—the local > local axis.

Jerry Wareham, a veteran of public television who is now CEO of WVIZ, Cleveland, has pointed out that many local stations (maybe as many as twenty of them) produce their own local arts and cultural magazine programs. There is *Artbeat* (Chicago), *EGG* (New York), *Arts Alive* (Oklahoma), *Boston Arts*, *Applause* (Cleveland), *Backstage Pass* (Detroit), and many more. If all the component pieces of these programs —reports, reviews, interviews, feature stories, mini-docs—were stored in a common video server, and if any station with access to the server could complement its local coverage by making use of items placed in the server by other stations, then everyone would gain. Local programs would be enriched, local stories would get wider dissemination, and audiences would be able to compare their own community's cultural life with those of other communities around the nation. The programs would still be locally produced and locally hosted. It would not be a case of PBS or a single large station enforcing its own tastes and priorities on other stations.

This local > local axis is potentially as powerful as the local > national axis. It could be applied to many different forms of programming, including public affairs, nightly news shows, ethnic and minority programming, and more. And television need not be the only platform on which this principle would operate. The *Horizons* Web-SPAN concept referred to earlier is another very obvious application, another way in which public television can capitalize on its localism, and on the newfound need of local stations to create multi-platform content in partnership with community institutions.

AN AGENDA FOR ACTION

These are some of the ways in which public television can emerge from the morass of media noise with a more distinctive voice. What these suggestions have in common is the need to build on the system's presence in, and access to, virtually every community in America. And that, in turn, depends on the stations' ability to transform themselves into powerful community institutions, the engine-rooms of community portals. It depends equally on the stations' willingness to allow their national programmers to develop a schedule that is more focused, less comprehensive, emanating much more directly from public broadcasting's known strengths and latent abilities.

No one knows, at this stage, how much of public television's programming will eventually be transmitted in High Definition (HD), or how much of its activity will revolve around platforms other than radio and television (probably quite a high percentage on both counts). No more is it known for certain what role the digital frequencies will play. (Might they even become an anachronism if they could be exchanged for a comprehensive "must carry" cable law?) But what is certain is that public television will have to produce and coproduce content on a scale undreamed of five years ago. Much of it will be local; some of it will be national. Much of it will be developed around local roots, some of it will continue to concentrate on subject areas in which public television has a special expertise, such as pre-school programming, science, the arts, and in-depth public affairs.

Confronted with such a formidable agenda, there is a natural tendency to wring one's hands and ask where the funding will come from. Faith is not enough. It brings us back to the chicken-and-egg situation of the community portals. As with the local partnership models that are necessary to demonstrate the potential of community portals if demand is to be created within the community, so it is with national programming. Only by demonstrating what public television can do nationally on the basis of its strength in localism will a demand for this kind of programming be created. If there is no demand, there will be no funding. But it's a reasonable bet that the demand is there—dormant, just beneath the surface, waiting to be harnessed for action.

APPENDIX:
LIST OF THOSE CONSULTED BY THE DIGITAL PROMISE PROJECT

Mason Adams, Actor, Member of Actors' Equity, Screen Actors Guild and American Federation of Television and Radio Artists

Dr. Scott Aikens, Digital Media Consultant, KQED

Maxwell L. Anderson, Director, The Whitney Museum of American Art

Diane Asadorian

Wayne Ashley, Ph.D., Manager of New Media, Brooklyn Academy of Music

Cynthia J. Atman, Ph.D., Director, Center for Engineering Learning and Teaching, University of Washington

Douglas L. Bailey, President, FreedomChannel.com

Ruzena Bajcsy, Deputy Director, The National Science Foundation

William F. Baker, President, WNET, New York City

Benjamin R. Barber, Director, Walt Whitman Center, Rutgers University

Henry P. Becton, Jr., President, WGBH, Boston

Charles Benton, Chairman, Benton Foundation and Public Media, Incorporated

John W. Berry, President-elect American Library Association

James H. Billington, The Librarian of Congress

Mary Bitterman, President, KQED, San Francisco

Jonathan D. Blake, Senior Partner, Covington and Burling, Washington, D.C.

Leo Bogart, Author, Sociologist

Derek Bok, President Emeritus, Harvard University

Sissela Bok, Author, Center for Population and Development, Harvard University

John Brademas, President Emeritus, New York University

Molly Corbett Broad, President, The University of North Carolina

Les Brown, Journalist

David Brugger, Former President, America's Public Television Stations

Bernice Buresh, Writer

Sheila P. Burke, Under Secretary for American Museums and National Programs, Smithsonian Institution

Kathy Bushkin, Senior Vice President, AOL Time Warner and President, AOL Time Warner Foundation

Robert N. Butler, M.D., President and CEO, International Longevity Center
Colin G. Campbell, Former President, Rockefeller Brothers Fund; Chairman, PBS
Laura Campbell, Associate Librarian, Library of Congress
James W. Carey, Professor, Columbia University Graduate School of Journalism
Marta Cehelsky, Executive Officer, National Science Board
Anthony B. Chapman, Director, Internet & Broadband, Thirteen/WNET New York
Peggy Charren, Founder, Action for Children's Television
Larry Chernikoff, President, Chernikoff and Company
Elizabeth G. Christopherson, Executive Director and CEO, New Jersey Network
David Clark, Director, Television Operations, Corporation for Public Broadcasting
Marshall Cohen, Senior Vice President, AOL Time Warner
Jeffrey I. Cole, Director, Center for Communication Policy, University of California, Los Angeles
Jonathan R. Cole, Provost and Dean of Faculties, Columbia University
Michael Connet, Senior Analyst for Strategic Planning & Next Media, Kansas City Public Television
Robert T. Coonrod, President, Corporation for Public Broadcasting
Frank Cruz, Chairman, Corporation for Public Broadcasting
Cathy N. Davidson, Vice Provost for Interdisciplinary Studies, Duke University
Bill Davis, Former Senior Vice President, National Public Radio
Sharon S. Dawes, Director, Center for Technology in Government, University at Albany/SUNY
James Day, President, Publivision
Philippe de Montebello, Director, Metropolitan Museum of Art
Mary A. Dempsey, Commissioner, Chicago Public Library
Everette E. Dennis, Felix E. Larkin Distinguished Professor, Fordham University Graduate School of Business; Chief Operating Officer, International Longevity Center-USA, New York City
Brewster C. Denny, Former Chairman, The Century Foundation
John Diebold, Chairman, The Diebold Institute for Public Policy Studies, Inc.
Senator Christopher J. Dodd, D-CT
Kenneth M. Duberstein, The Duberstein Group, Inc.
Senator Richard J. Durbin, D-IL
Julius C. C. Edelstein, Senior Vice Chancellor Emeritus, City University of New York
Prof. Marc Eisenstadt, Chief Scientist, Knowledge Media Institute, The Open University (UK)
Eli N. Evans, President, Charles H. Revson Foundation, Inc.
John H. Falk, Ph.D., President, Institute for Learning Innovation
Jonathan F. Fanton, President, John D. and Catherine T. MacArthur Foundation
Joseph Farrell, Professor of Economics, University of California, Berkeley
James Fellows, President, Central Education Network and The Hartford Gunn Institute
Charles Ferguson, Author and Designer, "Frontpage"

Harvey V. Fineberg, Provost, Harvard University
Charles Firestone, Executive Director, Communications and Society Program, The Aspen Institute
William W. Fisher, III, Professor of Law, Harvard University
Joel L. Fleishman, Senior Advisor, Atlantic Philanthropic Service Company
Max Frankel, Former Executive Editor, *The New York Times*
Jerry Franklin, President, Connecticut Public Television and Radio
Marion R. Fremont-Smith, Senior Research Fellow, Hauser Center for Nonprofit Organizations, Harvard University
Craig Fugate, Bureau Chief, Division of Emergency Management, State of Florida
Steve Futernick, Senior Vice President, Strategic Development, Connecticut Public Broadcasting
Ellen V. Futter, President, American Museum of Natural History
Peter Galison, Mallinckrodt Professor of the History of Science and of Physics, Harvard University;
Leonard Garment, Of Counsel, Verner, Liipfert, Bernhard, McPherson & Hand, Washington, D.C.
Michael Gildea, Assistant to the President, Department for Professional Employees, AFL-CIO
John Goberman, Executive Producer, "Live From Lincoln Center"
Debbie Goldman, Alliance for Public Technology and Communications Workers of America
Tom Goldstein, Dean, Columbia University Graduate School of Journalism
Jack Golodner, President, Department for Professional Employees, AFL-CIO
Louis M. Gomez, Associate Professor, Center for Learning Technologies in Urban Schools, Northwestern University
Martín Gómez, Executive Director, Brooklyn Public Library
Lynne M. Grasz, President and CEO, Grasz Communications
Richard R. Green, President and CEO, CableLabs
Vartan Gregorian, President, Carnegie Corporation
Frank Gumper, Vice President—Public Policy Development, Verizon Communications
Jacob S. Hacker, Junior Fellow, Harvard University
Barbara R. Hamlin, Director, Foundation/Government Underwriting, Thirteen/WNET, New York City
Patricia Harris, Research Director, WGBH, Boston
Kathryn Hauser, Vice President, Information Technology Industry Council
Richard Heffner, Host/Producer, public television's The Open Mind; University Professor of Communications and Public Policy, Rutgers University; founding General Manager, Channel 13 in New York City
Stephen Heintz, Former President, DEMOS; President, Rockefeller Brothers Fund
Randy J. Hinrichs, Group Research Manager, Learning Science and Technology, Microsoft Research
Howard Holzer, Vice President for Communications, Metropolitan Museum of Art

Karen Brooks Hopkins, President, Brooklyn Academy of Music

Reed Hundt, Senior Advisor for Information Industries, McKinsey and Company; Former Chairman, Federal Communications Commission

Josh Isay, Morris, Carrick & Guma

Jay Iselin, President, Marconi Foundation at Columbia University

Bill Ivey, Chair, National Endowment for the Arts

Senator James Jeffords, R-VT

Ralph M. Jennings, General Manager, WFUV, Fordham University

Al Jerome, President & Chief Executive Officer, KCET, Los Angeles

Alex Jones, Journalist, Director, Shorenstein Center, Harvard University

Marvin Kalb, Joan Shorenstein Center on the Press, Politics and Public Policy, Harvard University, Cambridge, MA

Eamon M. Kelly, Chair, National Science Board

Henry C. Kelly, President, Federation of American Scientists

William E. Kennard, Former Chair, Federal Communications Commission, Senior Fellow, The Aspen Institute

Richard Kimball, President, Project Vote Smart

Larry Kirkman, President, The Benton Foundation

Ann Kirschner, President and CEO, Fathom.com

Kevin Klose, President, National Public Radio

Katharina Kopp, Ph.D., Senior Associate, The Benton Foundation

Bill Kovach, Chairman, Committee of Concerned Journalists in Washington

Nancy C. Kranich, President, American Library Association, New York University Libraries

Erwin G. Krasnow, Attorney, Verner, Liipfert, Bernhard, McPherson, and Hand, Washington, D.C.

Donna N. Lampert, Lampert & O'Connor, P.C.

Kevin Landy, Counsel, Committee on Governmental Affairs, U.S. Senate

John J. Lane, Television News Executive

Congressman John B. Larson, D-CT

David Laventhol, Publisher and Editorial Director, *Columbia Journalism Review*

Edward Lazowska, Bill and Melinda Gates Chair, Department of Computer Science and Engineering, University of Washington

Paul LeClerc, President, The New York Public Library

Frank Leonard, Author, Futurist

Richard C. Leone, President, The Century Foundation

Gerald Lesser, Professor Emeritus, School of Education, Harvard University

Nathan Leventhal, Former President, Lincoln Center for the Performing Arts

S. Robert Lichter, President, Center for Media and Public Affairs

Senator Joseph I. Lieberman, D-CT

Dr. David B. Liroff, Vice President and Chief Technology Officer, WGBH, Boston

Tom Lix, President, Public Interactive

Mark Lloyd, Executive Director, Civil Rights Forum on Communication Policy; National Coordinator, People for Better Television

Glenn D. Lowry, Director, The Museum of Modern Art
Carolyn J. Lukensmeyer, Founder and President, AmericaSpeaks
Mark Luker, Vice President, EDUCAUSE
Robert MacNeil, Writer, formerly MacNeil-Lehrer NewsHour
C. Peter Magrath, President, National Association of State Universities and
    Land-Grant Colleges
Deanna B. Marcum, President, Council on Library and Information Resources
Congressman Edward J. Markey, D-MA
Stephanie Pace Marshall, Ph.D., President, Illinois Mathematics and Science
    Academy
Thomas R. Martin, Ph.D., Professor of Classics, College of the Holy Cross
Thomas Matzzie, Web Editor, AFL-CIO
John W. McCarter, Jr., President and Chief Executive, The Field Museum, Chicago
William J. McCarter, President Emeritus, WTTW/Chicago
Michael McCaskey, Chair, The Chicago Bears
Allison McDonald, Deputy Director, Foundation/Government Underwriting,
    Thirteen/WNET New York
Peter McGhee, Vice President for National Programming, WGBH, Boston
Christia Mercer, Associate Professor of Philosophy, Columbia University
Honorable Bob Michel, Hogan & Hartson, L.L.P., Washington, D.C.
Ellen Mickiewicz, Director, DeWitt Wallace Center for Communications and
    Journalism, Terry Sanford Institute for Public Policy, Duke University
Martha L. Minow, Professor, Harvard Law School
Pat Mitchell, President and CEO, Public Broadcasting Service
Mark Moore, Director, Hauser Center for Nonprofit Organization
John R. Morison, President and General Manager, WHRO, Norfolk, Virginia
Lloyd Morrisett, Chairman Emeritus, Sesame Workshop
Amy L. Nathan, Senior Counsel, Office of Plans & Policy, Federal Communications
    Commission
Susan Ness, Commissioner, Federal Communications Commission
Charles Nesson, Director, Berkman Center for Internet & Society, Harvard Law
    School
Mortimer H. Neufville, Executive Vice President, National Association of State
    Universities and Land-Grant Colleges
A. Richard Newton, Dean, College of Engineering and the Roy Carlson Professor
    of Engineering, University of California, Berkeley
Eli Noam, Director, Columbia Institute for Tele-Information, Columbia University
Paul T. O'Day, President, American Fiber Manufacturers Association
B. Robert Okun, Vice President, National Broadcasting Company, Washington,
    D.C.
Bruce M. Owen, Author, President, Economists Incorporated
Marc Pachter, Director, National Portrait Gallery, Smithsonian Institution
Everett C. Parker, Adjunct Professor, Fordham University, Director of Communication,
    United Churches of Christ

Thomas E. Patterson, Bradlee Professor of Government and the Press, Kennedy School of Government, Harvard University

Ancil H. Payne, Former President, King Broadcasting Company

Roy D. Pea, Director, Center for Technology in Learning, SRI International, Menlo Park, California

Robert Pepper, Chief, Office of Plans and Policy, Federal Communications Commission

Alvin H. Perlmutter, Television Producer, Sunrise Media LLC

Trevor Potter, Attorney, Wiley, Rein, and Fielding, Washington, D.C.

Michael K. Powell, Chairman, Federal Communications Commission

Monroe Price, School of Social Science, Institute for Advanced Study

Austin E. Quigley, Dean of Columbia College, Columbia University

Miles Rapoport, President, Demos and Founder, DemocracyWorks

William T. Reed, President & CEO, Kansas City Public Television

Gail Reimer, Executive Director, Jewish Women's Archive, a virtual home for Jewish women's history

T. Randall Riggs,Global Education and Training Manager, Agere Systems

Marita Rivero, Vice President and Radio Manager, WGBH, Boston

Sharon Percy Rockefeller, President and CEO, WETA, Washington, D.C.

Susan Rogers, Consultant, Susan Rogers Project Management & Consulting

Gregory L. Rohde, Assistant Secretary, National Telecommunications and Information Administration, U.S. Department of Commerce

David H. Rose, Co-executive Director, CAST-Center for Applied Special Technology

Peter Rosen, President, Peter Rosen Productions, Inc.

Peter Rosenblum, Associate Director of Human Rights Program and Lecturer on Law, Harvard Law School

Stephen M. Ryan, Partner, Manatt, Phelps, and Phillips, LLP

Robert Sachs, President & CEO, National Cable Television Association

Stephen Salyer, President, Public Radio International

Daniel J. Schmidt, President & CEO, WTTW, Chicago

Martin E. Segal, Chair, New York International Festival of the Arts; Chairman Emeritus, Lincoln Center for the Performing Arts

James J. Sharpe, Director, Distributed Learning Technology, IBM Learning Services

Congressman Christopher Shays, R-CT

Beverly Sheppard, Acting Director, Institute of Museum and Library Services

Laura Lee Simon, Past Chair, Trustee Emerita, Co-chair, Strategic Planning, Connecticut Public Television and Radio

Norman M. Sinel, Partner, Arnold and Porter, Washington, D.C.

Richard Norton Smith, Executive Director, Gerald R. Ford Foundation

William M. Snyder, Founding Partner, Social Capital Group

Sanford Socolow, Former Executive Producer, CBS Evening News with Walter Cronkite

Richard Somerset-Ward, Senior Fellow of the Benton Foundation

W. J. Spencer, The Washington Advisory Group, LLC

Frank Stanton, President, CBS Inc., 1946–73

Senator Ted Stevens, R-AK

Gary Strong, Director, Queens Public Library

Brigid W. Sullivan, Vice President for Special Telecommunication Services and Children's Programming, WGBH, Boston

J. Colin Sullivan, Manager, Corporate Communications, Emperative

Mike Sullivan, Executive Producer, "Frontline," WGBH, Boston

Cass R. Sunstein, Karl N. Llewellyn Distinguished Service Professor of Juris Prudence, University of Chicago

Paul Taylor, Executive Director, Alliance for Better Campaigns

Jack Thorpe, Colonel, U.S. Marine Corps, Retired

Sean Treglia, Program Officer, The Pew Charitable Trusts

Andries van Dam, Thomas J. Watson, Jr., University Professor of Technology and Education and Professor of Computer Science, Brown University

Susan Veccia, Project Manager, National Digital Library Program, Library of Congress

Richard C. Wald, Former Senior Vice President, ABC News; Fred W. Friendly Professor, Columbia University Graduate School of Journalism

Laura Walker, President and CEO, WNYC Radio, New York City

Mary L. Walshok, Ph.D., Associate Vice Chancellor, University of California, San Diego

Rita Weisskoff, Author and Educator, Children's Media Consultant

Kevin Werbach, Editor, "Release 1.0," EDventure Holdings

Marilyn L. Wheaton, Director, Cultural Affairs Department, City of Detroit

Richard E. Wiley, Senior Partner, Wiley, Rein, and Fielding, Washington, D.C.

Anthony Wilhelm, Program Director, Communications Policy, Benton Foundation

Tom Wolzien, Senior Media Analyst, Sanford C. Bernstein & Co.; former Vice President, NBC News

The Woodlands Group, Robert Stump, Co-ordinator

William A. Wulf, President, National Academy of Engineering

Daniel Yankelovich, Author and Sociologist

James Yee, former Executive Director, Independent Television Service

Gary Zarr, Director, Marketing, American Museum of Natural History

Jonathan Zittrain, Faculty Co-Director, Berkman Center for Internet & Society; Assistant Professor of Law, Harvard Law School

ABOUT THE AUTHORS OF THE REPORT

LAWRENCE K. GROSSMAN is a former president of NBC News and PBS, advertising agency owner, holder of the Frank Stanton First Amendment Chair at the Kennedy School of Government, and senior fellow and visiting scholar at Columbia University. He currently serves as a trustee of Connecticut Public Broadcasting and various nonprofit health organizations. He is a television columnist for *Columbia Journalism Review* and a Dupont-Columbia Journalism Award juror. He is the author of *The Electronic Republic: Reshaping Democracy in the Information Age,* a Twentieth Century Fund Book (Viking/Penguin, 1996).

NEWTON N. MINOW is former chairman of the Federal Communications Commission, PBS, the RAND Corporation, and the Carnegie Corporation of New York. He was a board member of CBS and the Tribune Company and is a life trustee of Notre Dame and Northwestern Universities. He is coauthor (with Craig L. LaMay) of *Abandoned in the Wasteland: Children, Television and the First Amendment* (Hill and Wang, 1995), an influential book on television and children. Senior counsel to Sidley & Austin, he is also the Annenberg Professor of Communications Law and Policy at Northwestern University.

Both Mr. Minow and Mr. Grossman have undertaken this project on a pro bono basis.

ABOUT THE AUTHORS OF THE DIGITAL PERSPECTIVES BACKGROUND PAPERS

WAYNE ASHLEY is the first manager of new media at the Brooklyn Academy of Music in New York, where he oversees *Arts in Multimedia*, the BAM/Lucent Technologies artist-in-residency program. He produces content for BAM's website and new media events for the Lepercq Space. He has worked as program director of Open Studio at the Seattle Arts Museum, an NEA/Benton Foundation-sponsored laboratory exploring the power of the Internet for communication and artistic expression. He recently produced "Before and After Geography," a web documentary featuring the work of choreographer Ralph Lemon, designed and built by digital artists Vivian Selbo and Carl Skelton, and is curating an exhibition of new media from Australia as part of the BAM Next Wave Festival 2001.

LES BROWN has covered the electronic media as a journalist since 1953 variously for *Variety,* the *New York Times,* and the magazines he founded in the 1980s, *Channels* and *TBI* (Television Business International). He is the author of seven books, among them *Televi$ion: The Business Behind the Box* (Harcourt Brace Jovanovich, 1971) and *Les Brown's Encyclopedia of Television* (Gale Research, 1992). He has been a presidential fellow of the Aspen Institute, a Poynter fellow at Yale University, and a resident fellow of the Freedom Forum Media Studies Center at Columbia University. Currently, he is a columnist for *TBI*, an international consultant, and an associate professor at the Fordham Graduate School of Business where he teaches a course on the broadband revolution.

CATHY N. DAVIDSON is the Ruth F. DeVarney Professor of English, vice provost for interdisciplinary studies, and founding codirector (with Karla F. C. Holloway) of the John Hope Franklin Institute at Duke University. She is past president of the American Studies Association and the former editor of the journal *American*

Literature. Author or editor of over a dozen books, she recently has published the award-winning *Closing: The Life and Death of an American Factory* (Norton, 1998), a collaboration with photographer Bill Bamberger.

EVERETTE E. DENNIS is executive director and chief operating officer of the International Longevity Center in New York City and Felix E. Larkin Professor of Media Industries at Fordham's Graduate School of Business. He was founding president of the American Academy in Berlin and founding director of the Media Studies Center at Columbia University, where he organized a technology studies laboratory and an advanced fellows program. He has been a professor and dean respectively at the University of Minnesota and the University of Oregon and is author or editor of thirty-eight books about media issues and industries.

MARION R. FREMONT-SMITH joined the Hauser Center at Harvard University as a senior research fellow in 1997 to direct a research study of the accountability of the philanthropic sector. She has served as assistant attorney general and director of the Division of Public Charities in Massachusetts and as a research director for the Russell Sage Foundation. She has been a partner of the Boston law firm of Choate, Hall and Stewart since 1971 and in 1997 became senior counsel to the firm. Her current research is directed toward documenting existing state and federal laws governing the duties of trustees and directors of nonprofit organizations and the methods of enforcement.

JOHN GOBERMAN is executive producer for television at Lincoln Center, where he has produced *Live from Lincoln Center* and a companion series, *Backstage/Lincoln Center,* as well as more than 150 full-length nationwide live telecasts. He is also the producer of Symphonic Cinema, consisting of the classics *Alexander Nevsky, Scenes from Ivan the Terrible,* and *A Symphonic Night at the Movies.* He coproduced the theatrical film, *Distant Harmony: Pavarotti in China,* and has made films for museums across the country, ranging from the Metropolitan Museum of Art to the Ringling Museum of Art. For his work on public and commercial television, he has received nine National Emmy Awards, three Peabody Awards, six Sigma Alpha Iota awards, and the first Television Critics Circle Award for Achievement in Music. He was cited by *Symphony Magazine* as one of the fifty most important people who have made a difference in the history of American music. He is currently at work on a film about music at the White House.

MARTÍN GÓMEZ is executive director of Brooklyn Public Library, the nation's fifth-largest library system. He has been instrumental in establishing the Brooklyn Public Library Foundation to raise private funds for library programs. He also helped to create an online wide-area network providing free public access to the Internet at Brooklyn's sixty branch libraries. His current focus is to strengthen the library's ability to improve literacy levels for children and young adults and to prepare the library for the digital age.

RICHARD KIMBALL is president of Project Vote Smart, an organization comprised of citizens who provide reliable political information by researching the backgrounds and records of over forty thousand candidates for public office through the project's website www.vote-smart.org, the Vote Smart hotline, and Voter's Self-Defense Manuals. He has been deputy press secretary for Walter Mondale, press secretary for Daniel Patrick Moynihan, an Arizona state senator, and chairman of Arizona's Corporation Commission.

ANN KIRSCHNER is the president and chief executive officer of Fathom, an interactive knowledge website. Before cofounding Fathom with Columbia University, she headed up new media for the National Football League (NFL), overseeing the introduction of new programming ventures in emerging technologies such as interactive television and the Internet. She is the founder of nfl.com, superbowl.com, and Team NFL on America Online. She also served as president of Comma Communications, a telecommunications and interactive consulting firm, cofounded Satellite Broadcast Networks and PrimeTime 24, and was the director of new business development for Westinghouse/Group W Cable.

CRAIG L. LAMAY is associate dean of the Medill School of Journalism at Northwestern University. Formerly editor of the *Media Studies Journal* and a fellow at the Annenberg Washington Program in Communications Policy Studies, he has written for the *New York Times*, the *Washington Post*, the *Los Angeles Times*, the *Wall Street Journal*, the *Chicago Tribune*, *Time*, and other publications. He is author or coauthor of twelve books, most recently (with Ellen Mickiewicz) *Democracy on the Air* (DeWitt Wallace Center for Communications and Journalism, 1999). Along with Newton N. Minow, he coauthored *Abandoned in the Wasteland: Children, Television and the First Amendment* (Hill and Wang, 1995).

MARK LLOYD is the executive director of the Civil Rights Forum on Communications Policy, a project of the Tides Center created to bring civil rights principles and advocacy to the communications policy debate. He also serves as the national coordinator of People for Better TV, a diverse coalition working to establish clear guidelines on the public interest obligations of broadcasters. Previously, he worked as general counsel to the Benton Foundation and as a communications attorney at Dow, Lohnes & Albertson in Washington, D.C. He has nearly twenty years of experience as a broadcast journalist, working at NBC and CNN. He is the recipient of several awards for his writing and reporting, including an Emmy and a Cine Golden Eagle. He is chairman of the board of directors of the Independent Television Service (ITVS).

THOMAS R. MARTIN is the first Jeremiah O'Connor Professor in Classics at the College of the Holy Cross. As one of the founders of the *Perseus Project* (Yale University Press, 1996, 2000), he has helped to create CD-ROM and online resources for studying ancient Greek history and culture. He is the author of *Ancient Greece: From Prehistoric to Hellenistic Times* (Yale University Press, 1996, 2000) and coauthor (with Lynn Hunt et al.) of *Making of the West* (Bedford Books, 2001).

SUSAN A. ROGERS is a freelance project manager and consultant in Cambridge, Massachusetts, specializing in projects involving organizational change and new technologies. Her clients include universities, museums, and other non-profit organizations. From 1995 to 1998 she managed the development of the Harvard Business School's enterprise-wide intranet and online course delivery systems and built an eighty-person information technology (IT) department responsible for in-house product development and customer service. She has twenty-five years of experience in IT and higher-education administration. She has participated in nonprofit boards and governance including senior management roles in institutional planning, fund raising, construction management, and operations.

RICHARD SOMERSET-WARD is senior fellow of the Benton Foundation in Washington, D.C. From 1963 to 1984 he was on the staff of the British Broadcasting Corporation, ultimately working as head of music and arts programming. Since 1984, he has lived and worked in New York City. Beside his work for Benton, he is a consultant to the National Gallery of Art in Washington, D.C., and an active writer and producer for television. His most recent film, *Ginevra's Story,* starring Meryl Streep, won the Gold Camera at the 2000 International Film and Video Festival in Chicago. He is the author of *Connecting Communities* (Benton Foundation, 2000) and the background paper for *Quality Time? The Report of the Twentieth Century Fund Task Force on Public Television* (Twentieth Century Fund Press, 1993).

LAURA WALKER is president and chief executive officer of WNYC Radio, the first nonmayoral appointee to New York public radio, and is responsible for ushering WNYC AM and FM into a new era as independent public radio stations. She began her professional career as a journalist and producer at National Public Radio, where she received a prestigious Peabody Award for Broadcast Excellence. She later joined the staff of Carnegie Hall, where she launched the award winning series *AT&T Presents Carnegie Hall Tonight.* She spent eight years at Sesame Workshop (formerly Children's Television Workshop), where she headed the development department and later the organization's efforts to establish the cable television channel, Noggin. She sits on the boards of Public Radio International, the Brooklyn Philharmonic, and Public Interactive.

Mary L. Walshok is associate vice chancellor for public programs and dean of university extension at the University of California, San Diego. In this capacity, she is responsible for UCSD-TV, a regionally focused broadcast station, as well as the university's self-funded continuing education and outreach programs, which represent an annual budget in excess of $30 million and involve more than fifty-thousand participants annually. A professor of sociology, she has also written extensively on work, education, and the new economy, including the book *Knowledge Without Boundaries* (Jossey-Bass, 1995).

Rita Weisskoff is a writer and educator with a special interest in using the power of popular media to support children's growth and development. She has extensive experience working with creative teams to design and integrate educational content into entertainment vehicles for children, including several preschool series currently on air and online: *Dragon Tales* and *Timothy Goes to School* (PBS) and *Little Bill* (Nick Jr. and CBS); and *Ghostwriter* (PBS, Nickelodeon, and Noggin), a television-based literacy project for older children. From 1983 to 1988 she was vice president and director of the Children's Advertising Review Unit of the Council of Better Business Bureaus, responsible for the self-regulation of advertising in children's media. She also taught in Connecticut public schools and universities for eleven years.

ABOUT THE PROJECT STAFF

EDITH C. BJORNSON is a consultant to not-for-profit and for-profit organizations in new media. She was formerly vice president for programming at Westinghouse Broadcasting and Cable, and vice president and senior program officer of the John and Mary R. Markle Foundation. She is a member of the board of trustees of the New York New Media Association, Connecticut Public Television and Radio, and is a life trustee of the HealthCare Chaplaincy.

HENRY GELLER was general counsel of the FCC from 1964 to 1970. Upon leaving the FCC he was associated with the RAND Corporation and the Aspen Institute until 1978, when he became assistant secretary of commerce for communications and information (and administrator of the National Telecommunications and Information Administration) in the Carter administration. In 1981 he became director of the Washington Center for Public Policy Research and a professor of practice at Duke University. From 1989 through 1998 he was a communications fellow at the Markle Foundation.

CRAIG L. LAMAY is associate dean of the Medill School of Journalism at Northwestern University. Formerly editor of the *Media Studies Journal* and a fellow at the Annenberg Washington Program in Communications Policy Studies, he has written for the *New York Times*, the *Washington Post*, the *Los Angeles Times*, the *Wall Street Journal*, the *Chicago Tribune*, *Time*, and other publications. He is author or coauthor of twelve books, most recently (with Ellen Mickiewicz) *Democracy on the Air* (DeWitt Wallace Center for Communications and Journalism, 1999). He is coauthor (with Newton N. Minow) of *Abandoned in the Wasteland: Children, Television and the First Amendment* (Hill and Wang, 1995).

ANNE G. MURPHY is president of Linkages, a consulting company that specializes in public policy and the arts and humanities. Prior to establishing her own company, she was director of the American Arts Alliance, where she served as the national voice for the nation's professional arts community in

279

matters of public policy, legislation, and public relations. Earlier in her career she held senior positions at the Public Broadcasting Service and the National Endowment for the Arts. She serves on the board of overseers for the Corcoran Museum of Art.